Dav

John Neff
on
Investing

JOHN NEFF

ON

INVESTING

JOHN NEFF

with

S. L. Mintz

JOHN WILEY & SONS, INC.

New York • Chichester • Weinheim • Brisbane • Singapore • Toronto

Published by John Wiley & Sons, Inc.
Published simultaneously in Canada.

This publication is designed to provide accurate and authoritative information in regard
to the subject matter covered. It is sold with the understanding that the publisher is not
engaged in rendering professional services. If professional advice or other expert
assistance is required, the services of a competent professional person should be sought.

Library of Congress Cataloging-in-Publication Data:

Neff, John (John B.)
    John Neff on investing / John Neff with S.L. Mintz.
        p.   cm.
    Includes index.
    ISBN 0-471-19717-3 (alk. paper)
        1. Investment analysis.   2. Investments.   I. Mintz, Steven L.
    II. Title.
    HG4529.N43   1999
    332.6—dc21   99-16345

Printed in the United States of America.

10 9 8 7 6 5 4 3 2 1

To Lilli
My wife of 45 years
My best friend
Mother of our children
And my staunchest supporter

ACKNOWLEDGMENTS

I AM INDEBTED to my family: Lilli and our children, Lisa and Stephen, for their support, interest, and understanding during the time-consuming period when this book was developed. I constantly and perhaps excessively used them as a sounding-board for different parts of this book and they were always willing and enthusiastic participants.

My collaborator, Steven Mintz, really did the heavy lifting in organizing my thoughts, accomplishments, and convictions into the chapters that make up this book. His patience, diligence, work ethic, and amiability were very much appreciated.

Another responsibility, in addition to managing the Windsor Fund, I shared with Bob Doran, Duncan McFarland, and Nick Thorndike over a 16-year period was managing partner of Wellington Management Company LLP, an investment advisor now managing upwards of $200 billion of discretionary assets. Their level of integrity, good judgment, dedication, sense of humor, and accomplishments were constant companions as we tried to lead Wellington in the never-ending quest to be an outstanding investment organization.

Over the years, both good and bad, I basked in the warmth of constant encouragement and support from Jack Bogle, Jack Brennan, and other Vanguard directors. Despite the occasional rough patches we suffered, I never had the feeling that I didn't have the confidence of this outstanding group of individuals.

All of Windsor's success would not have been possible without the remarkable team that contributed so mightily over my tenure. Chuck Freeman, my successor, made a stellar contribution over 26 years. He was sharing and the epitome of intellectual honesty that resulted in such coups as Tandy, Citicorp, and Chrysler as well as many others. Both Jim Averill and Jim Mordy over a ten-year period flushed out in admirable fashion typical Windsor fare.

I had the good fortune to have a trio of superb mentors that aided me along the way. In college at the University of Toledo, Dr. Sidney Robbins, head of the Finance Department and professor of the only two undergraduate finance courses I took, opened my eyes to the fascinations of the investment business and convinced me that I could make a contribution therein. Arthur T. Boanas, a Yorkshire man, who came to the United States after World War II, took me under his wing in my first job out of college and with endless patience and encouragement schooled me in the wonderful world of common stock investing. Paul M. Miller, one of the founders of Miller, Anderson and Sherred, an investment advisory firm now part of Morgan Stanley Dean Witter, and Chairman of the Board of Trustees of the University of Pennsylvania for eight years, through subtle, understated example helped me to mature a bit later in life.

I have had the good fortune to have outstanding helpmates over the years. Janet Ragusa took dictation and with customary tirelessness, accuracy, patience, and good cheer pounded out a rough draft of the hundreds of letters to the Vanguard Directors that make up the journal that accounts for about half of this book. Darla Knoll, administrative assistant extraordinaire for some 20 years, made me better than I am by keeping me organized and managing my affairs effectively. In my semi-retirement, Fran Kelly has looked after me with tender loving care.

Three people have encouraged and occasionally harangued me over the past couple of years to do this book: Charlie Ellis, who paid me the fine compliment of writing the Foreword to this book; Bill Hicks who helped with Windsor Fund out of the embryo; and Gene Arnold who sent me a bevy of messages to "get on with the book." To all of these people, as well as to many others who have displayed wisdom and friendship over the years, I am sincerely grateful.

J. N.

CONTENTS

CONTENTS

PART THREE
A MARKET JOURNAL

FOREWORD

JOHN NEFF IS the investment profession's investment professional. Nobody has ever managed a large mutual fund so very well for so very long a time. And no one is likely to do so ever again.

The record of his management of the Windsor Fund for more than 30 years is truly astounding. During an era when professional investment managers' returns have increasingly lagged the market averages, John Neff delivered an annual *average* that exceeded the "market" rate of return by more than 3 percent. (His results were actually 3.5 percent ahead of the market. After expenses, the *net* rate of return, over one-third of a century, averaged 3.15 percent *higher* than the market—year after year after year.)

Consider what his record really means, given the great effect of compounding (which Albert Einstein regarded as one of humanity's most enlightened ideas). Compounded over 24 years, 3 percent per year will *double* the original investment. John Neff achieved *more* than 3 percent for *more* than 24 years!

A sweet extra advantage for the tens of thousands of investors who have benefited from John Neff's splendid performance is almost unknown. Contrary to the reasonable expectation that to achieve higher returns, investors must accept more risk, the investment risks taken by John Neff were *lower* than the riskiness of the overall stock market. John would remind us: "That's just one of the several good reasons for being a contrarian investor!"

A true statement, but not the *whole* truth. John Neff is too modest to cite the main reason he was so effective as a "contrarian," or independent-minded investor: *Discipline*. John Neff was able to go against the tides of conventional market opinion because he knew more about the companies in which he invested. In addition to being original, independent, and *very* rational in his evaluations, John knew more because he worked longer and harder.

When John Neff received the worldwide investment profession's highest award, one of his "secrets" was revealed. At home (or wherever he might be visiting), every Saturday at 1:00 P.M., John retires to the privacy of his room to read—again—every word in every issue of *The Wall Street Journal* for the preceding week of business. This is only one evidence of the remarkable self-discipline with which this unique professional prepares himself for the very competitive work of professional investment management.

John engages most vigorously in meetings with securities analysts—both those at his own firm and those at the leading stockbrokerages. After cheerfully challenging their assumptions, analyses, and projections, he always makes his own independent price judgment. For the unprepared, meeting John Neff can be a "disaster." Those who meet Neff's standards appreciate that John answers his own phone ("Neff!"), and he always gives as good as he gets, or better, in both information and insight. Neff's rigorous discipline in "doing his homework" has one important consequence: His portfolio's turnover and the cost of transactions are kept to unusually low levels. Correcting errors—and, of course, making errors—is costly to investors. So are the taxes levied on short-term profits. John skillfully works to minimize both.*

John is not only the profession's professional investor, he is an exemplar as a "servant fiduciary"—always centered on his chosen responsibilities as investment manager for the families and individuals who have entrusted their savings to the mutual funds he manages.

The best investment decision I ever made† was to buy—25 years ago, on maximum margin—the so-called "Capital" shares of the Gemini duo-fund. A duo-fund (no longer allowed) was a special class of mutual funds

---

* John is a Trustee of the University of Pennsylvania. (He was never a student there, but he has taught in the university's Wharton Business School.) When asked to manage the equities of the university's endowment, he took it on *pro bono* for 16 years and delivered a strong performance. The university's endowment fund increased from $170 million to $1.8 billion. John has also served for many years as one of three Managing Partners of Wellington Management Company. His investment acumen complements his business acumen.

† My *most profitable* investment decision was different. More than 20 years ago, my partners and I invested in Berkshire Hathaway. That was a rational decision, but it was based more on faith in Warren Buffett than on knowledge.

in which half the money invested at the initial public offering got all the dividends, and half the money invested got all the appreciation or capital gains. In the then-prevailing bear market, stocks were far below their past valuations, and investor sentiment was and had long been consistently negative. This scenario created great opportunities for a contrarian investor, particularly one specializing in "value" stocks, which had been particularly hard hit. Gemini's Capital shares had, of course, borne the brunt of the bear market and were selling at a serious discount. If the market recovered, the Capital shares would rise with disproportionate rapidity—roughly, twice as fast—because of the duo-fund structure. If value stocks returned to normal relative valuations (a reasonable expectation among those who recognize the powerful tendency of stock market valuations to "regress to the mean"), a portfolio managed by John Neff would enjoy at least a quite favorable environment. And that superior performance could soon eliminate the then-current market discount.

John was recognized as a superior investment manager who could be expected to outperform the market (as he had done again and again). So, I had five complementary forces ready to work hard together for me: John Neff, value stocks, mean regression, a current market discount, and nearly two-for-one leverage on the upside. Still, the key factor in this investment decision was the sure knowledge that John Neff would have structured the portfolio and selected its holdings with extra care and attention to *risk*.

Emboldened by the conviction that America was being "sold short" by investors, I made a "worst case" estimate of the risk of a further drop in the market. The most I could imagine was another 20 percent. If this figure was correct, the rational course of action would be to borrow the maximum 30 percent of margin through my stockbroker and plunge deeply into purchasing the Capital shares of Gemini.* The stock market went up; the Capital shares went from a discount to a premium; value stocks became the market's darlings; the leverage of a duo-fund worked its wonders; and John Neff continued to outperform his peer group. All five forces locked in together, and a sixth, margin leverage, ensured my sons' education expenses.

Luckily for me, in many ways, my relationship with John Neff goes way back. When I first met him in Philadelphia 35 years ago, I knew

---

* Special and continuing thanks to Jay Sherrerd, who first pointed out, 25 years ago, "You can get Neff at a discount."

two things almost instantly. First, he was very smart, well informed, and serious about knowing more. Second, I liked him and I liked the cut of his jib. A few months later, John Corcoran, investment strategist for Donaldson, Lufkin & Jenrette (DLJ) was giving an erudite discourse on the investment opportunities available in different sectors of the market. While all the other professional fund managers in his rapt audience were cheerfully focused on how much some particular stocks could go up, the meeting was brought to an awkward halt by Neff's blunt question to Corcoran: "John, what about *risk?*"

That cinched it for me: Here was a truly independent thinker.

I've been listening to John Neff on every possible occasion ever since—as a share owner in the mutual funds he manages, at professional meetings sponsored by the Association for Investment Management and Research (AIMR), at portfolio manager seminars sponsored by DLJ, and, quite happily in recent years, in his role as a Director of Greenwich Associates.

A cheerful confession: From the very beginning, I strongly encouraged John to write this book—partly so I could read *John Neff on Investing*, partly so my sons and friends could, and partly so any serious student of the profession could benefit from the best thinking by this great investor.

CHARLES D. ELLIS

Greenwich, Connecticut
June 1999

PREFACE

IN THE SPRING of 1998, I taught a graduate seminar on investing at the Wharton School in Philadelphia. A very lively group of students sparked extensive reflection on my part. Aspects of my life fell
together in answer to dozens of questions about the nature of the investment process and why I chose the path I followed. This book con-
tinues my conversation with these students.

A book is a one-sided conversation, to be sure. But, like a good conversation, it can express a point of view in an informal manner, unen-
cumbered by charts and graphs that often clog books on this subject. If
we shared a compartment on a long train ride, what you read in these
pages is what I'd tell you about investing. I have highlighted the ideas
that seem most enduring to me after three decades at Windsor, rather
than supply a laundry list of topics related to investing. You can find
other books for that.

Teaching invited many questions about my own learning curve. I'm
not sure where it began, exactly. I joined the U.S. Navy and studied aviation electronics before I dreamed of trading stocks, much less managing the largest equity mutual fund in the United States—the status
Windsor held until the doors were closed to new shareholders in 1985.
Perhaps my career started before I learned to count. I was always a stubborn little fellow, which my mother expressed very succinctly: "John
Brown," she declared, "You would argue with a signpost." She was not
only right, she was prescient. My whole career, I have argued with the
stock market. Happily, as the Windsor Fund's record shows, I won more
arguments with the market than I lost.

Wherever learning curves begin in this mercurial business, they never seem to end. That's the marvel, and also the heartbreak, of the stock market. You can line up more experts than you can shake a stick at, but none can predict with certainty what investors really want to know: How will the market do tomorrow, or next week, or next year? An inexhaustible flow of new information produces outlooks no one has seen before. An early Greek philosopher, Heraclitus, observed that a person cannot step twice in the same river, because the river changes constantly. Nor, in the same sense, can an investor step twice in the same market, because the market changes constantly.

Hang around long enough, though, and you will begin to recognize the market's personality. It is irrational and unsentimental. It is cantankerous and hostile. At times, it is forgiving and congenial. The market has good days and bad days, good years and bad years. You can't predict them, and they can reverse course with stunning speed. But you can learn to cope with them and improve your odds. In the bargain, you can make good money.

Contrarian that I am, the format for this book is intentionally unorthodox as books on investing go these days. It is not about Hail Mary passes; it's about grinding out gains quarter after quarter, year after year. My kind of investing rests on three elements: character, goals, and experience. Therein lies the three-part structure. Part One (My Road to Windsor) is about my character, Part Two (Enduring Principles) portrays goals and mechanics, and Part Three (A Market Journal) records how events played out during the last quarter-century of my Windsor career. All were written with an eye to smarter investing, whether you trade one stock a year or a stock a day (I don't recommend the latter).

It seems pertinent at this juncture to add a note about the performance of value investing in the late nineties. Many so-called value funds have suffered a rough road. As a contrarian, I say that's to be expected. When better to write a book about out-of-favor investing than when it's out of favor? Being out of fashion ultimately enhances opportunities on the other side. On my watch, Windsor weathered trying times more than once but still managed to spring back with championship results.

Individual investors enjoy a key advantage over professionals in one critical respect. You can pick and choose stocks and bide your time unflustered by the fierce and often corrosive quarterly performance sweepstakes, especially in hostile market climates. Value investing (with a focus on low price–earnings ratios, as I practice it) demands sober reflection. Scarce to begin with, sober reflection gets even scarcer as bull markets progress.

Eventually, good stocks of good companies with solid earnings and low price–earnings ratios receive the attention they deserve. With patience, luck, and sound judgment, meanwhile, you keep moving forward. That's the nature of the investment game: now and then a windfall, but mostly a four-yard gain and a cloud of dust. My investment style can give investors a lucrative edge over the long haul. But if you can't roll with the hits, or you're in too big a hurry, you might as well keep your money in a mattress.

JOHN NEFF

Valley Forge, Pennsylvania
June 1999

Windsor vs. the S&P 500 (1964–1995)

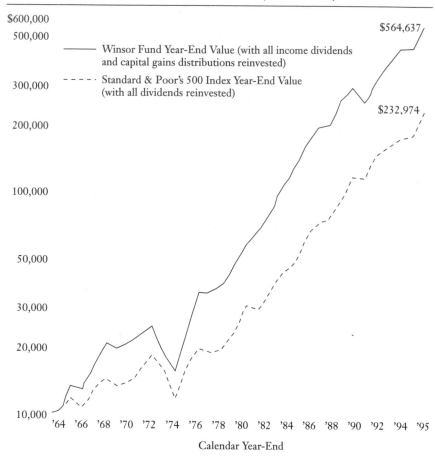

Windsor Fund Year-End Value (with all income dividends and capital gains distributions reinvested)

Standard & Poor's 500 Index Year-End Value (with all dividends reinvested)

$564,637

$232,974

Calendar Year-End

TOTAL RETURN PERFORMANCE SUMMARY PERIODS
ENDING OCTOBER 31, 1995

	Cumulative		Average Annual	
	Windsor	S&P 500	Windsor	S&P 500
5 Years	+154.2%	+121.1%	+20.5%	+17.2%
10 Years	+268.4	+319.8	+13.9	+15.4
15 Years	+902.3	+696.0	+16.6	+14.8
20 Years	+2,314.6	+1,352.4	+17.3	+14.3
Lifetime*	+5,546.4%	+2,229.7%	+13.7%	+10.6%

* Reflects tenure of Portfolio Manager, John B. Neff.

PROLOGUE

CITI SAGA

MOST INVESTORS FEARED for Citibank in May 1991. Amid real estate problems galore, and on the heels of cleaning up disastrous loans to developing countries, Citi's prospects were bleak. Billions of dollars had been set aside to cope with bad real estate loans and to correct enormous problems, but monumental hurdles remained. Other banks were recovering from similar problems; still, the headlines blasted Citi, and regulators swarmed over its books. Continental Bank's specter lurked in the background, reminding investors that venerable banks here today might vanish tomorrow. The stock price plunged almost daily. Critics besieged Citi's energetic chairman, John Reed, who was in the fight of his life with his job on the line.

At Windsor, after weighing Citi's situation carefully, we decided this was a good time to buy.

It wasn't as if Windsor owned too few Citi shares. The bank had drawn our attention in 1987, when we were seeking to replace our stake in J. P. Morgan following a very successful run-up in the stock price. Citi shares at the time were changing hands for between 7 and 8 times earnings, down from a heyday when the former chairman, Walter Wriston, briefly transformed Citi into a growth company. His efforts actually squeezed out growth of 15 percent a year. For a time in the early Seventies, Citi belonged to the very stylish Nifty Fifty, a list of household-name growth stocks that had captivated the stock market. When Citi's growth rate settled down and lost its grip on investors, Windsor swooped in. We experienced a much rougher ride than we had bargained for.

Citicorp exercised Windsor's contrarian streak from the start. Citi's important sizzle in 1987 was a steep discount to prevailing price–earnings ratios. This discount reflected genuine apprehension about loans to Latin American countries—aggravated, at least in Mexico's case, by the downward spiral in oil prices. Preoccupied with these concerns, the stock market overlooked an important perspective. Forced by banking regulations to set aside reserves in case these loans failed, Citi's earnings in 1985 and 1986 bore severe burdens. Other investors paled at the losses. We reached a different conclusion: Citi's earnings were very conservatively stated and probably would be higher.

By 1988, it looked as if Citi would reward our faith. A year after posting record losses, the bank was on the road toward record profits. And then recession hit, and its impact on widespread overdevelopment of commercial real estate was especially severe. Developers went bust, leaving banks on the hook with nonperforming real estate loans. Pressed to replenish their capital, banks routinely unburdened themselves of these loans at 50 cents on the dollar, or even less. In a smart move that raised eyebrows at the time, Citi held on to its loans rather than fold.

Despite this litany of crippling problems, Windsor steadily increased its stake in the downtrodden financial services sector. But things got worse, particularly for Citi. Through interactions with Reed, mainly because I offered a piece of my mind from time to time as Windsor's stake mounted, I grew to appreciate his determined, round-the-clock hard work. I also developed some concern for him personally. Tough as things were, I advised him not to give up golf. Introducing him, on one occasion, to an investment audience, I confessed to early confusion about Reed's first name. With so many reports in the media referring to "beleaguered John Reed," for a long time I thought that "beleaguered" was his first name.

Ignoring the pundits, we bought more shares of Citi in early 1990. Real estate woes notwithstanding, we believed that Citicorp had an extraordinary consumer position that would eventually win recognition in the marketplace. We noted that the problems primarily afflicted the bank's commercial real estate business. Earnings on the consumer side

were posting hefty gains. The dominant credit card business was outstanding, and Chairman Wriston's legacy—a firm foothold in the developing world—was starting to contribute to the bottom line. Figuring
that real estate would rise again, as it always does, we saw the potential
for making a bucket for shareholders. Citi wasn't making any money in
1990, but that was only because the bank was setting aside reserves related to real estate. Despite a tough environment, the rest of the business
was earning as much as the real estate segment was losing.

Nevertheless, Citi dashed our hopes again. As 1991 progressed, only
Citi, among Windsor's banks, failed us on the earnings side. So we did
what seemed logical. With an average cost of $33 a share and a going
price of $14 a share, we bought more shares.

The price continued to decline as 1991 wound down, and the media
lambasted Citi on a regular basis. "Citi's Nightmares Just Keep Getting
Worse," a *Business Week* headline blared in October 1991. In December,
Institutional Investor magazine conveyed Wall Street's sentiment in a feature story accompanied by a full-page photo of a dead fish. A lot of people thought Citi was about to go bankrupt; Ross Perot reportedly sold
Citi shares short. Claims that the picture was worse than Citicorp por-
trayed in its financial statements prompted desperate action on the pub-
licity front. To quell rumors, the bank had to announce publicly that it
had not flunked an exam imposed by regulators.

At that point, Windsor owned 23 million shares; a half-billion dollars
of shareholders' assets were at risk. Meanwhile, Congressman John Din-
gle, Chairman of the House Banking Committee, hinted that Citi might
become technically insolvent, and stories circulated about a run on one
of Citi's Asian branches. The price kept on sliding to nearly $8 a share
in late 1991.

I wouldn't say these were jubilant times, but we kept the faith. I never
really came to the point of thinking about selling the shares before earning a satisfactory return. Even after all the bloodletting, we figured that
the company's franchise was largely intact. With steep reductions in
costs, the path toward stronger earnings looked clear to us. In our view,
earnings would come tumbling out after 1991 as real estate problems diminished. Citi struck us as being somewhat in the same position as
BankAmerica in 1987. A later turnaround increased Bank America's
price more than eightfold.

We endured the slings and arrows, and the outcome eventually
brought sweet vindication and very handsome returns. By early 1992,

earnings and stock price were visibly on the road back. Our stake was profitable before calendar year-end, and Windsor's neck-out stance eventually garnered returns well worth the wait.

Windsor's roller coaster experience with Citi underscored a crucial point: investment success does not require glamour stocks or bull markets. Judgment and fortitude were our prerequisites. Judgment singles out opportunities, fortitude enables you to live with them while the rest of the world scrambles in another direction. Citi exemplified this investment challenge. To us, ugly stocks were often beautiful. If Windsor's portfolio looked good, we weren't doing our job. Citi wasn't the first such stock, and it certainly wasn't our last.

PART ONE

~

MY ROAD TO
WINDSOR

"Industry, perseverence, & frugality make
Fortune yield."

Ben Franklin

1

~

JOURNEY EAST

A FREEZING MORNING, in early January 1955, marked the start of my investment career. Picture a 23-year-old ex-sailor and newly minted college graduate at the Toledo entrance ramp to the just-completed Ohio Turnpike, thumbing a ride to New York City. This un-celebrated debut sounds strange nowadays to legions of job candidates seeking prestige and lavish signing bonuses right out of school. No one offered to pay for a bus ticket, much less airfare and a fancy hotel. I set out with an overnight satchel, a snack, and twenty dollars in my pocket. Hitching was the only way I could afford to get to New York in time for a series of job interviews the following day.

Maybe I looked unthreatening to drivers in those early days of inter-state highways. Cars were somewhat less plentiful, and crime was con-siderably less on drivers' minds. For whatever reasons, hitchhikers enjoyed more sympathy. I didn't wait long before getting on my way. I don't remember much about the conversation, but, given the Ohio-to-New York route, there naturally were a few comments about the 1954 World Series. The then New York Giants had swept the Cleveland In-dians in four games. As a lifelong Detroit Tigers fan, I kept the loss in perspective.

I knew more about baseball than about investing. The meager extent of my accumulated market wisdom at that time came from a couple of college classes on the subject. I was neither prepared nor inclined to preach the merits of investing, which probably was just as well. In those days, for most Americans, October 1929 and the Great Depression still chilled impressions of the stock market. The Dow Jones Industrial

Average had finally returned to its 1929 highs—after twenty-six years. When asked about my purpose, I just said I was going to New York to look for a job.

For a portion of the long stretch across Pennsylvania, I rode with a former journalist-turned-truck driver who had spent time in South Texas, near Corpus Christi, where I'd gone to high school. We were both exiles, in a sense, although my exile was self-imposed. He blamed his departure on a run-in with a Texas political boss named George Parr, a man credited with unearthing votes that helped sway the Lyndon Johnson ninety-four-vote election majority against Coke Stevenson in the 1948 U.S. Senate race. That contest was so close that a few hundred votes the other way might have changed the course of Presidential history. As it turned out, pundits tagged the future President with a cynical moniker that stuck: Landslide Lyndon.

After 16 hours and 600 miles, my fifth ride left me at a truck depot in Jersey City close to midnight. My triumphant arrival in the Big Apple required a long dark walk and public transportation, and only the night desk clerk greeted me when I checked into the 34th Street YMCA. The accommodations lacked the charm of the Y in Grand Rapids, Michigan, where I'd lived after high school while working two jobs at a time, but I had made it to New York, more or less on time. I only needed enough sleep to stay sharp through the four job interviews I'd lined up for the following day.

Bombshells and Ticker Tapes

New skyscrapers have altered the financial district, and the Information Age has transformed the floor of the New York Stock Exchange since my job search in early 1955, but the intersection of Wall and Broad looks much the same as it did then. The Exchange still dominates one corner; across from it sits Federal Hall, where George Washington swore the first Presidential oath of office. The third imposing building houses the bank that J. Pierpont Morgan built. Its façade still bears the scars left by an anarchist's bomb that rocked Wall Street one busy Thursday in September 1920.

A subtler but more far-reaching explosion has shaken Wall Street since I embarked on an investment career. For nearly a decade after the Second World War, Wall Street was a sleepy and antiquated business. Negotiated commissions were undreamed of, as were electronic trading accounts that allow individual investors to buy and sell stock in an instant. Stocks changed hands only through orders submitted by cadres of male stockbrokers acting on behalf of wealthy individuals, families, and a few trust departments. Indeed, many of the brokers were members of wealthy families or were connected to them in some way. Barred from owning common stocks by conservative rules enacted in the wake of the 1929 Crash, most pension funds and other institutional investors stuck mainly to bonds and the safest stocks. There was no mutual fund industry to speak of.

Few people had a television set, much less home computers and CNBC with instant access to prices and trading volume. To keep tabs on the stock market in 1955, investors relied on genuine ticker tapes. More often than not, the tapes moved haltingly; they printed out ten characters, then stopped, then printed out ten more characters. At this pace, tapes routinely fell behind trading activity, even though volume seldom exceeded 5 million shares a day—as many shares as might be traded in a single hot or not so hot stock these days. Orders to buy or sell stocks were noted by hand on slips of paper. Pneumatic tubes carried the slips to back rooms for fulfillment. To show price changes on the Exchange floor, reporters adjusted serrated dials fixed to a post. When orders flew, keeping up was a challenge. Off the Exchange, most brokerage firms employed "chalkers" or "posters" who erased the old quotes and chalked in new ones when they changed.

The mighty investment banks of today were not household names outside New York's financial district. To those in the know, so-called "wire houses" dominated Wall Street. These houses had offices in other cities, and they transmitted their buy and sell orders by wire. Merrill Lynch was the largest wire house, and its recommendations always had an impact. If Merrill commanded its troops to advise customers to buy Penn Central Railroad, orders for a half-million shares nearly swamped back-office capacity. In the hinterlands, such as Toledo and Cleveland, strong independently run regional brokerage houses dominated whatever action ensued.

In retrospect, I'd say that my decision to go to Wall Street mirrors the investment philosophy that ultimately served me well during my whole career. The investment business was undervalued and out of favor in 1955. The best and the brightest job seekers usually headed for great companies like Ford Motor or General Electric, in hopes of becoming captains of industry some day.

I entertained no such ambition. Instead, an article in *Barron's* guided me to training programs at four national stockbrokerage firms: Merrill Lynch, Blyth & Co., Smith Barney, and Bache & Co. Besides my own confidence in my prospects as a stockbroker, I carried an introduction from a finance professor who had persuaded me to consider an investment career. Had it not been for Professor Sidney Robbins, I would have presumed that success in the investment business required a personal fortune and an Ivy League diploma.

An Auspicious Beginning

I chose an exciting time to launch an investment career. Notwithstanding a tarnished reputation, stocks were starting to recover their luster. Confidence in the growth prospects for such leading stocks as Union Carbide, Dow Chemical, Minnesota Mining & Manufacturing, and Eastman Kodak, propelled their prices to record highs. Restored faith in the soundness of common stocks encouraged investors to surrender sure income for the chance of collecting capital gains, not to mention significant dividend income as well.

The economy was strong and prices were stable as the postwar era took shape. In the year just ended, the U.S. gross national product came in just shy of $400 billion, a new high. As an indication of prosperity, golfers flocked to links in record numbers. According to U.S. golf statistics for 1954, 3.8 million golfers played on approximately 5,000 courses spread over 1.5 million acres. The fourth year in the second half of the 20th century also marked a sixth year in a row without significant price increases. Economists noted the contrast with a 44 percent price decline in the aftermath of World War I. All signs were positive. Shipments of every commodity were strong, and *The Wall Street Journal* reported, on January 3, corporate executives were planning to expand plants on the strength of optimistic forecasts.

Reflecting these encouraging signs, the first day of trading in 1955 pushed the Dow Jones Industrial Average to 408.89, a new record. Bethlehem Steel, Chrysler, General Motors, Eastman Kodak, and Standard Oil of New Jersey all advanced on January 3. Five million shares changed hands—a mere trickle by today's standards, but, in 1955, the highest volume in almost five years. DuPont jumped 4 points, to 171½. As I reached New York, enthusiasm abounded.

My round of interviews posed no insurmountable hurdles. A two-year hitch in the Navy, a couple of finance courses, and experience as a shoe salesman at a leading men's clothing store in Toledo, Ohio, supplied sufficient preparation, I thought. At each stop, I sat through batteries of tests and interviews aimed, presumably, at learning whether I had the right stuff. I was not intimidated, insulted, or overwhelmed. Afterward, I thought I had done fairly well. I didn't wait around, though, for gilded invitations. Before I learned what impressions I had made in New York, I headed back toward home to interview for a position at the National City Bank of Cleveland. For a more pleasant trip and to make sure I arrived on time, I treated myself to a Greyhound bus ticket. A group of truck drivers on board sang all night long.

I was not a big hit in New York. Instead of extending job offers, Merrill Lynch and Blyth turned me down flat. Smith Barney invited me back for more tests and interviews. Concluding that my voice lacked the requisite authority, Bache offered to consider me for a securities analyst position instead of a stockbroker. Bache's offer did not sit well with me at first, but eventually I realized I was better suited to securities analysis and portfolio management than to pushing stock for a living. Stockbrokers make a good living, if they do things right, but they spend most of their time handholding and less of it plying their trade. Stockbrokers' routine can become stultifying and controlled, and I need to be intrigued. And if I was going to become a securities analyst, Cleveland was just fine with me—and with Lilli, my wife of four months, who had lived in Toledo all her life. I agreed to join the bank.

Whether it was recompense for my chilly reception or not, I can't say. But Wall Street suffered a stiff comeuppance right after I departed for Cleveland. On January 6, a Thursday, following the Federal Reserve's decision to raise margin requirements on stock purchases from 50 percent to 60 percent of the purchase price, the Dow Jones Industrial Average slid 2.2 percent. It was the worst drubbing of shareholders since the outbreak of the Korean War five years earlier, *The Wall Street Journal* reported the next day. And matters got worse before bottoming out on January 14.

Although these events formed a backdrop to my debut as a professional investor, I scarcely noticed them at the time. My considered opinions and a coherent strategy—and, some might say, a measure of arrogant self-confidence—still lay ahead of me.

2

~

GRUBBING IT OUT

MY INCLINATION TO buy out-of-favor stocks comes naturally, but by itself doesn't account for beating the market. Success also required lots of perseverance. You have to be willing to hang in when prevailing wisdom says you're wrong. That's not instinctive; more often than not, it goes against instinct.

Perseverance conjures up my memory of the basement furnace in our home in Grand Rapids, Michigan. I could not have been more than five years old, but I remember my grandfather stoking that furnace. He'd shovel the coal onto a treadmill-like device, which fed the flame. It was a hot, dirty job, but my grandfather stuck with it until the job was done. I always admired him for keeping us warm in the dead of Michigan's winters.

The more I delve into my past, the more I see lessons that ultimately played out in my choice of career. Perseverance, sympathy for the woebegone, frugality, stubbornness, and integrity, together with an inclination to flout convention and a penchant for rigorous analysis—these qualities formed the building blocks of a successful investment strategy.

Shortcuts usually grease the rails to disappointing outcomes. Too many investors appear to believe that the way to make money in the stock market is to hop on the line that moves fastest, from a Sputnik-driven craze for electronics in the late Fifties to the tech boom in the Nineties. Indeed, a handful of stocks reward investors handsomely each time, but many vanish. Easy come, easy go.

Growing up never taught me that success comes automatically. My parents' marriage probably never had a chance. They divorced when I was four years old. My mother, born Barbara Brown in Mount Pleasant, Michigan, wed my father before finishing high school. She married him, she later confessed to me, chiefly to escape her parents. Two years later, on September 19, 1931, she had a son.

Before the marriage failed completely, we moved around some. In Detroit, my father sold automotive lubricating equipment to gas stations and repair shops. If this was my parents' plan to start fresh, it didn't work. We parted company. My mother and I went in one direction, my father in another. Fourteen years would pass before I saw him again. In one of life's bitter ironies, my mother had no place else to go but back to her parents' home in Grand Rapids, with a toddler in tow.

Our home with the basement furnace was on Madison Avenue, in Grand Rapids. My mother's father supported us there on his income as a life insurance salesman. Previously, in the Twenties and early Thirties, he had run a manufactured gas business in Mount Pleasant, Michigan, and, later, in Bryan, Ohio. This business transformed coal to gas in days before natural gas was widely available. In the Great Depression, people still needed gas for warmth and cooking, but that did not prevent the company from sinking along with many other businesses. Even sturdy utilities and, for that matter, mutual funds perished in the Depression simply because of too much debt taken on during the late Twenties. Nevertheless, thanks to my grandfather's tireless efforts to keep us afloat, the Depression left no particular impression on me. We lived reasonably well all the time in Grand Rapids, amid its strong Dutch and Polish communities. That didn't particularly help me, however. Neff is a German name.

Eventually, we moved to neighboring East Grand Rapids, an upscale suburb. I attended the first and second grades in an East Grand Rapids school about two miles from our home. A fire hydrant six houses up the street divided Grand Rapids from East Grand Rapids. This municipal boundary prevented me from going to a perfectly good school closer to home. Even then I habitually compared and analyzed alternatives.

Miss Fritz, who lived nearby, taught first grade. Thanks to her comment on my report card, I learned the meaning of "pugnacious" at an early age. I was never inclined to back down from an argument, even when confronted by the mantle of authority. My mother, in fact, used to claim that I ought to be a lawyer because I would argue with a signpost. She was probably right. In the long run, I did the better thing; I argued with the stock market.

My grandfather took my absent father's place in our household until he became ill in 1939. I was in second grade when he died. Afterward, my mother, my grandmother, and I moved to Mount Pleasant, Michigan, in the center of the state. We were not completely without resources, thanks to modest savings and some life insurance proceeds. Unfortunately, my grandmother did not invest her nest egg wisely. She used a portion of my grandfather's estate—maybe all of it—to set up her son, my Uncle Dodds, in the supermarket business.

Of Entrepreneurial Stock

I grew up in a family of entrepreneurs. Uncle Dodds was not the first in my family, on either side, to start a business. John George Neff, born 1834 from good old Pennsylvania stock, dating back to the colonial period, taught for a time before taking up work in a brickyard. In short order, he bought the brickyard—maybe a very early leveraged buyout, if he borrowed the money to pay for it. After generating enough income to breed horses and purchase a genteel homestead in 1873, John George sold the business to his sons, including my great-grandfather Benjamin Franklin Neff. These three brothers operated the brick factory near Bryan, Ohio.

My mother's aunt and uncle, surnamed Plumb, were successful entrepreneurs. They formed a chain of supermarkets in and around Grand Rapids back in the Thirties, when this form of retailing was in its infancy. It was called Food City, and I still remember those stores from my own childhood. They weren't great big supermarkets by today's standards. As a matter of fact, they weren't much larger than a modern deli department. When prices and promotions changed, a sign painter arrived. I would watch him paint specials on the window. The flourish he applied to the price of celery was amazing. Besides an opportunity to see an artist at work, or the closest approximation in my neighborhood, bargain shopping made a lasting impression on me. I've never bought a stock unless, in my view, it was on sale.

My mother worked as a secretary for Wolverine Spice, a wholesaler owned by Food City. Uncle Dodds managed a grocery store in the Food City chain. That's where Dodds got his training in the grocery business. But before he got his chance to run Food City, my great-aunt and great-uncle split the company in half, taking a few stores in western Michigan and leaving the Grand Rapids locations to their partners. Eventually, in the early Sixties, their son sold the shares for cash to Allied Supermarkets, a Detroit supermarket chain. Cash was a wise choice; Allied eventually went bankrupt. Meantime, Dodds apparently approached my grandmother about providing start-up money for a store of his own, and she complied. Any success was short-lived. It's hard to say whether the business started to slide and Dodds started to drink, or vice versa. In the end, the sequence did not matter. Dodds succumbed to alcohol, the company went bankrupt, and three more lessons were impressed upon me at a young age: (1) when it comes to money, emotional attachment can fool you; (2) just because a company is down it is not always a wise investment, and (3) excessive drinking was not a business or a personal virtue.

Though I was the product of a broken home, I never knew it. Tireless efforts by my mother and grandmother fostered a very comfortable atmosphere insofar as I could tell. Thanks to their unflagging support, my self-confidence flourished along with behavior that earned a demerit for poor self-control in the fifth grade. My inclination to flout convention in later years probably reflects how well my grandmother and mother preserved it in our fatherless household. In any event, not having lived for very long with my father, I grew up scarcely conscious of his absence.

As for a father figure in the household, Uncle Dodds in his own way helped fill the gap. We shared a fascination with maps, many of which he provided, and, together, we mulled the significance of the 1940 census. To this day, I remember that the 1940 population of Grand Rapids was 164,592. Uncle Dodds showed me how to find exotic cities. Locating Budapest, for some reason, was a marvelous revelation. On Saturdays, 11 cents bought a ticket to the movies. For the price of admission, we'd see one or two short comedies and at least a couple of shoot-'em-up westerns with Gene Autry or Roy Rogers. They stumbled into a mess every time. Dire as their predicaments became, they always wriggled out.

On two occasions in grammar school, the stock market came into view. I have no idea why, but we studied the stock market in the sixth grade at McKinley Grade School in Bay City, Michigan. It was just one of many special projects. (We also studied Alaska with the same ardor, but I haven't been to Alaska yet.) The more active exposure occurred even earlier, while I was a fifth grader in Grand Rapids. During recess that school year, we participated in the usual array of activities: tag, tossing baseballs, and the like. Once in a while, we traded baseball cards. Because the cards were in short supply, bidding for the most desirable cards could go sky-high—three, four, or five cards in exchange for one! Total mania on the playground ensued. It was the strangest thing, very bizarre. As the cards became a form of currency, emotional momentum gripped us all. One person bid in the expectation he could sell it to someone else for a higher price. Here I was in the fifth grade, and the temptation to overpay seemed obvious. It has stuck with me, ever after, that the cards that enjoyed the biggest runups eventually tumbled the farthest. Maybe not right away, but usually sooner rather than later.

Besides the few sketchy details of the first lesson in markets that I can remember, I also recall a fascination with the prospects for earning money without having to actually work—or so it seemed. You had to figure out which baseball cards were going to attract the most attention, and buy them before the crowd. More amazing still, going after an out-of-favor card sometimes generated the buzz that made it valuable. This, at any rate, was something to think about on predawn paper routes and other odd jobs that garnered my spending money. From the age of 11, I earned all my own spending money and bought my own clothes.

Around the time I finished fifth grade, in 1941, my mother met an entrepreneurial Texan named Jim Hutton. After a two-week courtship, they married and we moved to Tawas City, then Bay City, and then again to Detroit. Jim had kicked around in the oil fields in Michigan, where he involved himself in a bidding process for winning royalty rights under prospective future oil wells. At the time, this was very mysterious and somewhat alluring to me. He'd go out and bargain with the farmers and landowners for permission to explore their land. If he bought a stake, he could keep it or sell it to someone else, at least in theory. Or he could wait for the land to be drilled and possibly discover oil. In practice, however, his ship never came in. Instead, he ended up taking defense jobs that were plentiful, if not well paying, during the World War II years, when wage levels were frozen.

During the summer of 1944, I caddied by day and delivered papers at night. I took home $40 a week—not a bad wage for a twelve-year-old. I earned almost as much as adults who worked full time on assembly lines. Caddying at the exclusive Detroit Golf Club meant carrying clubs and advising golfers now and then for local personalities, including Mayor Jeffries of Detroit. I also caddied occasionally for Edgar Guest, the first syndicated poet in many newspapers—and maybe the last one, for all I know. I wouldn't have thought poetry could cover the tab for membership, but he managed to play lots of golf. He was a cheery guy to accompany for a loop, which is what we called 18 holes, but not generous when it came to tips. A quarter was a good loop and 50 cents was very good. Once in a great while, I got 75 cents or a dollar, but never from Edgar Guest.*

A larger thrill awaited me. When golfer Gene Sarazen played the course, I caddied for an amateur in his foursome. This was just nine years after Sarazen secured a tie in the Masters Tournament by belting a legendary 235-yard fairway shot that landed in the cup for a double eagle. I still recall the smoothness of his swing, whether he was driving half the length of a par five or lofting the ball toward a nearby green.

Eventually, my stepfather's home state exerted an irresistible tug. To Jim, Texas was the Promised Land, so, in November 1944, we moved to Corpus Christi, where he planned to continue to seek his fortune. How or why he picked Corpus Christi I don't know. He was from the middle of the state, around Waco, where his family had a ranch. We auctioned off what we couldn't cart south on our small trailer, including some of my prized belongings. Although I put my toys and games on display in our basement, they attracted no customers. As a consequence, I had to give them away—a harsh, early lesson in market dynamics.

We headed by car for Texas, nonstop. When we reached Corpus Christi, we took up temporary residence in a motel while waiting for a developer to finish construction on our somewhat modest three-bedroom house (purchased for all of $5,500) on the city's outskirts.

The Iceman Cometh

In high school, I worked in a convenience store with an icehouse attached. The icehouse held cakes of ice that I would pop into an enormous grinder to produce shredded ice, which we'd sell, mainly for picnics. When the owner left for one reason or another, he put me in charge of the business. I was cashier, stock clerk, and bottle washer. I also deboned fish, and, in addition to my lavish pay of 50 cents an hour, the owner gave me all I could eat, including ice cream. It was a good deal.

My real father was completely out of my life. Only his mother, a librarian in Bryan, Ohio, stayed in touch. She sent me a book on Christmas and a book on my birthday. The *Complete Book of Marvels*, written by

---

* At a Chrysler board meeting in the summer of 1998, I was invited to a dinner given in honor of two retiring directors, Bob Lutz and Tom Denname, at Bloomfield Hills Country Club. Somebody asked me if I'd ever played the course. No, I said. The last time I played golf in Detroit was in 1944, when caddies were allowed to play on Mondays.

adventurer Richard Halliburton,* was my version of *Star Wars*. I must have read it a dozen times; each new reading tapped into my youthful wanderlust and transported me to realms more exotic than central Michigan or East Texas. Inviting his audience to join him on his travels, Halliburton expressed perfectly my adolescent state of mind:

> Dear reader,
>
> When I was a boy in school my favorite subject was geography, and my prize possession my geography book. This book was filled with pictures of the world's most wonderful cities and mountains and temples, and had big maps to show where they were. I loved that book because it carried me away to all the strange and romantic lands. I read about the Egyptian pyramids, and India's marble towers, about the great cathedrals of France, and the ruins of ancient Babylon. The stories of such things always set me to dreaming, to yearning for the actual sight and touch of these wonders.
>
> Sometimes I pretended I had a magic carpet, and without bothering about tickets and money and farewells, I'd skyrocket away to New York or to Rome, to the Grand Canyon or to China, across deserts and oceans and mountains, then suddenly come back home when the school bell rang for recess.
>
> I often said to myself: "I wish my father, or somebody, would take me to all these wonderful places. What good are they if you can't see them?"

In due course, Jim assumed my real father's place, though globe trotting beyond the midwest was not a part of our agenda. He never made much of a success of himself until after I left home in 1949, but he worked very hard whenever he had an opportunity. Jim instilled in me a work ethic. He was a good man, firm in his ways—which was inconvenient at times. We could not utter a sound during Walter Winchell's radio program every Sunday evening around seven o'clock. Winchell captured world news in his distinctive manner. Every program started off the same way: "Good evening, Mr. and Mrs. North and South America and all the ships at sea. Let's go to press!" Then there would be this rat-a-tat-tat kind of delivery, one bulletin after another. You could hear him turn over the news scripts he read from. Jim would not permit a sound when Winchell was on the air, as if we were listening to the voice of God. In his waning years, this voice of God took to hawking stocks of dubious quality.

---

* Richard Halliburton, *Complete Book of Marvels*, Bobbs-Merrill (1941), Indianapolis, 316 pages.

I loved the radio. In high school, I could seldom listen to a teacher for more than ten minutes without my thoughts wandering. I never entirely fit in, though I never felt my peers looked down on me. Besides a mild case of social ineptness, I was not a very accomplished student. My northern voice sounded unique, I was told. It had a high-pitch but I could project well. I can remember being on some local radio shows and dramatizations. I read announcements at Corpus Christi high school, the only high school in a metropolitan area with, in those days, a population of 120,000.

As a naval installation and seaside resort during the war years, Corpus Christi was a bit different from more remote Texas backwaters. Year-round mild weather and six or seven naval air stations meant sailors were in view at all times. In school, being a Yankee caused me no real grief, although schoolmates who noted my Yankee accent tagged me with a peculiar moniker: "Brooklyn." As a means of escape, listening to radio was superb. How vividly, how successfully, I formed images conveyed by the sound of a voice. I could listen hour after hour, and often did. Those images weren't spoon-fed like car chases in action movies. Left to the mind's eye, *Mystery Theatre* cast a spell on me. But I was a sucker for movies, too, and saw them as often as I could slip away.

My mother would have liked me to be theatrical, and she tried to bake into me a flair for performance. San Antonio was the "big city" if you lived in Corpus Christi, and I remember going there one time with Jim, my mother, and my half-sister Heidi to see skater Sonja Henie give an exhibition.

My mother was a big movie fan. Subscriptions to *PhotoPlay* brought new issues regularly for many years, and my mother rarely missed the chance to get me to listen to Jimmy Fiddler, a popular Hollywood radio reporter in the Forties. He followed Winchell on Sunday nights. My own extroversion has surfaced since, but in high school I was backward socially and a little shy. I was not motivated to perform, except now and then when someone suggested I might not be up to a challenge. I finished in the second 25 percent of the class, not a distinguished record by any stretch. By then, I was on the way to becoming what I am today: an amalgam of Michigan substance and Texas b.s.

With no lingering appetite for Corpus Christi or for more schooling, the day after graduation I hopped a Greyhound bus back to Grand Rapids, where I still had family and, more importantly, my most enduring memories.

3

~

BASIC TRAINING

FROM THE GREYHOUND bus station in Grand Rapids, I headed straight for the apartment doorstep of my great-aunt Lou, my maternal grandfather's sister. She and her husband, Al Plumb, the Michigan supermarket owners, took me in, but not for very long.

That they took me in at all probably reflected my Aunt Lou's relentless determination to pump me for family gossip. For this purpose, I was the perfect pigeon, despite my mother's coaching to keep my mouth shut in matters concerning, and especially not concerning, Aunt Lou. But you can't fight human nature. Straight as an arrow, and always inclined to share my opinion, I replied in dutiful fashion to all inquiries from older members of my family. This quickly worked to my detriment. Aunt Lou squeezed all she could learn from me almost before I had a chance to sit down in her richly appointed, and somewhat stuffy, Victorian living room. After that, my days—two days, to be precise—with Aunt Lou and Uncle Al were numbered.

After a lapse of some five years, and just two days after finishing high school, I sought shelter with these maternal relatives. My presence could not have been a hardship. The Plumbs were as near to manor-born as anyone on either side of my family. They had servants, who were summoned to the dinner table by a bell. I slept in a spare bedroom meant for a maid.

Uncle Al had started in the hardware business in upstate Michigan with his father in the early 1890s. Three years later, they barely survived the panic of 1893, an inflection point of note that helped fuel the great conflict between mostly Republican advocates of the gold standard and William Jennings Bryan's free-silver Democrats. This was the issue that culminated in Bryan's famous speech at the 1896 Democratic convention, where he railed against crucifying Americans on a cross of gold. He lost, the Democrats lost, and the gold standard prevailed. I don't think anyone was crucified. For me, in any event, Uncle Al represented a link to that frantic period in 1893 when markets succumbed to groupthink. Similar patterns of mass behavior have precipitated inflection points time and again in my own career. Each time, they have created lucrative investment opportunities.

After a couple of nights with the Plumbs, they deposited me on the steps of the Grand Rapids YMCA. My room at the Y, though hardly spacious, was larger than my accommodation at the Plumbs. I found it entirely pleasant, notwithstanding a morals raid that nabbed two denizens of my floor after I had been there a while. Those were days when local authorities considered it their business to pursue homosexuals.

Except for this interruption, calm prevailed at the Y. It housed a large group of students attending a nearby for-profit business school, Davenport by name, in downtown Grand Rapids. There were a couple of dozen classrooms and no dormitories, so the Y served that purpose. They were all contemporaries and dedicated to finding careers—all in all, a good atmosphere for me.

Next door to the Y, a city library became my new home. I read the paper there every day, and along with news of the Korean Conflict, then heating up, a small business section began to catch my eye. I went job hunting in 1949, just as the economy was suffering its first postwar recession—not what one would call great timing. Far from anticipating the bountiful decades that followed, employers in those days were bracing for the Depression to resume. Images of unemployed factory workers and bread lines were still etched in their memories.

I eventually encountered Carl Hartmann and, later, Eugene Christenson, nicknamed "Chris" or sometimes "Swede." Both attended Grand Rapids Junior College about two blocks from the Y. I could hardly talk to girls without tripping over my words, but Carl was well versed. He was a few years older and possessed measures of social maturity that I lacked, at least on the dating circuit. Carl had already served a stint in the military and regaled anyone who would listen with tales of his military experience. He introduced me to a girl and even lent me his car for our date in greater Grand Rapids. On several occasions, he invited me for a weekend trip to his home, about 40 miles away. His two married sisters urged me to spend more time in the company of girls.

Nothing was more foreign to me in those days than the investment business. While some of my contemporaries were being educated at fancy business colleges, I was learning about money at the other end of the spectrum. The Y manager hired me to tend the basement soda fountain and snack bar several nights a week. Billiards and a Ping-Pong table drew an audience at the steep price of 60 cents an hour. Meantime, I'd sell sandwiches and mix milkshakes. Carl had a girlfriend who worked in the cafeteria next door, and she often hit me up for news of the errant Carl. I'd learned my lesson from Aunt Lou: Loose Lips Sink Ships. Carl's girlfriend got no information from me.

Carl and I, together with two Davenport students from upstate Michigan, moved out of the Y and into an apartment together. When school ended, the students fled, and I moved back to the Y. That's when I met Chris, who offered a steady diet of object lessons in the folly of reckless living. Chris lived a bit too high on the hog for someone of his modest means. Though charismatic, he followed a perilous course, constantly in debt and scrambling to keep afloat.

A promoter by nature, Chris sold new and used cars. But a paycheck did not prevent him from falling behind in his rent to the Y. That was Chris—entertaining and usually broke. I lost track of Carl, but crossed paths with Chris from time to time. He remained a promoter. In the Sixties, he toured the country with a jet-powered car.

Music Man

The local employment office fixed me up with a string of temporary jobs, which I supplemented by working at the soda fountain at night. The jobs ranged from pouring cement to bottling juices. As for training for the investment business, nearly half of my income went straight into savings. Finally, I ended up at a company called American Musical Instruments, better known as AMI. It manufactured jukeboxes, a very popular item in that era when pop music was coming to the fore but phonographs were scarce. I started as a shipping clerk.

Jukeboxes were marvelous inventions. They were colorful, their parts rotated, lights flashed. As a clerk, I showed promise. I also grew bored very rapidly. Though I expressed a preference for a more challenging position with a shot at advancement, my requests fell on deaf ears. Because no one showed any inclination to confer a promotion on me, I skipped a couple of days of work to sell an encyclopedia door to door. In two days, I found enough prospects to resign my post at AMI. They said, "Not so fast" and offered me a more challenging job—this time, with some career potential. Over the next few months, I rotated through several different areas of the business, including the machine shop where parts were manufactured and the assembly line where the jukeboxes were assembled. Without so much as a college degree, I felt good about my prospects in the music business. And, true to my frugal nature, while earning $60 a week I was leaving almost half of it in the bank.

My new life on a factory floor took an unexpected turn when, after about nine months at AMI, my father reappeared. I had not seen him since I was four years old, and, as a practical matter, lacked even a scant memory of him. Our only contact in the interim was a watch he sent me for high school graduation.

After learning from my mother of my situation in Grand Rapids, he wanted to make amends with the son he had parted company with 14 years earlier. Maybe his concern had to do with failure to provide child support part of that time. He never explained that lapse; I could only surmise that he figured my mother's parents could afford to take my mother and me in, and it's likely there was some animosity too. My mother took frequent opportunities to stress that he owed me all that money. I was not sure that life with father would suit me at that juncture, and neither was my mother. She arrived in Grand Rapids the same time my father did, to broker any deal likely to affect the course of my life.

My mother carefully orchestrated the reunion. I spoke with my father by phone, but didn't see him until all three of us met one evening for dinner. If there was bitterness or anger, it was not obvious to me. But I had heard many times from my mother about my father's drinking problem. He seemed to be one of those hard-driven drinkers who felt better about himself when he drank. Apparently, others liked him better also. By all accounts, he could be quite entertaining after a few drinks. He enjoyed recalling one famous binge that landed him in Philadelphia's annual Mummer's Day parade on New Year's Day.

For all his flaws, my father, John F. Neff, was a very intelligent and perceptive man, and an excellent salesman. He knew how to appeal to my entrepreneurial zeal, just surfacing at AMI. For my part, I was intrigued with the prospects of joining Neff Equipment, a company I could reasonably expect to run some day, which was how he pitched the proposal. There were entrepreneurs on both sides of my family, so I guess it rubbed off on me in some fashion. Before I leaped, however, my cautious nature intervened. I paid a visit to Toledo, where I met my second family.

My half-sister Judy, then about 10 years old, enjoyed discovering an older brother. My stepmother was somewhat less enthusiastic. As the legacy of his first marriage, I was a possible rival for my father's attention. She and my father were married in 1938, five years after my parents split up. He was drinking much of the time, and she kept him from going off the deep end. In 1945, he received a small inheritance after the death of my grandmother (the librarian in Bryan, Ohio, who had sent me books throughout my childhood). He sobered up, joined AA, and put the cash to work in a new business that distributed lubrication equipment and air couplings manufactured by Aro Equipment, a company my grandmother's brother had started in 1931. Though closely held by some of my Neff cousins, its shares were traded in New York on the Curb Exchange, the hurly-burly forerunner of the American Stock Exchange.

I elected to cast my lot with my father. I returned to Grand Rapids long enough to pack my bags and give notice at AMI. Losing me was not the worst thing that ever happened to the company, even though I'd give a full day's work for a day's pay. We said farewell on good terms. I didn't want to burn that bridge, just in case life with father did not live up to expectations.

In September 1950, I started work for my father's company, Neff Equipment Co. Meanwhile, he exchanged his two-bedroom house for a three bedroom model, just to give me a place to stay. Obligation might have been a motive, but perhaps not the most important one. I was his only son, and as his business flourished, he was thinking about posterity.

The business did well because automobile dealers, service stations, and auto repair shops all needed air compressors to drive lubrication equipment, lifts, pneumatic tools, and the like. With cars proliferating, there was no shortage of demand. Thanks to my father's talented salesmanship, we also began selling equipment to farmers in Ohio and just across the border in Michigan. In a real coup, he bid on and snared sales contracts from Rossford Ordnance, a U.S. Government procurement facility near Toledo. When the Korean Conflict heated up, Rossford stepped up its demand for compressors and other industrial equipment that my father was glad to sell to them.

I accompanied my father and his two other salesmen on sales calls. He was persuasive. He seldom left a customer without an order—if not for a big-ticket compressor, then maybe for an attachment or a fitting that secured attachments to the compressors. When urgent calls came in, I jumped on the truck with my Uncle Jack, who handled installation and maintenance. One time, we delivered a compressor to Tecumseh Products in Tecumseh, Michigan. We got top dollar because they needed it right away.

Working for my father at least taught me that you don't need glamour to make a buck. Indeed, if you can find a dull business that makes money, it is less likely to attract competition. Also, merchandise well bought was merchandise well sold. He bargained with his suppliers for several discounts off list, which placed him in a good cost position with his customers. Using much the same bargaining prowess years later, I was able to negotiate friendly prices for stocks.

I was not cut out, however, to sell lubricating equipment. The novelty soon wore off and aggravations increased, chiefly because of my father. I was probably not the easiest of sons to deal with, admittedly. But he was a difficult man. Over the slightest infractions, he harangued people who worked hard for him. His behavior did not fit my definition of civility. Though ethical and honest, at the same time he was extremely demanding and not especially sympathetic. To some degree, I inherited his tendency to be demanding. I can be difficult. But my father was not very happy, and bitterness added sting to his demands.

It took me a while to work up enough gumption to quit. To my amazement, he accepted the news well. In fact, I continued to live with him while working as a new car salesman, a job I found through the local newspaper. Lee Motors, a Ford dealership owned by the Tank Brothers, presumably recognized in me a mix of inexperienced exuberance and the ability to be educated. When I approached, they recognized a promising neophyte, and I got to sell a product I could relate to somewhat better than lubricating equipment.

I was draft age, however, and, for the war going on in Korea, I was top-drawer draft bait. Before the Selective Service called my name, I volunteered for a 24-month stint in the Navy. Having served in my high school's Naval Reserve unit, signing up for real service was fine with me—and certainly more appealing than being in the ground troops embroiled in the Korean Conflict. My naval enlistment affected my father more visibly than either my decision to join his company or to leave it. It seemed the height of irony that when I took leave of the man who had not seen me for 14 years without much evidence of regret, he wept over my departure. He implored me not to join the submarine service, and in that I complied. He never explained his aversion to submarines. I guess he was claustrophobic.

Before I embarked, he made me a memorable offer. If I would purchase publicly traded shares of Aro Equipment, he would make good on any loss. I was no stock market wizard, but even I could recognize an offer too good to refuse. I gathered up my savings and bought shares of Aro Equipment. On my way to join the Navy, I became a participant in the stock market for the first time.

I proceeded to naval boot camp in Great Lakes, Illinois, a naval base with the distinction of being remote from both oceans. It also had a golf course and access to Chicago for the one liberty we were granted after finishing boot camp. This phase, including airman's school, lasted five months before the Navy, in its wisdom, shipped me off to an aviation electronics technicians' school, where I squeaked by in lackluster fashion. I actually flunked a portion of the twenty-eight-week program and spent a week repeating it. Finishing uncomfortably close to the bottom of my class, I collected the booby prize: assignment to Norfolk, Virginia, along with 40,000 or so other sailors. There was no love lost between the Norfolk community and the cadres of aimless young men in sailor uniforms. An apocryphal sign—often talked about, but I never saw it—warned sailors and dogs to keep off the lawn in the city park.

Having distinguished myself so indifferently in aviation electronics, the Navy saw fit to enroll me next in the advanced aviation electronics technicians' school. So much for military intelligence, a famous oxymoron.

By the time I completed advanced aviation electronics technicians' training, I'd spent the better part of a year in classrooms. That, plus boot camp and airman's school, consumed about 14 months of a 24-month enlistment. The Navy put my education, such as it was, to work by assigning me to a fleet carrier air group. We maintained Corsairs, a gull-wing fighter plane from the Second World War, but the Navy was replacing them with an early generation of fighter jets called Panthers. As it turned out, I spent the rest of my military career in Jacksonville, Florida, working first with the propeller-driven Corsairs, and eventually with the Panthers. By the time I was fully qualified to service a Panther, I was mustered out. During 24 months in the Navy, I never got on board a ship.

The Navy paid us every two weeks, and the first night after payday six or seven poker games sprang up. By the following night, there were only one or two poker games. Much like money in the stock market, poker money migrated to the most proficient and well financed players, a group that usually included me. Observing occasionally, I noted how sailors who ultimately went home with cash in their pockets played consistently and with good knowledge of the odds. They were not lured into action for big pots unless the numbers were on their side. If those sailors applied the same philosophy to stocks, some of them are successful investors today.

Common or Preferred?

Somehow I acquired a booklet on investing, and long hours of lollygagging between work details gave me plenty of time to peruse it. I read about common stock and preferred stock. Without any indication whether my Aro Equipment stock was common or preferred, I wrote to my father and asked which type I owned. I owned common shares, which, I learned, rise and fall in price with the company's performance. This was my introduction to the theory and reality of how shareholders garner the lion's share of potential rewards, as well as the risks of loss.

My nascent interest in stocks marked the earliest sign of my investment career, although the outcome was still far from obvious to me or to anyone else. At the same time, it was abundantly clear that a combination of frequent boredom and tongue-lashing from boatswain mates made a military career untenable. To avoid similar experiences in civilian life, I finally figured out that it was time to give college a try. In this spirit, I enrolled in two correspondence courses offered by the United States Armed Forces Institute, better known as USAFI. My quick grasp of freshman English and an introduction to psychology emboldened me to think I might succeed in college, despite my undistinguished academic track record in high school. One weekend, a buddy and I hitchhiked from Norfolk to nearby William & Mary College, which administered college aptitude tests. The results left little doubt that I could handle college.

Discharged in January 1953, and elated to be free again, I drove from Jacksonville, Florida, to Toledo in twenty-four hours. Three days later, I was a college student at the University of Toledo and living, for the second time, in my father's house. The GI Bill picked up the tab for tuition and some living expenses, and selling shoes in a top-drawer haberdashery brought in additional income. For 30 hours a week, on top of a full academic load, I was a shoe-dog. This job had two excellent benefits: I could buy shoes and other menswear at a friendly price, and my employer allowed me to study when I wasn't selling or stocking shelves. I could usually put about one-half of this time toward reading and studies.

Meantime, I met Lillian Tulac, of Hungarian descent. I was less tongue-tied by then, and succeeded in stealing her attention away from a professional Triple-A baseball player, among other suitors. We managed to overcome some differences about religious faith. Lilli is a devout Catholic; as plans proceeded for a wedding, it turned out that I was never baptized. Baptism is just a procedural matter, of course. We could have addressed that. But I had larger doubts. Some things have to be taken strictly on faith, particularly religion. I couldn't quite bring myself to that. Nevertheless, we dated for 12 months before becoming engaged, and were married in September 1954.

I Meet a Mentor

An inventory of my skills on entering college revealed a relentless curiosity, facility with numbers, an ability to express myself, and firm self-discipline. Although I finished high school awash in ordinary grades, college became a lark. My grades rarely fell below an A, and I was graduated summa cum laude, with highest honors. The sharp contrast with earlier academic experience, so far as I could tell, lay in a degree of maturity, motivation, and courses that sparked my interest—especially two taught by Sidney Robbins, professor of finance and investment.

Dr. Robbins had come to the University of Toledo from New York's Columbia University. He was a confirmed disciple of Benjamin Graham and David Dodd, deans of the school of fundamental analysis. Eventually, Dr. Robbins returned to Columbia, where he finished his academic career. So devoted was he to finance education that he preferred writing about investment opportunities to speculating. Back in the Thirties, he stumbled on a few issues of perpetual warrants—the right to buy stock at any time in the future at a fixed price. Ordinarily, warrants come with expiration dates. But in the Depression's bleak market, companies had to stretch the rules to attract fresh capital. An investor who owns one of these warrants today (if any still exist) could purchase the stock for a price target set sixty years ago, or sell the warrant at a price that would reflect future price expectations for the stock. Provided the issuer survived the Depression, it's a safe bet that its perpetual warrants would carry a hefty premium today. Although Robbins immediately spotted this value, instead of buying all the perpetual warrants he could gather up, he wrote about them for *Barron's*.

My major in college was Industrial Marketing. By accepting credits for my time spent in Navy classrooms, the program left me free to take courses that appealed to me. An interest in stocks drew me to Professor Robbins's investment course. This was where the fundamentals of investing were revealed to me: sales, earnings, operating profits, cash flow—you name it and Sidney Robbins taught it. His enthusiasm and his profound understanding of investment attracted me to his mentoring. And he persuaded me that membership in the professional investment community is not necessarily confined to wealthy offspring of elite families.

A more engaging introduction to finance and investment is impossible to imagine. Not unlike his mentor, Ben Graham, a playwright in addition to his legendary investment credentials, Dr. Robbins entertained a broad range of interests. In the middle of presentations about finance, diversions carried him in other directions. We'd end a class sometimes as crammed with information about the Apollo Theatre in Harlem or about Gilbert and Sullivan as with new insight about cash flow. Stunningly, it was all-consuming.

Thanks to a full course load for 24 straight months, plus some service credits, I completed my undergraduate degree in two years. Although I took only two courses related to finance and investment, both from Dr. Robbins, I collected the school's award as outstanding student of finance. Toledo offered scarce opportunity, however, for an ambitious young man seeking a place in the stock business. I might have worked for Electric Autolite, which manufactured components for Chrysler, or for half a dozen smaller auto parts suppliers populating the Toledo area. On the strength of Sidney Robbins's encouragement and his connections on Wall Street at Bache & Company, I headed east, to New York.

4

~

BANKER'S HOURS

NO ONE ON Wall Street was clamoring for my services in January 1955, so I accepted an offer to join National City Bank in Cleveland. Besides its virtues as Cleveland's most prominent financial institution, the Bank was a lot closer to Toledo, Lilli's hometown.

Armed with my native skepticism, the teachings of Sidney Robbins, and a dog-eared copy of *The Great Crash*, John Kenneth Galbraith's engaging account of events leading up to the 1929 market meltdown, I marched into the professional investment arena more full of myself than full of ideas. The Bank put me to work as a securities analyst in its Trust Investment Department, a unit formed in the depths of the Depression to safeguard personal and corporate assets against erosion.

No sooner had I arrived than the department threw six new industries in my path. The Bank had only six analysts, so we divided the investment universe by six. Almost before I could find my way to the watercooler, I was expected to render intelligent assessments of the chemical industry, the drug industry, the auto and auto parts industries, the rubber industry, and banks and finance companies. Delving into this wide span of American industry gave me an ideal background that served me well through my career. This was open season for learning about the investment process—so open, in fact, that credit files and investment files sat within reach of each other. Before banks had to install so-called "firewalls" to keep inside information from leaking out, all that prevented us from capitalizing on this information were the ethical standards each of us had been weaned on.

To say I loved my new challenge would understate my enthusiasm. After kicking around aimlessly, I had hit the jackpot on the career chart. Every detail fascinated me. Autos came easiest. I had always had sympathy for four-wheeled creations. My father was a car nut, so I guess the affinity was in my genes. Early in 1955, car making was a good industry in America, and it commanded attention from Wall Street and from regulators. FTC and Justice Department officials were worried that General Motors was too big and dominant, according to a headline in *The Wall Street Journal*. A few days later, the giant auto maker launched a $525 million stock offering.

Chemical and drug companies were tougher to analyze than car companies. I didn't have a great background in science. I had taken chemistry and physics in high school, but not a hint of science in college. To overcome being stone cold in that area, I studied chemicals, product mixes, and polyvinyl chlorides and their precursors. I indulged my hunger for details and emerged quite comfortable about dealing with chemical processing. All this nitty-gritty can have a pronounced impact on stock price. Chemicals, in those days, were considered growth industries, and their stock prices fetched price–earnings ratios higher than the market's average.

Technology was not and never became my strongest suit. But after untold hours spent immersed in annual reports and other records of performance that emphasized remote details, I got the hang of technological companies. Besides poring over financial reports, I studied trade publications, and even a few technical manuals, in an effort to understand the processes that drove these businesses. The information sank in, apparently. During a tour of Eastman Kodak, when it was still an important chemical company with many products other than those used to develop photographic film, I peppered the guide with questions. "Well," said one of the executives accompanying us, "you obviously have a degree in chemical engineering." I took it as a compliment.

My first year at the Bank exposed me to lesson after lesson about what constitutes a sound company strategy. But that wasn't all I learned. A trip to Ford inadvertently nurtured my ambition to become more than a securities analyst. On my first tour of a Ford engine plant, a veteran auto analyst was to accompany me. He arrived in a dilapidated car that hardly belonged on the road. In his dotage, I realized, he could not afford a better car than mine.

A Wobbly First Step

Let it be on record that my first market call as a professional investor was wrong. About six weeks after I had started, I became edgy about stock prices. After a whopping 45 percent advance in 1954, the mighty Dow Jones Industrial Average looked—to me, anyway—too high and headed for a fall. Others took heart from the market's resilient recovery after the scary slide in January, but I failed to share their optimism. A series of new highs looked a bit frothy to me, despite news reports that steel, aluminum, rubber, petroleum, and shoe company officials (covering most of the important industries then) were projecting healthy growth ahead. I warned my boss to brace for a sharp reversal, or what I would later call an inflection point.

As a newly minted securities analyst, my voice did not carry much weight. No one scrambled to adjust the portfolios we managed. Lucky for me. Had someone said, "Okay, John, what should we do?" I'd have drawn a blank. I had no strategy to recommend. Happily for everyone, my warning went unheeded. Without faltering again in 1955, the market continued its upward swing and ended the year up more than 17 percent. The Dow Jones Industrials finished 1955 at 488.4, a record level.

Rescued from embarrassment by judgment that was more penetrating if not wiser than mine, I stormed up the learning curve with redoubled enthusiasm. Using every source available, I devoured information in search of fresh market insights. What a time it was for new inventions, new ideas, new trends. In the mid-1950s, nearly every day brought news of something that had not been seen before, from General Electric's first studio for color telecasting to Scripto's "liquid lead pencil," the forerunner of ballpoint pens.

Average daily trading volume zoomed during my first year on the job. True, it amounted to only a fraction of the daily activity now, but, in those days, record-setting trading activity marked investing as a growth industry—a far cry from the desperate doldrums that stretched back to the Depression era. Trading days had arrived as investors abandoned a mentality that stressed income and preservation of capital over capital gain. Of ten stocks that comprised the Big Board's most active list on February 1, 1955, the first day of my first full month in the business, shares of only three are still traded now: American Airlines,

General Dynamics, and Exxon-Mobil (known then as Standard Oil of New Jersey). The latter two, I might add, have changed dramatically through mergers, acquisitions, and divestitures. The rest of the stocks on that day's most active list have either merged with larger companies or disappeared altogether. Radio Corporation of America, the most prominent, was later sold to General Electric. Others included Hupp Corporation, Chance Vought Aircraft, and two railroads, Pennsylvania Railroad and Chicago Minnesota St. Paul & Pacific.

As for American Bosch, the most active stock on the first day of February 1955, a mere 225,000 shares traded hands amid total volume of 3.5 million shares. Although minimal by today's standards, the volume was enough to tax that era's fairly primitive investment technology. We had no quotron machines or any other desktop means of instant market access. So we would go to lunch and stop in at Bache & Company, a local branch of the New York investment firm. All kinds of flotsam and jetsam hung out in the "peanut gallery," as we called it; you could always find someone dozing in one of the chairs. Still, this was a marked improvement over market information methods when I was in Toledo, an even more remote backwater. To post the ticker-tape prices in full view, chalkers would walk around the room erasing the earlier entries and substituting the new prices for traded stocks. Most chalkers, not surprisingly, were attractive young women whose dimensions made keeping tabs on stock prices a pleasant task.

At the bank, I started doing statistical sheets, which resembled Value Line reports but had considerably more data. Information was not as varied or comprehensive as the financial printouts are nowadays, but we would dig out information and report it. There was no source other than our own legwork, but by building a statistical sheet, we could create a company's past record. It was arduous and painstaking labor but it yielded superb training. Even today, I can't think of a better way to start to understand a company's performance than by poring over its results with pencil and paper.

Natural Questions

As we studied companies close-up, questions naturally occurred, so we would call on management and ask the same kinds of questions that I ask now: Why is the margin deteriorating? Why are administrative expenses rising faster than sales? Why is the dividend payout ratio slipping?

Answers to questions were not always readily apparent. On the strength of a final quarter in 1954, the chief executive of U.S. Industries had proclaimed a bright future. Not bright enough, it turned out. Two decades later, U.S. Industries became one of my worst disappointments at Windsor. A later chief executive was promising prosperity ahead when I sold Windsor's last shares in 1975, after losing nearly half of the investment.

Bulletins that textile maker Kayser Inc. had bought another company, Catalina, prompted Kayser's deal-hungry management to couch further plans in language that sounds familiar today. "Company officials have several times indicated that they will continue to examine new merger or acquisition possibilities," *The Wall Street Journal* reported on February 3, 1955, "with an eye to good management, good earnings records, and outstanding product names. No moves in this direction, however, are understood to be in prospect at present, although merger rumors appear to have been behind the recent wide swings in the common stock." Two decades and a few deals later, Kayser-Roth helped enhance the Windsor Fund's value.

A company called Reynolds Spring changed its name in 1955 to Consolidated Electronic Industries, a harbinger of the frothy "'tronics boom" then starting to take shape. By the late 1950s, the clamor for technology had taken full flight, in part a result of frenzied reactions to the Soviet Union's launch of Sputnik. At the boom's peak, the merest hint of electronics goods sent a stock price skyward, leading some companies to adopt names ending in variations on "tronics" for no more reason than that their machine tools ran on electricity—not unlike today's "com" speculative bubble.

It would have been out of character in those days for any department of the National City Bank to get caught up in the lure of hypergrowth. Founded 16 years before the Civil War by two veterans of The Fireman's Insurance Company, National City Bank had remained intact through more than a century of market panics and crashes. In 1933, amid thousands of bank closings nationally, it was the only bank in Cleveland that met deposit obligations with 100 cents on the dollar. Depositors in other local institutions settled, at times, for 5 cents on the dollar, and some banks simply closed their doors permanently.

A Modest Paycheck

My starting salary at the Bank was relatively modest, even by 1955 standards. In my first year as an investment professional, I pulled down a fat $4,200. (Forty-three years later, the Bank and the local newspaper paid me twice that princely sum for a morning keynote address.) Fortunately, Lilli and I were accustomed to living cheaply—though sometimes a little too cheaply for her taste. I did not endear myself to her when I insisted that she return a few wedding gifts that had no practical value to us. I remember a chafing dish was one of those casualties. Accordingly, we hung onto our savings and never invaded principal.

Although thrift now seems embedded in that idealized era, not everyone lived as we did. I always had the feeling that no one else at the Bank lived on just their salary. When we had our first child, Patrick, I had to carry Lilli up a flight of stairs to our attic apartment. Soon afterward, we bought a house (half of a duplex) for $10,200. That seemed like a good deal. By making double payments, we garnered enough equity in 1960 to buy a real house of our own, with four bedrooms and three baths.

Despite our modest circumstances, my new post exposed us a bit to the Bank's social circles. Its history intertwined with the interests and estate of Mark Hanna, a 19th-century industrialist who owned interests in mining and railroads. In the late 1930s, some years after Hanna's death, there was a phone call between the Bank's new chairman, Lewis B. Williams, and George Humphrey, an official of M. A. Hanna & Company and, later, President Eisenhower's Treasury Secretary. "Accomplish just two things and you'll never hear a word from us," Humphrey told Williams. "Increase earnings every year, and raise the dividend."[*]

Given the Bank's long heritage, socializing meant rubbing elbows with Cleveland's well-heeled upper crust. Our top executives and new hires out of college essentially belonged to that ilk, although rumor had it that the Bank's president, Sidney Congdon, educated himself after he had completed the tenth grade. With this exception (if the rumor was true), my colleagues were all to the manor born. Lilli and I obviously were not. The first neighborhood we lived in was blue-collar, and most of our neighbors were our seniors by at least 30 years. I'm sure I lacked

---

[*] "National City 150 Years: 1845–1995," No author, National City Bank, Cleveland (1995), p. 29.

some sophistication and maturity at 25 years of age, but I was educated and not shy about sharing my opinions with anyone.

Early in my tenure, our social schedule picked up—not least because I was a pretty good pitcher for the Bank's vaunted softball team—but we never made the Bank's A-list. Not that Lilli or I cared. I was not inclined to play by their rules. Instead of bankers' pin stripes, I wore sport coats.

Though arduous, work went swimmingly. My knack for investment analysis bloomed. I took in great chunks of data, put them in some sort of order, and judgments emerged. Enough were right to win a string of rapid promotions. As time passed and I became more conversant in stock selection, the Bank's stodgy trust investment committee eventually warmed to my ideas. Normally, investment reports ran an exhaustively detailed six or seven pages. But after reviewing the prospects for instant color photography, I conveyed the case for Polaroid on a single page. Much to the surprise of my colleague Bill Roe, my succinct argument won a place for it on the Bank's list of stocks approved for investment. Better yet, instant color photography took off as I had predicted, and Polaroid stock snared hefty gains. Years later, however, the stock faltered and has never quite recovered.

Meanwhile, in night school, I was pursuing a graduate degree in banking and finance from Western Reserve University, now Case Western Reserve. It took three and a half years to complete the program—almost twice as long as my undergraduate degree had required. Going to school and working for the Bank tested my energy, but I had a superb dovetailing of instructors from the academic world and from the real world. They included Federal Reserve employees and other local business leaders.

The most significant part of my education, post Sidney Robbins, was gleaned from talented cohorts at National City Bank. The Bank's investment department had surprising depth and experience. Bill Roe, who joined the Bank shortly before I did, approached investment with a shrewd and open mind.

Art Boanas, a thoughtful mentor, always brought a fresh view to investing. An economist by training, Art was brilliant and quirky and contrarian to his marrow. He came to the Bank by way of a post at the Federal Reserve. In contrast with Sidney Robbins, he assigned no particular importance to Graham & Dodd. He professed no interest in what they had to say about securities analysis, but that did not prevent him from sniffing out the kinds of investments they might have recommended.

Besides conveying his overarching economic perspective—a mix of classical economics and skeptical views of human nature—Art schooled me in the principles of contrarian investing. Given my penchant for arguing with signposts, I took rapidly to arguing with the marketplace. We fought the same intellectual battles, sometimes together and sometimes challenging each other. A genial Englishman who had patrolled the moors of Yorkshire as a teenager during World War II, Art nevertheless exemplified, for me, intellectual ruthlessness. Ideas and judgments about markets or stocks are easy to defend when they reflect prevailing opinion, but going your own way is a lonely task that pits an investor against conventional wisdom and often against his or her own inner voice. When you follow a contrarian path, Art often said, "The investment community can make you look bloody wrong." A decision will look wrong the next day if you can buy the same stock for less—the very opposite of an investor's most fundamental aspiration. But that's how it goes outside the friendly confines of received wisdom. To bolster his own confidence, Art adhered to a simple proposition: "I'm not fighting another person," he said. "I'm fighting the market, just one person against the market." This approach appealed to oddballs like us.

Too True to Be Good

Art's drawback as a securities analyst was a weakness for ideas that were simply too clever or too advanced for the Bank's stodgy mindset. At one point, he investigated the prospects for titanium investment and wrote an extraordinary, detailed report building a very favorable case—long before anyone dreamed of titanium golf clubs. Art was right many years later, of course, as events turned out. But there was never the slimmest chance that the investment committee would go for it. You need to take a stand in this business, but you also have to be realistic about investment horizons. Shrewd investors usually take that message to heart.

It's not surprising that Art grew frustrated. During my eight years at National City Bank, I always enjoyed the company of excellent investing talent and experience. Sadly, it wasn't put to the best use. The Bank mainly looked to fill trust portfolios with recognizable stocks that would remain there until an investor's demise, whereupon the basis would be written up for tax purposes. Opportunities to exchange a stock that was past its prime for another that had growth or value potential often passed us by.

This approach to investing, in my view, was hitting behind the ball. The Bank's Trust Investment Committee had the power to approve or veto all investment ideas. Notwithstanding the Committee's willingness to embrace Polaroid and a handful of other forward-looking recommendations, its hidebound hierarchy usually precluded any kind of creative stock picking. You'd have to go to the Committee to secure approval for the stock you worked on, and it was headed by a not-so-benevolent despot of a bond man who had no special instinct for stocks other than risk aversion. In my judgment, all he did was reflect what had already been acknowledged in the marketplace. There was no overbought stock he did not love. Given this approach, it did not take me long to figure out that I would never get to practice my skills as I saw them. It was not enough to be prudent. You needed to apply some imagination and flair, and both were often outside the Trust Investment Committee's purview.

Tending my personal portfolio allowed me to try out my ideas about investing. Soon after joining the Bank, I combined my shares of Aro Equipment, which my father had encouraged me to buy, with my savings, and amassed about $3,000. By managing this grubstake and adding small amounts periodically, I increased it to $20,000 in less than four years. By the time I got to Windsor, in 1963, it was nearly $100,000.

Despite my growing discomfort with the Bank's backward-looking investment style, I became head of securities analysis for the Trust Department in 1958. Now somewhat more mature, at 27 years old, I was the Bank's youngest officer. From that post, I watched growth stocks zoom in the late Fifties only to tumble earthward again in 1961. Meantime, ironically, I turned down an invitation from the Wellington Management Company, manager of the Wellington Equity Fund, as Windsor was known in its earliest days. I was at the Bank about six years when Wellington called me on the recommendation of the Chrysler analyst contact, who praised my talents as an auto industry analyst, a slot Wellington wanted to fill. I explained to them that I already had too much of my career invested in a broader base. After following a wide array of industries, I thought that I'd find just one too limiting.

By the time President John Kennedy was inaugurated in January 1961, despite my vote cast for Richard Nixon, I was pretty certain a move was inevitable, and even Lilli was reconciled to moving east, if necessary. For someone who harps on the value of hard-core analysis, I have to confess that my first and only job change relied on a less than rigorous analysis of alternatives. After starting with a handful of names, I eventually narrowed the list to three mutual fund management firms: Dreyfus, National Investors, and Wellington.

I didn't know a great deal about mutual funds except that they seemed to make some considerable sense in bringing the people's capitalism to the troops—but at a hefty price for rank-and-file investors, I thought at the time. Sales commissions routinely snared 8 percent of an investment, up front. Nevertheless, I did recognize, in all three management companies, an investment mindset much more entrepreneurial than the Bank's.

During cold calls to Dreyfus and National, I announced that I was thinking about a change and sampling opportunities. Speaking with them, I thought the rapport was good. But ultimately, we never saw eye-to-eye.

On the strength of previous contact, I also called Wellington. Its equity fund, Wellington Equity, had plunged dramatically since it was introduced in 1958. This time, they weren't looking for just an auto analyst. They wanted someone with ideas for potentially rescuing the beleaguered Wellington Equity fund, which foundered in its fifth year of existence amid the dramatic 1961–1962 inflection point. The opportunity seemed broad enough, and there was nowhere interesting to go at the Bank. So, with enthusiastic support from Lilli, who was no doubt relieved that New York was not our destination, I packed my bags and headed for Philadelphia.

5

~

BAPTISM BY FIRE

IF ANYTHING, WHEN I arrived in 1963, the Windsor Fund was in worse shape than I had anticipated. Much like stocks that have proven to be my best investments, six-year-old Windsor was downtrodden, woebegone, and out of favor.

The team in charge had lost its sense of direction. In 1962, a devastating year for many investors, Windsor's performance was down by 25 percent. With shareholders bolting for the exits, more money was flowing out of the $75 million fund than was flowing in. More ominous still, Windsor, known at first as the Wellington Equity fund, was beginning to tarnish the company's flagship $2 billion Wellington Fund. Having gone public in 1960, Wellington Management Co., the investment advisor, also had to worry about its own stock price.

Never mind the Wellington Fund's hard-earned reputation. Launched in 1928 by Walter Morgan, a native of Pennsylvania's anthracite coal region, the Wellington Fund had survived the 1929 Crash and the Great Depression, a distinction few funds could claim.

The original Wellington had done quite well, thanks to combining stocks in its portfolio with bond investments. Serving as a pretty good anchor to windward, bonds kept Wellington out of trouble when stocks declined. This ran counter to pre-Crash strategy touted by many gilt-edged promoters from Jesse Livermore to Goldman Sachs. Popular funds not only hitched their wagons to stocks, they borrowed heavily to boost performance. As a consequence of excessive leverage, many of them vanished in the aftermath of 1929. Wellington, thanks to its conservative make-up, flourished.

For a period after World War II, during the heyday of balanced funds and risk aversion—Wellington was one of the largest mutual fund around. Common stocks were not optimistically valued. Investors weaned on the Depression era cared almost exclusively about preservation of principal and current income. Stock price appreciation, last touted in the heady days before the Great Crash, held scarce appeal. To attract risk-averse investors to stocks, dividend yields in those days often exceeded bond yields.

Sewell Avery, the postwar chairman of Montgomery Ward, comes to mind. By worshiping at the altar of historical parallel, he did in a great company. Fearful of expansion in the teeth of a depression that seemed inevitable to many timorous postwar observers, Avery restrained the retailer's growth. Meanwhile, across town in Chicago, rival Sears Roebuck added stores full speed ahead, and eventually reduced once-great Montgomery Ward to a marginal competitor.

As the 1950s progressed and stocks returned to the footlights, balanced funds fell from favor. Although a handful of balanced funds persisted, they lured fewer takers at the equity race track. Proliferating stock funds became sexy as the somewhat stodgy Wellington flagship floundered. That's when John Bogle started urging Walter Morgan to expand Wellington's horizons, author Robert Slater reported.[*] Morgan resisted, fearful that stock funds eventually would suffer the same fate that befell them following the 1929 Crash. But after much urging and steep declines in its share of the mutual fund market, Wellington decided to join the action by creating the Wellington Equity Fund, as Windsor was named at its outset.

An initial public offering raised $33 million, one of the three largest mutual fund underwritings on record at the time. It had taken the original Wellington Fund 17 years to reach the same level, Slater noted. For three years, Windsor outperformed the S&P 500 by healthy margins. Wellington Management, and Bogle in particular, basked in the Wellington Equity's bright prospects.

But after the market spun downward in mid-1961, Windsor fared far worse. In 1962, as the S&P slid 8.7 percent, Windsor lost a quarter of its shareholders' investment. My predecessor, Windsor Fund portfolio manager Bob Kenmore, who held only nominal authority, was out of the picture before I had a chance to meet him. Real authority rested with the

---

[*] Slater, Robert, "John Bogle and the Vanguard Experiment," Irwin Professional Publishing, Chicago (1997), p. 22.

investment committee—a group not unlike their hidebound counterparts at the Bank. But these folks knew something had to change if Windsor was to persevere.

Owing partly to poor investment judgment and an administrative hierarchy that hindered swift reaction to market developments, Windsor had taken its lumps twice—first on the downturn, and afterward on the rebound. Bad enough that the market hammered Windsor's vulnerable collection of small growth stocks. In this respect, Windsor had lots of companionship.

Market Overboard

In classic fashion, frantic efforts to correct the underperformance only compounded Windsor's plight. Windsor had succumbed to infatuation with small supposed growth companies without sufficient attention to the durability of growth. In early 1961, the market emphasized these goods. Like managers of similar portfolios, Windsor participated at first in the glory of dubious growth stocks. Instead of banking those ill-gotten gains, Windsor rode the stocks too long and got killed. Worse, panicked management sold its beleaguered growth stocks at the bottom and shoveled the proceeds into "safe" stocks. You don't bounce back by owning highly recognized goods, simply because they didn't go down as much. This strategy might have stemmed losses had the market slide continued, but when the pendulum swung back again, Windsor fell far off the pace. In 1963, the S&P gained 22.8 percent as Windsor lagged behind by more than 10 percentage points.

Like other mutual funds in that era, the Wellington Fund and the Wellington Equity Fund relied chiefly on cadres of stockbrokers to put shares in investors' hands. For that to occur, however, missionary mutual fund sales reps (called wholesalers) based in 12 cities circulated throughout the country. Their job was to persuade stockbrokers to put their investors' money into the Wellington funds.

As word of Windsor's subpar performance resonated, its crippling effects spilled over onto Wellington Fund sales. By 1963, the wholesalers were screaming for better results. Windsor Fund directors were desperate for ways to rescue Windsor. To make matters even worse, a handful of Wellington shareholders filed a lawsuit charging management with expropriating Wellington's name and reputation. The suit was settled in part by changing the equity fund's name to Windsor.

By the time Wellington hired me as a securities analyst, the mandate was clear: Forget hitting the gong. Just fix performance to the point where it won't damage Wellington.

Soon after I joined Wellington but before moving to Philadelphia, I visited Joe Canning, a Wellington wholesaler in Cleveland. He invited me to lunch and, of course, I accepted. He was more intellectual than many sales guys, but hard driving also. He warned me that when I reached Wellington's home office, someone would tell me that the wholesalers made too much money. Then he emphasized the need for attractive investment products, without which he and his counterparts would labor. I took it all in while noticing, on his wall, photos of members of the Wellington Management Investment Committee. I decided then and there that one day my picture would join theirs.

The Windsor portfolio when I arrived held all kinds of shabby stuff reflecting recent fads and fashions that eventually littered the marketplace. They were similar to much of what turns up in momentum funds that seek, foremost, the current fashion: biotech stocks when the biotech sector is hot, oil stocks when the oil patch is flourishing, or Internet stocks when everything ending in .com commands investors' attention. A resemblance to the "tronics" boom in the late Fifties is easy to see. In that technology-driven market, any name that hinted at a technology connection drove prices higher.

Then, as now, this approach amounts to hitting behind the ball instead of anticipating market climates six to eighteen months ahead of the investment crowd. Poor performance often occurred as a consequence of a technical orientation that tried to predict peaks and troughs in stock charts. It assumed that where a stock has been implies where it is going. Many funds used charts to divine future stock prices. When I was interviewed at Dreyfus, my tour included the chart room, replete with all kinds of electronic gadgets and readouts. Playing the technical or momentum game always has seemed misguided to me.

Lilli accepted the move east with her characteristic resolve. Given my ambition and my choice of career, she had figured that an eastward move probably was inevitable. Compared to New York, Philadelphia at least seemed more like Ohio. We had three children by then: Patrick, Lisa, and Stephen. While they completed the school year in Ohio, I settled pro-tem in Philadelphia. The first place I called home was a fleabag hotel downtown. Soon I moved briefly to another YMCA. After three weeks under that roof, I moved into an apartment with a couple of fellow analysts who were bachelors at the time.

Meanwhile, I started hunting for a house. Most that I saw were decent enough, but none surpassed our house in Cleveland. Lilli came down twice to aid in the search. On one of her visits, we drove through a neighborhood of impressive looking homes—Georgian colonials, I was told. The trouble with them, said our real estate agent, was water. The area had a saturated past; in other words, the houses sat square in the midst of a floodplain. For that reason, the agent advised us against it. Given my sensibilities, tattered goods didn't bother me so long as the fundamentals were acceptable. So I took the warning as an invitation to look inside. It had a big foyer, a spiral staircase, four bedrooms, and three baths. It suited us perfectly. We lived there for 21 years without regret.

The powers-that-be when I arrived at Wellington started with Walter Morgan. Although he inhabited the white-shoe world by the time I met him, he was not to-the-manor-born, either. He was an accountant from the Wilkes-Barre region of Pennsylvania—the anthracite country, as locals labeled it, to call attention to its rich coal deposits. John Birmingham and Ed Mennis were portfolio administrators of long standing. Both had been with the company for many years—most of their working lives, in fact. Ed, who had a PhD, practiced the economic side and drew the road map of the economy. He had also covered the autos and other specific industrial areas as an analyst. A method that he used, along with seven other Wellington analysts, garnered information on the economy with a sampling technique. He would then determine the capital expenditures at some 200 companies under Wellington's analytical coverage. From these data, he determined, more readily than less industrious competitors, the real outlook for capital expenditures in the year ahead.

Besides Birmingham and Mennis on the investment side, there was a senior man, A. Moyer Kulp, in his seventies at the time. Kulp, Morgan, and Joe Welch, with a legal background, constituted Wellington's original trio of managers. I belonged to the next generation, along with John Bogle, who succeeded Morgan as chairman.

Make Yourself Valuable

As the newest securities analyst on the block, my responsibility at Wellington was broadly delineated. But in an organization that clearly needed lots of help, there was just one mandate: Make yourself valuable.

According to lore, this was a venerable tradition at Wellington. After Bogle arrived in July 1951, goes the popular account, Walter Morgan stuck him in a corner and told him to make himself valuable until a suitable assignment came along. By the time I joined Wellington, Morgan was grooming Bogle as his successor.

Initially, I stepped in as the liaison with Wall Street. I would trek up to New York and knock on doors, pick up ideas, write memos. Imbued with a great deal of curiosity, I'd visit the impressive Wall Street offices with a lot of oak paneling, and I thought I was going to meet God's gift to the investment community. It wasn't long before I discovered that the analytical skills at work in the paneled offices were no better than mine, and were often worse. Each time I traveled to New York, I stopped in at different places to try to capture whatever viewpoints, insights, or opinions those sources would share.

All told, I enjoyed an ideal apprenticeship for a future portfolio manager. The education broadened my horizons in ways that continued to pay off for the next three decades, exposing me for the first time to airlines, savings and loans, finance companies, and a wide industrial spectrum. I learned about companies by frequently attending securities analysts luncheons. I saw as many companies as possible because I never knew when they might come into view, either because of price declines or new fundamentals.

I would gather and summarize investment information. I'd write memos of my Wall Street sojourns and circulate them to decision makers at Wellington. I was their eyes and ears, as they characterized my role. In short order, I also performed broad securities analysis, such as multi-industry companies. This time, I had a real chance of trading shares opportunistically—a refreshing change from stodgy bank days.

As part of an early make-yourself-useful exercise, I became an expert in a multi-industry company called Textron. Textron was a conglomerate, the sort of investment that later proved very lucrative. With my varied exposure, I could take a company with industrial exposure and bring it into some sort of useful perspective that went beyond the range of a typical analyst who was focused on just one or two industries at most. Textron had evolved from a textile company under the control of an entrepreneur named Royal Little. An ex-commercial banker, Rupert C. Thompson, succeeded Little and assembled a fascinating mix of companies reflecting many components of the economy. Textron competed in automotive supplies, consumer durables, and machine tools, among other segments. Its most memorable product, for me, was the Huey helicopter. After an analysis of its fundamentals, I recommended the stock, and we bought it.

It did not occur to me then, but I conclude now that the fund's directors were testing me for something bigger. Meantime, I started comparing Windsor's style, performance, and strategy to competitive equity mutual funds.

The analysis amounted to nothing more than a systematic overview of the Fund's dismal results. It wasn't rocket science. But to directors shell-shocked by the fund's poor performance and hungry for direction, my assessment put matters into a sensible perspective. If I had to make sense of a portfolio today, I'd follow the same basic approach.

Scrutiny of Windsor's poor performance revealed a common theme: Windsor paid extraordinarily high price–earnings multiples on the way in. When the cost of admission features such multiples, continuation of unusual growth is usually needed to realize worthwhile appreciation.

It is critical to understand that a stock's price reflects two underlying variables: (1) earnings per share and (2) the multiple of earnings per share that the market attaches to it. Thus, two stocks both may earn $2 a share. But if one is perceived to be growing faster, the stock price normally garners a higher multiple to encompass expectations of higher earnings later on. If the multiples are, say, 15 times earnings and 30 times earnings, then the shares of each stock will change hands for $30 and $60, respectively. By capturing growth in earnings and the expansion of a market multiple, shrewd investors cash in. Too many of Windsor's stocks, unfortunately, got caught instead in a downdraft; steep declines in market multiples were set off by hints of slower growth rates.

Shifts in performance or in investor sentiment can trigger outsized consequences—up or down, depending on whether price–earnings multiples expand or contract. My predecessors at Windsor witnessed the downside. A marked margin of error in analysis of the difference between unusual growth and an earnings plateau produced crippling effects. Such shifts are all it takes to pummel a portfolio. I've seen them all: a hint about earnings underperformance relative to expectations, a rumored lawsuit, results a penny short of Wall Street's estimates to name a few causes. Besides the stocks that posted poor earnings, market multiples also collapsed for many stocks that suffered no earnings deterioration.

Windsor's failures in the industrial products segment deserved special attention. In this blighted category, "adventuring" outside the quality zone was most unrewarding. Of 41 industrial stocks, scarcely 8 deserved to be called successful, and their successes were lackluster at best. The majority of extreme losers, it turned out, lent themselves to three generalizations:

1. Almost without exception, faulty company analysis deserved the blame. Fundamental targets were simply missed by extremely large margins.
2. Windsor had not overpaid for anticipated earnings—or even current earnings, for that matter. If earnings power had only been maintained, we might have at least retreated without losing money. Our perspective was so poor in this adventure segment that, in most cases, substantial earning power deterioration occurred.
3. We displayed a gratifying ability to realize mistakes and salvage values from situations that subsequently deteriorated, in some cases to the vanishing point. Virtually every elimination of a loser was a good sale.

To prevent similar imbroglios from recurring, I advised fund directors to restrain stock selections in the industrial products segment to predictable companies in predictable industry climates, where Windsor might capitalize on special abilities in economic analysis. These targets would be less dramatic but more assured—essentially incorporating the conservative Wellington philosophy in the Windsor growth fund.

Restraint did not rule out room in the portfolio for future champions. But it imposed a severe burden of proof on depth and quality of analysis, involving a full understanding of competitive factors with qualitative checks. Then, as now, I assigned great weight to a judgment about the durability of earnings power under adverse circumstances.

Without actually making matters any better, this explanation of the Windsor Fund's performance at least lent clarity to the situation and corralled directors in my camp. Whatever their bent, I was a straight shooter. I supplied answers and bolstered them with facts. This, I suppose, was a marked improvement over wishy-washy assessments that would have left directors as puzzled as before.

I must have passed the test. Within two months of delivering my analysis, and barely eleven months after my arrival, Wellington tapped me to become its first individual portfolio manager.

6

TAKING COMMAND AT WINDSOR

WELLINGTON MANAGEMENT ALTERED its method of managing the Windsor Fund in May 1964. The new style focused responsibility and authority on a single portfolio manager. The aim was to enhance flexibility and exploit fully the large and growing flow of financial information so the Fund would respond more quickly to the rapid changes that were reshaping the investment world.

That's how we depicted the new management structure, but when Wellington elevated me to portfolio manager, two key adjustments remained. I dispatched one right away.

From my first day at Windsor, I wanted to create impact by taking outsized positions where I saw promising returns. After eight years at the Bank and one at Wellington, I'd seen enough hitting behind the ball. By playing it safe, you can make a portfolio so pablum-like that you don't get any sizzle. You can diversify yourself into mediocrity. This sounds like heresy to many advocates of modern portfolio theory, but sticking our neck out worked for Windsor.

I wasted no time in executing my investment philosophy. In June 1964, Windsor already owned shares in a Pennsylvania company named AMP Incorporated, the same company that made news in 1998, when it fended off a hostile takeover attempt by Allied Signal Corporation, at a cost of embracing Tyco Industries as a white knight. Much as it is today, AMP was a quality manufacturer of connectors and was based in Pennsylvania's

Appalachia. If you put electronics units together, you have to connect them. AMP's business tended to be predictable and, in my view, was underrated by investors. I thought we should take a larger position.

Wellington had empowered me to take Windsor's helm, but old habits die hard.* My portfolio changes still required the Investment Committee's stamp of approval. The committee pronounced judgment on investment ideas when they met periodically. Seated together in those meetings, the committee members cast an imposing mien. Each member reinforced the others' doubts, often to the point where the only consensus was to table a decision or water it down. History had shown that this was no way to steer a mutual fund, especially during tumultuous times.

Rather than wait for the next meeting, I embarked on a new strategy. I approached three key committee members, one at a time. In one-on-one encounters, their collective countenance vanished, and they almost always deferred to my salvo of exhaustive, fundamental analysis. The first two gave AMP a green light without memorable objections or questions. The third and final member was Wellington vice president Ed Mennis. He heard me out, conceded that AMP stock was worth owning, but asked if we were allowed to own as much stock as I proposed without violating guidelines. Once I reassured him about the rules, he also ratified my decision. From then on, buy and sell orders essentially rested on my authority, although I always kept the three committee members apprised of my intentions, buttressed by my telling analysis.

The second adjustment took a little longer.

Seven securities analysts serviced the Wellington and Windsor Funds when I took over. But here was poor, old, woebegone Windsor stuck with a constituency that was not overjoyed with our lack of performance. Nevertheless, I was promised access to any analysts at any time. As things turned out, the promise of analytical support did not materialize. Put yourself in the analysts' position. While I was knocking at their door, asking for their time and perspective, Wellington also was knocking. Windsor was a $75 million fund; Wellington had $2 billion

---

* Board members often made valuable contributions. But I still recall one crusty old director who was in the shipping business with Mr. Morgan. At meetings he would bellow, "When are we going to have the cigars?" He would reach in a humidor on the conference table and grab about a week's supply—which for him was quite a few. When the discussion turned serious and his counsel was sought, he'd bellow "Well, what does management think?"

under management and it was the flagship. It wasn't hard to figure out which fund was going to command the analysts' attention.

After about six months of butting my head against the wall, I concluded that I would never get sufficient support from Wellington analysts. I wanted to investigate companies myself—and did, to some extent—but I lacked the time to cover as many as Windsor required. So I proposed a compromise: "Give me one analyst exclusively, and I'll surrender my nonexistent rights to the other six." Management agreed, and Bill Hicks became Windsor's first official, full-time securities analyst.

A Strategy Evolves

The Windsor 1964 annual report, the first during my tenure, was dated October 31, five months after my only promotion in 30 years. The best we could say was: We narrowed the performance gap. Windsor lagged behind the S&P 500 by 300 basis points.

Probably because the verdict was not yet in on my contribution as manager, the 1964 annual report did not mention me by name. It nevertheless reflected key hallmarks of my systematic efforts to appraise past performance and restore Windsor to a distinct and positive footing.

We had stiff competition. Although far fewer combatants populated the mutual funds landscape in 1964, the ranks were growing rapidly. Besides Windsor, I could have named only a handful of competitors of comparable size, all scrambling for the same type of assets. Investment styles were starting to surface, but the present degrees of specialization had not yet emerged.

The mutual funds field has grown more cluttered, but my motto has not changed: *Keep It Simple*. Toward simplifying Windsor, we narrowed the field of appealing investments into just two broad groups.

1. *Growth stocks.* These are companies with established and recognized growth characteristics, such as sharply rising demand for their products, modern technology, advanced marketing techniques, scientific orientation, or intensive research programs. They therefore offer above-average, long-term prospects for rising earnings and dividends.
2. *Basic industry stocks.* These companies afford a broad participation in the long-term growth of the American economy. Carefully selected companies of this character, at certain times, will

offer outstanding opportunities for increased income and profits. Also included in this general group are "special situations"—companies that are undergoing significant changes in their products, market, or management.

Brain surgery it's not, but I've always found that investors who skip elementary steps stumble sooner rather than later.

Size matters in the investment arena. A perennial question is asked by novice and seasoned investors alike: Should intelligent investors favor well-known large companies? Or: Should we throw in our lot with smaller, lesser-known companies?

Windsor's answer was "Measured Participation." This concept sounds esoteric, but the idea was really quite simple. We elected to measure our degree of participation in one stock against the relative risks and rewards we would expect to find in other market sectors. For example, no matter how attractive a particular oil stock looks, we have to ask ourselves whether a different sector of the market looks more promising.

A decade before experts started talking about asset allocation strategies, Windsor set out to shift assets between large, stable, fairly predictable companies and smaller companies whose products, markets, or services had more room to grow, but on a less sturdy foundation.

"Measured Participation" framed Windsor's efforts to classify, categorize, and analyze our portfolio performance. We assessed growth stocks and basic industry stocks on the basis of Quality, Marketability, and Growth and Economic Characteristics. We de-emphasized conventional breakdowns by industry. Applying these criteria to our two stock groups yielded stock groups that set the stage for Windsor's next three decades.

Seen through the lens of measured participation, reasons for underperformance became apparent. When the market began clamoring for quality growth stocks in the wake of the 1961–1962 decline, our blue-chip representation was lowest in our peer group. The Investment Committee, in its infinite wisdom, had hung onto many hard-hit stocks rather than sell under duress, and had used scarce cash to purchase safe stocks that missed out when the most hard-hit stocks bounced back.

Because of my emphasis on stocks with a future instead of stocks with a past, my first full year as a portfolio manager started off with a bang. Windsor's dazzling 29.1 percent total return outstripped the benchmark S&P 500 by nearly 17 percentage points. The Fund's net asset value ended calendar 1965 at its highest level in Windsor's seven-year history. As we closed the books on 1965, assets managed stood within striking distance of the $100 million mark.

A less ebullient 1966 at least gave us the chance to test Windsor's performance in a down market. After crossing 1,000 during intraday trading in January 1966, the Dow Jones Industrial Average closed slightly lower. For my part, I do not recall being excited about the Dow's march toward 1,000. As I told *Newsweek* some years later, when the Dow was en route to another record level, "It's just a number."

To the dismay of the cheering investors who were primed for the Dow Jones Industrials to enter 1,000 territory and stay there, the market disappointed them for six years. Not until November 1972 did the Dow Jones close higher than 1,000, and not before it had slid again below 700.*

Despite real economic growth in 1966, an escalating war effort in Vietnam awakened the inflationary beast. After a long snooze, rising interest rates approached the century's highest levels. Reacting to inflationary jitters, investors dealt the market its third largest annual decline, to that date, since World War II. Windsor acquitted itself well. Measured participation kept us out of the worst regions amid the 10 percent decline by the S&P 500. When the dust settled, Windsor gave back 3.3 percent, one-third of the market's loss.

As noted in the 1966 annual report, Windsor shareholders enjoyed increased current income. Dividends from net investments exceeded those of any previous year and amounted to nearly double dividends paid in 1963.

We sustained better momentum than the market in calendar 1967. We posted a gain of 31.5 percent, compared to 23.9 percent for the S&P 500. Calendar year-end, we exceeded, by a wide margin, $100 million under management, concentrated among only 77 stocks.

Tsai Is Buying

Beating the market three years in a row sounds like cause for celebration, but the market's giddy climate in 1967 tempered our enthusiasm. The go-go era was in full swing, orchestrated by a handful of funds that

---

* The Dow Jones Industrials didn't close over 1,000 to stay until 1982. Thus, an investor who hitched a wagon to the Dow in January 1966 waited 16 years for a meaningful capital gain. When inflation over that span is considered, the investor suffered a 60 percent loss.

touted growth that outpaced Windsor. Our eight-point advantage over the S&P 500 seemed meager compared with a couple of Fidelity funds directed by Gerald Tsai, a hot growth manager who epitomized the meteoric go-go era when adrenaline funds, as I call them, held sway.

Mutual funds that Tsai managed ultimately flunked the test of time, but in the late Sixties he was the toast of Wall Street. Fidelity Trend and Fidelity Capital transfixed everyone, even the stockbrokers who sold Wellington Fund.

I remember one Windsor sales junket across upper New York State when we still relied on wholesalers, our missionary salesmen who beat the bushes to lure stockbrokers, and ultimately their customers, to Windsor. In company with a wholesaler named Bud Kator, we criss-crossed New York State and stayed in cheap, older hotels, mostly belonging to a real down-on-your-luck chain owned by long departed Milner Hotels. Bud was tight with every nickel—not a bad trait, ordinarily. But among the shortcomings that plagued these hotels, one room had a hole in the wall, right through the lathing. I'm not a great trappings man; an average YMCA then suited my needs. But Milner Hotels were even below my standards.

While we traveled cheap, every broker we met heaped lavish praise on Jerry Tsai. In the middle of a sales pitch, their eyes roved toward the ticker tape in search of Tsai's influence on small and obscure growth stocks. Such was his renown that mere rumors of his interest would trigger market activity. In our own trading room, like thousands of others across the country—and like the floor of the New York Stock Exchange itself—rumors flew in legendary whispers. "Tsai is buying . . . Tsai is selling." Much of his merchandise was overexploited and risky by my standards. Small companies with scant earnings were sold on the promise of great earnings ahead. The greater-fool theory ruled.

Caught up in the cult of these so-called "story stocks," investors lined up to buy shares in mutual funds loading up on companies that made gadgets and frivolous fashion accessories. Rumors fed reality by triggering price changes when the magic name was mentioned.

An idea and a promotion could attract thousands of investors who failed repeatedly to distinguish mere flaky ideas from a slew of near-frauds like National Student Marketing. This one was the brainchild of a man named Cortes Randell, who cobbled together a collection of businesses aimed at the youth market. Amid estimates that National Student Marketing commanded the loyalty of consumers with $45 billion in disposable income to spend on everything from tooth paste, posters, and beer mugs to expensive stereos and camera equipment, investors gobbled up its shares. As a conduit between manufacturers and the youth market, National Student Marketing eagerly distributed anything and everything. In just two years, it shot from less than $1 million in sales to $68 million.

Not shy in the least, Randell trumpeted his success in phone calls to investors from his private Lear jet. To sustain this blistering pace of growth, he launched or bought up businesses that made goods or provided services to the youth market, including, *Fortune* Magazine reported, a youth-oriented insurance company and a travel service, usually using high-flying stock as currency.

I remember a road show in Philadelphia for National Student Marketing, built largely on the premise that giving samples to college students created lifelong loyal customers. Like other adventures that began on the up-and-up but eventually were overtaken by slick promoters, National Student Marketing was not without merits. But by the time the road show reached Philadelphia in search of new investors, I recall how a broker who sponsored the presentation squirmed while Randell flogged the shares with cavalier abandon. Soon afterward, however, the house of cards started to collapse, eventually forcing a chagrined board of directors to boot Randell out. But even that remedy could not save the company.

To investors with shooting stars like National Student Marketing in their eyes, Windsor resembled a stick-in-the-mud during the late Sixties. We did not court delusions of grandeur nor cut our cloth to suit passing styles. We stuck with measured participation and realistic expectations, and we took some flak for our stance. One good friend who managed the local Philadelphia office of Goldman Sachs—a gilt-edged investment bank then as now—put it bluntly: Windsor, he said, was "just not with it." Those were his exact words. "Not with it."

I wasn't surprised by criticism. Anyone could feel the adrenaline pumping through go-go funds. In 1967, while Windsor edged the market by 7.6 percentage points, a respectable margin, Tsai and a handful of rock stars outpaced the market by even wider margins. In short spurts, they would rack up spectacular gains.

For about three years, performance investing held sway tenaciously. Three of Tsai's celebrated counterparts, Fred Alger, Fred Mates, and Fred Carr, rose to such prominence that David Babson, a religious buy-and-hold growth investor with a decent long-term track record, eventually blamed the industry's unraveling problems on too many Freds.

Capitalizing on short memories, a rising market, and celebrity status, go-go funds enlisted cadres of drooling investors. The capacity of investors to believe in something too good to be true seems almost infinite at times, especially when the market is crying for a sobering inflection point.

Near the very apex of the go-go craze, Wellington jumped in with both feet. It agreed to merge with Thorndike, Doran, Paine & Lewis (TDP&L), the firm that managed Ivest, one of the hottest growth funds around. Engineered by John Bogle, then heir apparent to Wellington founder and chairman Walter Morgan, the merger looked like a good blend of Wellington's sound reputation, administration, and distribution capacity with the hot hands behind high-flying Ivest.

Although my influence was on the rise, thanks to my making Windsor respectable, no one yet consulted me on matters of overarching business strategy. Windsor's and Ivest's investment styles diverged. I was sometimes a buyer for stocks they were selling. But I was not hasty in reaching a conclusion that they were misguided. I always honored other approaches until proven wrong. In other words, I hadn't completely closed my mind at the outset. I tried to learn from other schools of thought.

Privately, I suspected the potential for disappointment in this combination. On the other hand, go-go funds were stealing the lion's share of new investment in mutual funds while the Wellington Fund was suffering steady erosion in its share of the mutual fund market. Notwithstanding Windsor's improved outlook, Wellington needed a more dramatic product to boost its sagging near-term fortunes.

A contact at Bache & Company, the firm that had rebuffed my desire to become a stockbroker in 1955, advised Bogle to take a look at TDP&L. When I finally made a trip to Boston, I liked the new group. An unmistakable air of confidence surrounded them. It surfaced, for instance, when I met partner Bob Doran's secretary Olive—dubbed "the big 'O'." "The first thing I want to know," Olive asked me, "are you important in this company?"

Doran himself lacked quite the New England pedigree that his three partners exuded in spades. More than simply to-the-manor-born, they bore the bloodlines of the *Mayflower*'s passenger list. Thorndike's mother was a Lowell. Lewis's mother was a Saltonstall whose cousin, Everett, served as U. S. Senator from Massachusetts. Paine belonged to the family that spawned Paine Webber, the venerable Wall Street investment dealer.

Although Bogle initiated and engineered Wellington's merger with TDP&L, it was widely seen as a capitulation. *Institutional Investor* devoted a cover story to the merger in January 1968. The title said it all: "The Whiz Kids Take Over at Wellington." We were supposed to deliver depth in sales and administration, along with a long and venerable track record. They were supposed to be investment wizards.

A comparison of Ivest and Windsor certainly appeared to favor the whiz kids' approach at the time we merged. In the stretch leading up to 1968, Windsor neatly outdistanced the S&P 500, and Ivest neatly outdistanced Windsor. But soon thereafter, along with other high-flying adrenaline funds, Ivest ran into some rough weather.

Every tub rests on its own bottom, once inflection points are reached. Tsai would go on, with great fanfare, to launch his own Manhattan Fund in 1970, but the go-go era had run out of gas. Many investors who 12 months earlier had dreamed of making fortunes were lucky to collect 50 cents on the dollar. One by one, funds crumbled and vanished. After having been eclipsed by adrenaline funds for several years running, we persevered in the very testy 1969 market. Amid this wreckage came one of my better moments. I was in New York attending a popular annual mutual funds conference, and the very salesmen who 12 months earlier were ready to give Windsor up for lost, instead initiated a spontaneous and glowing ovation when I was introduced. Windsor's demise, Mark Twain would have said, had been greatly exaggerated.

While investors who had hitched their wagons to go-go practitioners nursed their wounds, this era's collapse created splendid investment opportunities for Windsor as we entered 1970.

PART TWO

ENDURING
PRINCIPLES

"Ponder, then act."
Sir Winston Churchill

7
〜

Elements of Style

Investment strategies abound for making money in bull markets, bear markets, adrenaline markets, or you-name-it markets. During the nineties alone, investors witnessed nearly every market climate, from doldrums in 1991 to a frenzy for Internet stocks in 1998. A new century will unveil more variations and, no doubt, new advice on ways to navigate them. Or, on the other hand, investors can throw in the towel and merely match the market, less fees, with an index fund.

Windsor was never fancy, fad-driven, or resigned to market performance. We followed one durable investment style whether the market was up, down, or indifferent. These were its principal elements:

- Low price–earnings (p/e) ratio.
- Fundamental growth in excess of 7 percent.
- Yield protection (and enhancement, in most cases).
- Superior relationship of total return to p/e paid.
- No cyclical exposure without compensating p/e multiple.
- Solid companies in growing fields.
- Strong fundamental case.

In a business with no guarantees, we banked on investments that consistently gave Windsor the better part of the odds. It wasn't always a smooth ride; at times, we took our lumps. But, over the long haul, Windsor finished well ahead of the pack.

Low Price–Earnings Ratio

I have earned several labels in my career. To some observers, I am a *value investor*. That venerable investment style has roots in the pioneering research by the legendary Benjamin Graham and David Dodd. Graham and Dodd demonstrated, in the depths of the Great Depression, that investors' least favorite stocks tend to outperform more fashionable alternatives. Other observers call me a *contrarian*, a rather vague label that suggests a stubborn nature. Personally, I prefer a different label: *low price–earnings investor*. It describes succinctly and accurately the investment style that guided Windsor while I was in charge.

For over three decades, on Windsor's behalf, I roamed the market's bargain basement where stocks with low price–earnings ratios normally abound. Through every imaginable market climate, we stuck religiously to our strategy. Carloads of research statistics demonstrate that low p/e investing works, but no evidence I have seen speaks more convincingly than Windsor's track record. During my 31-year tenure, we beat the market 22 times. By the time I retired, each dollar invested in 1964 had returned $56 vs. $22 for the S&P 500. As a total return, Windsor had chalked up a 5,546.5 percent gain, outpacing the S&P 500 by more than two-to-one. When we closed the doors to new investors in 1985, to prevent the fund from becoming unwieldy, Windsor was the largest equity mutual fund in the United States.

Low p/e ratio stocks populate bargain basements because their underlying earnings and growth prospects don't excite most investors. As a low p/e investor, you have to distinguish misunderstood and overlooked stocks selling at bargain prices from many more stocks with lackluster prospects. The distinction is not readily visible. It begins with a thorough grasp of what price–earnings ratios tell investors.

USING P/E RATIOS AS YARDSTICKS

Where price alone discloses nothing about the relative value of two or more stocks, the p/e ratio supplies a yardstick. In a supermarket, two dissimilar bags of chocolate chip cookies may tell shoppers how many bags of each they can afford to buy, but there's no offhand way to know which bag contains more cookies for the money. Price per pound unveils that information. In lieu of price per pound, p/e ratios express stock prices per dollar of earnings.

A p/e of 10 means that the stock price represents 10 times earnings per share. With a p/e of 20, the stock price represents 20 times earnings. In May 1999, the average p/e for the S&P 500 was around 28 times earnings, but p/e ratios of individual companies varied widely. A share of Microsoft changed hands for 79 times earnings; the p/e for Caterpillar, the farm equipment maker, was 12. A favorite of mine, Beazer Homes, was about 6 times earnings.

Thus, new Microsoft shareholders paid $79 per dollar of earnings. Caterpillar shareholders scooped up a dollar of earnings for around $12. Beazer shareholders paid $6 for each dollar of expected earnings.

For any company, p/e ratios are simple to find. Besides Value Line and other paid subscription services, newspaper stock charts normally include a p/e ratio with every listing, and any personal finance Website worth visiting posts them.

ALL EARNINGS ARE NOT EQUAL

Don't assume too quickly that Caterpillar necessarily gave its shareholders a better deal. Not all earnings are equal. Price–earnings ratios express more than historical earnings. Expected earnings are also implied, and they, in turn, reflect growth expectations. At the end of this daisy chain, therefore, the p/e ratio ultimately expresses the expected growth rate in earnings. Microsoft shareholders appear to believe that a much higher and predictable growth rate will leave them better off, sooner or later, than Caterpillar shareholders.

Woebegone regions have always lured me, for one very compelling reason: Swept up by flavors of the moment, prevailing wisdom frequently undervalues good companies. Many—but not all—that languish out of favor deserve better treatment. Despite their solid earnings, they are rejected and ignored by investors caught in the clutch of groupthink.

STRAIGHT LINES CAN THROW CURVES

Opportunities in low p/e stocks can be excellent. Most investors are great at extending straight lines. They have every confidence—or at least a dogged hope—that a hot stock or industry or mutual fund will continue on the same trajectory. Expecting more of the same invariably fuels adrenaline markets that culminate in disappointment when enthusiasm wanes.

Rather than load up on hot stocks along with the crowd, we took the opposite approach. Windsor didn't engage in the market's clamor for fashionable stocks; we exploited it. Our strength always depended on coaxing overlooked, out-of-favor stocks to move up from undervalued to fairly valued. We aimed for easier and less risky appreciation, and left "greater fool" investing to others.

This strategy gave Windsor's performance a twofold edge: (1) excellent upside participation and (2) good protection on the downside. Unlike high-flying growth stocks poised for a fall at the slightest sign of disappointment, low p/e stocks have little anticipation, no expectation built into them. Indifferent financial performance by low p/e companies seldom exacts a penalty. Hints of improved prospects trigger fresh interest. If you buy stocks when they are out of favor and unloved, and sell them into strength when other investors recognize their merits, you'll often go home with handsome gains.

The stocks Windsor bought usually had had the stuffing beaten out of them. Their p/e ratios were 40 to 60 percent below the market. Discounts of this magnitude grew somewhat harder to find as the Nineties' bull market progressed, but they did not vanish. The market's boundless capacity for poor judgment ensures a steady supply of out-of-favor candidates. To the extent that investors apply telling judgment about growth prospects and concentrate their assets where the promise is greatest, the world is their oyster. Even as breathless enthusiasm for a handful of tech stocks paved the fast track to riches in the late Nineties, some classic low p/e merchandise—banks, homebuilders, autos, and airlines—pitched in with heartwarming gains.

YOU DON'T NEED STUNNING GROWTH RATES

Absent stunning growth rates, low p/e stocks can capture the wonders of p/e expansion with less risk than skittish growth stocks. An increase in the p/e ratio, coupled with improved earnings, turbocharges the appreciation potential. Instead of a price gain merely commensurate with earnings, the stock price can appreciate 50 to 100 percent.

P/E Multiplicity

Current Market Price	Static P/E	Expanded P/E
Current earnings per share	$ 2.00	$ 2.00
Current market price	$26.00	$16.00
Current price/earnings multiple	13 : 1	8 : 1
Growth rate	11%	11%
Expected earnings	$ 2.22	$ 2.22
New price/earnings multiple	13 : 1	11 : 1
New market price	$28.86	$24.42
Appreciation potential	**11%**	**53%**

Growth rates and p/e ratios don't always orchestrate themselves so favorably. But the extra gain shown in the table above, courtesy of p/e expansion, is not far-fetched. Windsor landed results of this magnitude time and time again by wagering that overlooked companies would attract market attention. Over almost any period of time, that wager is far safer than betting, along with momentum investors, that high fliers will continue streaking to new heights.

Brand-name growth stocks ordinarily command the highest p/e ratios. Rising prices beget attention, and vice versa—but only to a point. Eventually, their growth rate can diminish as results revert towards normal. Maybe not in all cases, but often enough to make a long-term bet. Bottom line: I wouldn't want to get caught in a rush for the exit, much less get left behind. Only when big growth stocks fall into the dumper from time to time am I inclined to pick them up—and even then, only in moderation.

In Windsor's neck of the woods, the prospects for increasing an out-of-favor company's p/e ratio from, say, 8 to 11 times, always proved more promising than lining up in hopes of comparable percentage advances by companies that started with lofty p/e ratios. For a growth stock with a starting p/e ratio of 40 times earnings, comparable expansion would have to propel the p/e to almost 55 times earnings—to say nothing of sustaining it. Aside from late bull markets, in which good low p/e candidates were largely ignored while growth stocks' p/e reached strained and dangerous levels, Windsor's edge was usually formidable.

NEVER COUNT ON WINDFALLS

Such merits notwithstanding, a low p/e strategy won't create million-aires in a week's time—although I have enjoyed occasional positive surprises. Investors looking to parlay 100 shares of stock into an instant windfall should consider a riskier strategy than mine. Before you plunk your money down in hopes of making a faster buck, remind yourself that you may end up with only a fraction of your grubstake. Even if you know what to *buy*, not knowing when to *sell* can obliterate your gains.

Windsor was not fancy. As in tennis, I tried to keep the ball in play and let my adversaries make mistakes. I picked stocks with low p/e multiples primed to be upgraded in the market if they were deserving, and endeavored to keep losers at break-even levels. Usually, I returned home with more assets in the Windsor Fund than the day before. And I slept well—and still do.

Questions about earnings *quality* began to muddy the water around the time I surrendered the reins at Windsor. During the early Nineties, an unprecedented slew of mergers and acquisitions, refinancings, restructurings, and reengineerings jarred corporate balance sheets and added new twists to income statements. Meantime, as *The Wall Street Journal* and other financial media noted, widespread tinkering with financial results to ensure steady earnings progress cast additional doubt on the credibility of financial statements.

ACCOUNTANTS CAN'T OUTWIT HUMAN NATURE

Sprinting to keep up, accounting regulators and equity analysts cooked up alternatives to traditional earnings per share. New measures encompass earnings over and above the cost of capital, dilution of earnings per share resulting from generous executive stock options, and earnings before payment of interest on debt, taxes, and depreciation, better known by the acronym EBITD.

Some of these new measures may indeed stem deterioration of earnings quality; others only grease the rails. But because these measures don't mark a new development in human nature, a basic truth remains unchanged: Investor psychology undermines efficient stock markets.

If anything, a proliferation of accounting maneuvers and counter-maneuvers should ultimately favor investors who expend extra time and energy in search of dull stocks destined for greater glory.

Investors should always corroborate earnings, or other information a company distributes, with a reliable outside source or, at least, apply a test of common sense. If discrepancies arise, resolve them or understand them before you invest. When accounting shortcomings are exposed and earnings are revised sharply downward, searing declines in the affected companies' stocks are likely.

Fundamental Growth in Excess of 7 Percent

Growth evaluated in the marketplace at a very low p/e multiple forms the basis for intrigue. For Windsor's purposes, a low p/e multiple usually languished 40 percent to 60 percent below prevailing market multiples. Moribund or badly run companies deserved to languish, of course. Low p/e companies growing faster than 7 percent a year tipped us off to underappreciated signs of life, particularly if accompanied by an attention-getting dividend.

At the end of a fiscal year, growth consists of increases in the stock price plus dividends. As a practical matter, however, earnings garner most of the attention in the marketplace because increased earnings will fetch a higher p/e.

With future stock prices at stake, earnings prospects frequently ride a crest of speculation. Every "sell-side" securities analyst on Wall Street who follows a company puts out an earnings estimate, as do "buy-side" analysts who crunch numbers for their respective investment advisors. Merrill Lynch and other retail stock brokerage firms make their analysis available now to customers on line. Availability of research has become a competitive tool that ordinary investors can put to use.

A number of services gather up estimates and publish consensuses. This is prevailing wisdom in its most literal form. When news circulates that a company has missed an earnings estimate, it is normally being compared to a consensus. If the company's fundamentals remain strong, low p/e investors often recognize buying opportunities.

TRAILING EARNINGS PORTRAY THE PAST

To differentiate between (1) earnings that have materialized already and (2) expected earnings that are yet to come, Wall Street, in its infinite wisdom, has coined terms. The former are called *historical earnings* and include earnings in any past period. Earnings recorded in the most recent 12 months or four quarters are called *trailing earnings*. Price–earnings ratios are commonly expressed either in terms of trailing earning or future earnings.

It's impossible to predict with certainty what earnings will be in the future, but every securities analyst and portfolio manager gives it a shot. Typically, as calendar years pass the halfway mark, stock prices begin to reflect expectations for the following calendar year, 18 months hence, instead of the current year. Depending on the benchmark—trailing earnings, current-year earnings, or forward earnings—p/e ratios vary. When p/e ratios are used to assess stock prices, it is critical to know which earnings the price is being measured against.

FORWARD EARNINGS GLEAN THE FUTURE

In the absence of a crystal ball, forward earnings estimates boil down to educated guesstimates. Starting with historical and trailing earnings, an investor must visualize prospects for the company and the industry it belongs to.

Forward growth rates are exposed to surprises. The market, to say the least, does not like to be negatively surprised. At high p/e levels, stocks' key support is from expectation encouraged by past performance, which is visible in their historical growth rates. With so much expectation built in, any hint of falling short can have punishing results. The fact that a company merely fell one penny short per share is not the operative consideration. It implies that growth has slipped in some measure and future earnings will not be as rosy as expected. As many investors have learned the hard way, companies cannot double earnings each year ad infinitum. Just as a pendulum swings back toward the center, exceptional growth rates eventually descend toward the normal range. Experts use a fancy term to describe this process: reversion to the mean.

One brand of earnings is not inherently superior to another. Each has its use, and savvy investors use them all.

OFF BY A DIME, OFF BY A DOLLAR

For momentum investors, who pin their expectations to high growth rates, any slip in quarterly earnings performance can cause grievous results. There is little solace in missing targets by tiny amounts, even though accounting practices leave ample wiggle room. Most companies that are close to earnings targets should meet those targets—particularly when the stock price hangs in the balance. In high p/e territory, if lofty growth expectations are missed by an inch, it may mean that a company has really missed by a mile. Whatever the actual amount of the miss, uncertainty alone can mete out tough punishment, and creative accounting practices ultimately catch up to offenders.

Windsor steered clear of such precipices. Candidates for investment were required to show sturdy track records. Except for cyclical companies that had peaks and troughs, we preferred persistent increments of quarterly earnings. Looking ahead, we sought evidence of reasonable and sustainable growth rates poised to catch investors' attention in a sober marketplace. Growth rates less than 6 percent or exceeding 20 percent (our customary ceiling) seldom made the cut. Higher growth rates entailed too much risk for our appetite.

It's easy to start debates about appropriate time horizons for calculating earnings growth. Five years worked for us. We were always poised to react to events that occurred in a shorter time frame, but, ultimately, long-term financial results drove Windsor's long-term investment performance.

In most industries nowadays, five years is a long time for markets, prices, and competition to develop. In high technology, five years represents multiple generations. It may sound foolish to warn against using longer time frames to project earnings, but good reasons for that warning happen all the time. In adrenaline markets, investors chase gee-whiz stocks on the basis of unimaginable earnings. A market pundit once quipped, in an earlier period of tech stock supremacy, that some high-flying stock prices contemplated not only future earnings, but the hereafter as well. You don't have to look further than Internet stocks to reach the same conclusion.

Shareholders often wondered about Windsor's fondness for slow-growth commodity industries like cement and copper. Admittedly, this has always been a more difficult breed of investing, particularly in terms of timing. But if a confidence-generating case can be made for supply-and-demand relationships becoming more balanced and then even tight, the inevitable increase in product prices creates very dramatic profit increments, and, consequently, an opportunity for substantial earnings gains.

Yield Protection

Besides growth in earnings, annual growth includes another component: yield. Conventional appraisals of investment returns usually ignored the yield. We didn't.

The yield for any stock merely expresses the dividend as a percentage of the stock's price. For a $10 stock that pays an annual dividend of 50 cents, the yield is 5 percent. Along with p/e ratios, dividends and yields are quoted in daily newspaper charts and on worthwhile personal finance Websites.

YIELD IS RETURN THAT SHAREHOLDERS CAN POCKET

In addition to its other merits, a low p/e strategy often results in a superior dividend yield. While they are waiting for vindication on the outlook for earnings growth, low p/e investors usually bank a meaningful portion of the combined growth rate through yield alone.

In their 1931 opus, *Security Analysis*, Graham and Dodd stressed that yield is the more assured part of growth. Only time will tell whether earnings and growth rates meet expectations. But can you be confident about the yield? You can, unless a company lowers the dividend under extraordinary duress. In fact, good companies are much more apt to *increase* the dividend, which is like learning that your bank plans to increase its passbook rate.

Yield Perspective

	Low P/E	High P/E
Price	$20.00	$50.00
Earnings	$ 2.00	$ 2.00
Dividend	$ .50	$ .50
P/E ratio	10:1	25:1
Yield	2.5%	1%

Windsor outpaced the S&P 500 by 3.15 percentage points* a year while I was portfolio manager. That's an average figure, of course; in some years Windsor did much better, in a few years not so well. Yield played a formidable role. Without roughly 2 percentage points (200 basis points) a year that superior dividend return contributed, Windsor's edge versus the S&P 500 would have slipped to 1.15 percentage points. One of the noteworthy aspects of Windsor's record was an average annual growth in dividends from the accomplishing companies in the portfolio.

Low p/e and high yields normally go hand in hand. Each is the flip side of the other. That makes dividends (a component of earnings) high relative to the price. As shown in the table above, low p/e usually means high yield; high p/e means low yield.

I never quite understood why a 15 percent grower plus a 1 percent yield usually sold at twice the price–earnings ratio of an 11 percent grower with a 5 percent yield. Of course, there is a tax difference although pension funds, endowments and other non-profit entities are not taxed. Growth in earnings is not taxed until it is distributed as a dividend. But even when taxes are considered, yield players get the better bargain.

YIELD WON'T COST A CENT

Because stock prices nearly always sell on the basis of expected earnings growth rates, shareholders collect the dividend income for free.

---

* This was after expenses; before expenses, the difference was 3.5 percentage points. This reflects both superior performance and the low costs imposed on investors.

This advantage adds up year after year because when most investors, or Wall Street, or the media, make price comparisons, they don't include yield. Only the shareholders reap this benefit. A dividend increase is one kind of "free plus." A free plus is the return investors enjoy over and above initial expectations.

One of Ben Franklin's wise observations offers a parallel: "He that waits upon Fortune is never sure of a dinner." As I see it, a superior yield at least lets you snack on hors d'oeuvres while waiting for the main meal.

Historical yield advantages become tougher to duplicate as bull markets gather steam. But even in steamy 1998 and 1999, opportunities did not vanish entirely. Investors comfortable with real estate investment trusts (REITs) grabbed yields of about 7 percent—quite a striking margin over the 1.4 percent yield by the S&P 500. The world's number-one packaging company, Crown Cork & Seal,* paid a dividend representing a 3.4 percent yield. Before the German automaker Daimler-Benz swooped in, venerable Chrysler's yield was 5 percent.

Several solid bank stocks also offered fetching yields. While growing earnings at a 9 or 10 percent clip back in 1997, BankAmerica and First Union featured yields greater than 3 percent—nearly two percentage points superior to the market's overall yield.

YOU DON'T ALWAYS NEED YIELD

At Windsor, we didn't insist on yield all of the time. Our focus on yield left a great number of stocks out of reach, but did not preclude us from trafficking at times, in no-yield stocks. Our relatively prosaic, dull, conservative portfolio notwithstanding, we reserved the freedom to snare less recognized growth companies with 12 to 15 percent growth rates and little or no yield.

Intel, which had no yield, marked such a departure for us on two separate occasions. It was one of those miraculous growth companies that represents a lot of what is great about this country. We paid around $10 a share in late 1988 and sold in 1989 at around $18. The purchase in late 1994 at $57 was only about eight times prospective 1995 earnings. The growth rate would obviously slow down, but we looked for 15 percent

---

* I joined Crown Cork's board of directors in July 1999.

growth for this well-financed and extraordinary company. Intel manufactures microprocessors for personal computers, laptops, and workstations in virtually every office in America, except mine.

How could we afford to buy no- or low-yield stocks in Windsor and still maintain the positiveness of our long-term dividend growth stream? The answer was that growth could be moderated for a year or two if, in our judgment, capital opportunities were available in more exciting fare, or we needed to broaden our portfolio's diversification. One should not forget the magnitude of the inherent growth of the income stream in the corpus of the portfolio. This was most remarkably etched in Ford, our largest holding at one time, which had increased its dividend by almost 60 percent in just 6 months.

Additionally, we had the traditional recycling opportunity from successful investments that had been purchased at good yields. They matured into more average yields and were then replaced by other more standard, Windsor purchases with good yields. Characteristically, those trades gave us approximately 200 basis points more yield on our purchased equities than on those that were being sold.

Superior Relationship of Total Return to P/E Paid

In Windsor's lexicon, "total return" described our growth expectations: annual earnings growth plus yield. Without these growth expectations, real or imagined, rational investors (and we liked to think of ourselves as rational) do not buy equities. Thus, total return represented, in effect, what Windsor got when it bought a share of stock.

Total return supplied half of a ratio that summarized, very neatly, Windsor's competitive edge. The other half of the ratio, p/e, disclosed what we paid to secure the total return. As a way to measure the bang for our investment buck, total return divided by initial p/e could not have been more succinct. We just never found a catchy name for it other than "total return ratio."

Academicians probably don't celebrate this measure; it's a bit too unsophisticated by their lights. But I never found a better way to express total return relative to what we paid for it.

Windsor hunted for stocks with a cheapo profile: their total return divided by the p/e ratio was notably out of line with industry or market benchmarks. Discounts up to half the going price for growth turned up dozens of winners. To put it differently, we preferred stocks whose total return, divided by the p/e, exceeded the market average by 2 to 1.

Dramatic price erosion attracted Windsor to the trucking industry in 1984. A company named Yellow Freight caught our eye. Calculating its total return relative to p/e paid yielded this measure of Yellow Freight's appeal:

	Earnings Growth	Yield	Total Return	P/E	Total Return ÷ P/E
Yellow Freight	12%	3.5%	15.5%	6x	2.6

For many years, Windsor routinely snatched stocks whose p/e ratios equaled half of the total returns. As the Nineties progressed, this target became tougher to realize. By early 1999, S&P 500 earnings were growing long-term at an 8 percent clip. This, plus a 1.1 percent average yield, pegged total return at 9.1 percent. Meantime, the going p/e hovered around 27 times earnings:

	Earnings Growth	Yield	Total Return	P/E	Total Return ÷ P/E
1999 market	8%	1.5%	9.5%	27	.35

The bad news, currently, is that Windsor's old criteria are much harder to meet when p/e ratios lose sight of underlying growth rates. But investors can still seek the same relative advantage that Windsor enjoyed. A stock whose total return ratio exceeds .7 matches Windsor's traditional edge.

It's the Evaluation, Stupid

A slim total return for the S&P 500 underscores the point I hammered on at the *Barron's* roundtable in January 1999. How much were investors willing to pay for such meager growth rates? A heady price, by any previous standards.

As investors enamored of big growth stocks rationalized lofty prices, I suggested that fundamentals drive value, not blind faith in ever-rising markets. Rephrasing a theme of the 1992 Presidential election campaign, I expressed my perspective in very straight terms: "It's the evaluation, stupid!"

Far from erasing the merits of low p/e investing, bull markets add urgency, in my humble opinion. Hitching wagons to stocks with high p/e ratios invites disappointment—if not searing declines sooner or later—once a falloff in the growth rate restores sobriety. When that occurs, low p/e stocks hold value better and show more spunk in the aftermath. Just when low p/e investing seems to have become obsolete, the relative advantages, if anything, become more dramatic.

No Cyclical Exposure without Compensating P/E Multiple

Cyclical stocks normally comprised a third or more of the Windsor Fund. Auto makers, chemicals, and aluminums presented us, at times, with one money-making opportunity after another. Investors blew hot and cold on cyclical stocks, a pattern that low p/e shooters like us couldn't resist. Whereas growth stocks are expected to increase earnings steadily, the trick with cyclical stocks is to catch them at just the right moment—after one cycle has decimated the stock price, but before improved earnings become apparent to everyone. When purchases were timed right, Windsor began selling just as demand picked up.

When evaluating prospects for cyclical stocks, we had to recognize that earnings fluctuate under the best of circumstances. In place of five-year growth rates, our estimates of normal earnings guided our analysis. Normal earnings merely represented a best estimate of earnings at more fortuitous points in the business cycle. Other investors performed the same exercise, of course, but few were as willing to stick their necks out. Windsor gained an edge in cyclical stocks by staking out positions when big Wall Street firms were advising their clients to wait and see.

The very nature of cyclical industries induced us to buy the same companies over and over again, buying low and selling high. In the course of my term at Windsor, we owned oil giant Atlantic Richfield, for example, on six different occasions.

NEVER CAPITALIZE PEAK EARNINGS

A critical point about cyclical stocks deserves emphasis: A ceiling on their p/e ratios limits the upside. In the growth stock arena, at least in theory, p/e's can expand as long as earnings keep rising. Not so with cyclicals. As peaks in their cycles approach, the market correctly resists conferring higher and higher earnings multiples when it knows that troughs are on the horizon.

Timing is everything. No one can predict tops and bottoms with absolute certainty. Some cycles last longer than others. We protected ourselves by purchasing cyclicals only with prospective p/e ratios that scraped bottom. Now and again, ratios got worse before they got better, but, normally, even our losers retained most of their value. By getting on board early, when we were right we garnered the highest possible return on the upside.

A low p/e strategy typically makes maximum money six to nine months before cyclical companies report better earnings. Predicting that point will tax an investor's understanding of an industry's dynamics and of overarching economic considerations.

In 1997, Continental Homes was typical, when it was lost amid the ranks of misunderstood homebuilders. With the demand for housing on the rise and interest rates on a downward slope, a winning recipe seemed visible to me. Most investors, however, wanted evidence of dramatic earnings improvement. I didn't wait for that evidence. I bought the shares and sold them after the price tripled.

Solid Companies in Growing Fields

Typical Windsor fare featured good companies with solid market positions and evidence of room to grow. Laboring outside the spotlight, they were more vulnerable than America's great companies to investors' whims. That's what we liked; for that matter, we were good shareholders in management's eyes. When markets were least accommodating, we bought the shares. So long as the businesses remained sound, strategic plans were in place, and sufficient resources existed to weather difficult conditions, we counted on them to work their way back to center stage.

In addition to Windsor's cherished cadres of less known growth companies, first-tier companies occasionally stumbled into view. Bad news almost always overshadows good news, and even great companies can fall victim to investors' malaise. Thanks to such mood swings, during my 31 years, Windsor owned virtually the whole range of American industry, which sooner or later became available at low p/e ratios.

On the strength of its industry leadership, we built a compelling case for ABC Television in 1978. By our reckoning, ABC was the preeminent broadcasting company. Its success went well beyond highly publicized prime-time leadership. We noted important gains achieved in all other major programming—notably, parity with CBS in the highly profitable daytime segment. Beyond the network assets, ABC owned the most profitable TV station group and radio operations in the industry.

Remarkably, ABC was accorded the very lowest multiple in broadcasting—approximately five times 1978 earnings. Importantly, we regarded these earnings as good-quality earnings. The mix of programming costs was extraordinarily rich, which created enough flexibility in costs to offset an eventual showdown in network revenue gains. Thus, we had confidence in ABC's earnings in the face of the next cyclical test, and we expected its performance to occasion an important upgrade in its p/e multiple. In a longer-term view, we looked for 9 percent growth from ABC's existing operations, in line with the broadcast industry. We also expected ABC to lift its growth rate an additional 2 percentage points, thanks to smart use of cash flow. Without boosting the dividend, which seemed due for a boost to catch up with earnings, the yield was nearly 4 percent, for a total return of nearly 15 percent. We were targeting a p/e of 14 times, versus 12 times for the market. ABC deserved an Emmy for its subsequent performance. Our gains in 1979 ranged as high as 85 percent.

In mid-1982, availing ourselves of a downtrodden market's characteristic failure to identify worthy stocks, we applied ourselves to finding opportunities. At that point, most investors were running away from the oil stocks that had been embraced enthusiastically just a couple of years earlier. The situation invited Windsor's attention, but we had to be careful to sift out the weaklings from the companies with good, underlying strength.

DRILLING FOR EARNINGS

In this climate, Halliburton, an oil services outfit, satisfied Windsor's tried and true requirements. Halliburton had the premier position in the down-hole, cementing and stimulating areas where, along with its chief competitor, it accounted for the lion's share of this critical oilfield service. Nearly 85 percent of Halliburton's earnings were concentrated in these areas, where the customer needed a unique and readily available service.

Halliburton had a long record of not only providing the service, but without price gouging the customer even though such opportunistic practices were common. We believed that the footage drilled domestically would continue to grow, although at a reduced pace, and Halliburton was poised to benefit not only from increased penetration of its natural markets, but also from a trend toward deeper wells. The company had two construction subsidiaries that contributed 15 percent of total earnings in 1982 and stood to participate in a rebound. To us, Halliburton looked like a 16 percent grower with an almost 5 percent yield, available at a purchase price of less than 5 times earnings. *Outcome: This was a gusher. Halliburton shares fetched championship gains by mid-1983.*

Boeing, perhaps the epitome of a solid company in a growing field, represented something of a departure for Windsor in 1986. Its appeal was twofold: (1) we had never owned it before, and (2) not too surprisingly, the prevailing consensus had sharply eroded the price of the stock. It was a well-capitalized, well-financed premier entry in the world sweepstakes of commercial aviation, along with a much less important participation in the defense area. Earnings were likely to slide in 1986 by almost 25 percent. This decline was caused, temporarily, by fewer deliveries of the very profitable 747 aircraft, but also involved significant expenditures to try and snare new business in the defense arena.

Adding to the pressure, the company suffered out-of-control losses in the newly purchased Canadian de Haviland small aircraft division. The company's accounting was as conservative as its finances. We thought there would be a real breakout in earnings, not only in a recovery during

1988 to around the 1986 levels, but also in a further spring in 1989. This prediction was premised on very significant deliveries (almost double the 1987 pace) of the very profitable 747 in the new long-range 400 division. Despite uneconomic (to them) competition from the European consortium of the new Airbus 320 and prospective 340, we thought Boeing's outstanding relative position, further buttressed by a weak dollar, would serve the company very well in the burgeoning international commercial aircraft competition. The yield was only around 3 percent, but excellent finances, in combination with the earnings prospect, allowed for excellent increases in the yield as well. ***Outcome:*** *Boeing took off on schedule, garnering a 68 percent return for Windsor versus 24 percent for the aerospace group and 11 percent for the S&P 500.*

Strong Fundamental Support

Short of attempting to shoehorn a thorough treatment of fundamental analysis into a few paragraphs, I can offer brief perspectives on some of the measures that are most useful to me.

No solitary measure or pair of measures should govern a decision to buy a stock. You need to probe a whole raft of numbers and facts, searching for confirmation or contradiction. The goal is to develop credible growth expectations for a low p/e company or industry. Fundamental analysis consists largely of appraising corporate performance against industry or market benchmarks. Fundamentals consistent with benchmarks usually reinforce the unrecognized virtues of low p/e stocks; fundamental shortfalls may expose gaps that cripple prospects for p/e multiple expansion. Judgment lies in recognizing which way the fundamentals point. Conventional wisdom and preconceived notions are stumbling blocks as well as signs of opportunity.

My style of security analysis examines earnings and sales: (1) earnings growth drives the p/e and the stock price, and (2) dividends come from earnings. Ultimately, *growing sales create growing earnings.* Squeezing greater earnings from each dollar of sales (called margin improvement) can buttress a case for investing, but margins do not grow to the sky. Eventually, attractive companies must demonstrate sales growth.

Public companies post sales and earnings every quarter. Examine the relationship between sales in dollars and sales in units. Ordinarily, I favor dollars over units. Earnings are measured in dollars, not in units. The link is important because of what it communicates about pricing. If the growth of dollar sales outpaces the unit sales, rising prices can help fuel momentum. Taken in tandem with overall rising sales, rising prices often flag a opportunity. Low p/e merchandise poised to capture price increases often pays a tidy return.

Similarly, keep an eye on deliveries. When companies can't deliver goods as fast as they can take orders, it might suggest trouble. In 1998, when Boeing's assembly lines could not keep up with orders, the stock price suffered. On the other hand, when demand exceeds supply, companies can sometimes raise prices. Low p/e investors must discern whether earnings will return to normal and what sort of attention they will draw.

You must determine whether the backlog is due to a shortage of raw materials, too few skilled workers, or a technical glitch, to name three obstacles of different magnitude. A shortage of raw materials or a technical glitch may lend themselves to quick remedies, but if substantial numbers of skilled workers are wanting, there's no quick and easy way to fill that gap. The magnitude of the problem—or opportunity—has a bearing on how long it will take for the p/e ratio to respond.

GO WITH THE FLOW

In an era of rising doubts about earnings calculations, cash flow has assumed increasing importance. I don't take it quite as far as some securities analysts do. To me, cash flow consists of retained earnings* plus depreciation—an accountant's way of measuring how much wear and tear has diminished the value of a building or a piece of machinery. Companies record depreciation in their financial statements.

More exacting fans of cash flow go a step further than EBITD. A nifty acronym for their version is EBITDA (earnings before interest, taxes, depreciation, and *amortization*), pronounced more or less the way it's spelled. Leveraged buyouts typically rest on assessments of EBITDA, which suggest how much debt a company can sustain and still remain viable. For my purposes, retained earnings plus depreciation was always sufficient proxy for cash flow. When this figure is in hand, you must

---

* Retained earnings are net profits not distributed through dividends or other means.

reconcile it with two others that reveal how much cash the company will require to feed its capital requirements: (1) working capital and (2) capital expenditures. Any shortfall in cash flow must be financed in some fashion. Excess cash flow can provide capital for additional dividends, stock repurchases, acquisitions, or reinvestment.

The Washington Post Company represented a quality package of well-established media properties. Newspaper earnings, mainly from the *Post* itself, represented 40 percent; *Newsweek* Magazine brought in 30 percent, and *Post–Newsweek* TV and radio stations earned the remaining 30 percent. In addition to inherent growth of these businesses—aided by good markets for the *Post* and the broadcasting properties, and the ability to step out with new publications at *Newsweek*—there was a regular benefit of genuine excess cash flow each year. ***Outcome:*** *Windsor posted a 45 percent gain after 12 months.*

In another instance where cash flow guided our assessment, we added gasoline producer and refiner Amerada Hess in late 1988. At that time, it was still dominated by family ownership centering on the family patriarch, Leon Hess. The company had not fashioned a particularly good result in refining or in marketing. The exploratory side looked somewhat better, most notably in the North Sea near the United Kingdom. The company was probably more dramatically undervalued on the basis of its oil reserves than on the basis of traditional earnings, although we believed that more satisfactory earnings were due eventually. We paid $26 a share, and our target price, $40, amounted to less than 5 times the prospective 1989 cash flow per share. ***Outcome:*** *After Hess advanced 50 percent in less than one year, Windsor cashed in.*

RETURN ON EQUITY

Return on equity (ROE) furnishes the best single yardstick of what management has accomplished with money that belongs to shareholders. It constitutes a ratio of net income to the value of common stock. Using this benchmark, we added a significant property and casualty insurer to Windsor in 1981.

Crum & Forster occupied a special niche in the workers' compensation segment of the property and casualty insurance industry. In 1981, the company had garnered one of the best returns on equity in the industry, thereby enabling it to build shareholders' equity. This important strut supported our estimation of the company's growth rate. ***Outcome:*** *Strong gains in accordance with our expectation attracted a bid by Xerox Corporation, then bent on an ill-fated expansion into financial services. Our quick gain on the sale of our Crum & Forster stake was unfortunately offset by deterioration in the price of our Xerox shares.*

HOW WRONG CAN YOU BE AND STILL WALK AWAY?

Operating margin highlights the relationship between sales and what's left over after costs related to sales are deducted from sales. The nature of an industry ordinarily governs the margins. Successful software companies enjoy operating margins in excess of 40 percent; supermarkets settle for razor-thin margins. The operating margin gives an indication of a company's earnings margin of error to untoward events. If the operating margin is 20 percent and a bad turn of events knocks off 5 percentage points, a pretty good margin remains. In the low p/e spectrum (where going against the grain may invite bad news), a robust operating margin supplies hefty protection against negative surprises.

The pretax margin goes a step further. It highlights the relationship between sales and all costs other than taxes—a more telling source than the operating margin because it reveals whether costs unrelated to sales are hindering the overall business prospects. As an investor, that's a more refined indication of your tolerance for being wrong.

At day's end, all the techniques for finding low p/e stocks have one objective: compiling a salable record of accomplishment. Every stock that Windsor owned was always for sale. Unless other investors see the point you've been trying to make, you won't enjoy the reward you anticipated. Will a single stock fetch a friendly price when you're ready to sell it? There are no guarantees, but a low p/e strategy can tilt the odds in your favor.

8

~

THE BARGAIN BASEMENT

THE INVESTMENT PROCESS must begin somewhere. In my case, all ladders start in the dusty rag and bone shop of the mart, where the supply of cheap stocks replenishes itself daily.

FOLLOW LOW PRICES EVERY DAY

Keep tabs on stock prices posting new lows. This list changes every day. Two days after the Dow Jones Industrial Average closed above the 10,000 mark for the first time, the stock of 185 New York Stock Exchange companies sank to their lowest points in 52 weeks. On NASDAQ, 148 stocks etched new lows.

Low stock prices should never trigger automatic buy signals. For some of these companies, more dismal days lie ahead. But, in the course of my career, few days have passed when the new low list has not included one or two solid companies worth investigating. The goal is to find earnings growth capable of capturing the market's attention once the climate shifts.

Scan published stock tables for stocks changing hands at a price that is close to a 52-week low. Newspapers routinely list most stocks on major exchanges and indicate the price range during the previous year. Find out whether the price is moving up briskly from a low or is languishing nearby. Then find out why. This turf is not every investor's happy hunting ground. As a matter of fact, it's hardly anybody's, for the simple reason that many of these companies are poor performers. But a few may meet low p/e criteria. Dull though they are, the results can shine.

TRY THE "HMMMPH" TEST

The stock market news usually lists 20 worst performers from the previous day. They can be down from 8 percent to 30 percent, ordinarily. Whip through this list, as I do, and you'll find a familiar name now and then—a company you know something about. Some names I would not have expected to see on this list elicit an audible "Hmmmph." I hear myself. There's a question-mark tone that implies: "Does this stock bear further investigation?"

Barring evidence or knowledge of some fundamental deficiency, I'll see how these stocks measure up against low p/e criteria. Even if a stock doesn't make the cut, the next time it comes into view I'll have an edge versus the competition.

BAD PRESS CAN BRING GOOD NEWS

Unfavorable news flags my attention. About the time experts declare that low p/e has no future and that stocks *du jour* will rule forever, inflection points are drawing near. In February 1991, Windsor's poor showing in 1990 prompted a story in *Forbes* entitled "Tarnished Glory."*

A few months later, prospects looked brighter. "Stock Picking Style Returns to Success,"† *The Wall Street Journal*'s "Heard on the Street" column headlined. "Now that the old reliable 'value' style has snapped out of the doldrums, investors want to know what some leading bargain hunters are stuffing into their portfolios." In early 1999, the same phenomenon arose. After several prominent publications declared the demise of value investing, value bounced back. In July, Windsor topped *The Wall Street Journal*'s list of seven rebounding mutual funds it called "Comeback

---

* Richard Phalon and Michael Fritz, "Tarnished Glory," *Forbes*, February 4, 1991.
† John R. Dorfman, "Inside the Value Investors' Portfolio," *The Wall Street Journal*, May 22, 1991.

Kids."* Like Windsor, the next two funds on the list also were large cap value funds.

Ever conscious of the frailties of prevailing wisdom, I read the news with an eye to finding particular companies or industries on hard times. When I find one, I've got to decide whether the underlying business is actually sound and fears have been overblown. Windsor collected handsome profits by taking issue time and time again with prevailing opinion. Few such disagreements were more dramatically visible than when mammoth environmental liabilities threatened to swamp the insurance industry. Reflecting this gloom in the late 1980s, numerous property and casualty insurance companies slipped into Windsor's range. We particularly liked Cigna Corp.

Every Wall Street analyst but one predicted future liabilities of approximately $500 billion for toxic and environmental obligations. If such a blow occurred, it raised doubts about the industry's viability. Wall Street's propensity for groupthink fans these dire expectations. Too many sell-side analysts whisper in each other's ears, and few want to stick his or her neck out too far. There's not much of a reason to be a hero if being wrong can cost you your job. You can sum up the Street's psychology this way: Hope for the best, expect the worst. Meantime, don't stick your neck out.

Before questions about tainted landfills arose, asbestos underscored Wall Street's tendency to overreact. The full magnitude of those imagined costs never materialized, and prices of stocks thought to be affected by asbestos rebounded. With this precedent in mind, we took issue with expert opinion about environmental liabilities. Instead of focusing on the fate of the insurance industry if costs reached the predicted magnitude, we wondered about the impact once overreactions melted away.

Meantime, hoopla surrounding environmental liabilities obscured Cigna's very appealing managed care business. As current costs and reserves set aside to meet future environmental costs mounted, Cigna held its own, thanks to managed care's robust earnings.

This and a downtrodden p/e ratio looked very promising to us. As things turned out, the actual reserves that insurance companies had to establish represented a fraction of the Doomsday estimates. Cigna's share

---

* Pui-Wing Tam, "Seven Mutual Funds that Went from Loser to Winner," *The Wall Street Journal*, July 23, 1999 p. C1; Fund rankings by Morningstar Inc.

was a big number, to be sure, but well within the limits of Cigna's financial resources. *Outcome: In 1991, as environmental consequences abated, Cigna's shares advanced by 54 percent while other property and casualty insurers enjoyed, on average, a 45 percent gain. In the same period, the S&P 500 logged a 29 percent gain.*

MARKED PRICE DROPS CAN RAISE PROSPECTS

Windsor routinely picked off sound companies at steep discounts to higher prices. Here are some examples of prices Windsor paid relative to earlier peaks:

Purchases, July–October 1986	% Decline from 1986 High	1986 High
Atlantic Richfield	−25.0%	$ 21.00
Cigna Corp.	−24.9	191.00
Travelers Corp.	−23.3	70.00
Aluminum Co. of America	−23.1	111.00
Chrysler Corp.	−22.1	127.00
General Motors Corp.	−19.0	36.00
Standard Oil Corp.	−18.6	28.00
Great Western Financial	−18.4	23.00
Citicorp	−17.6	33.00
IBM	−17.1	149.00
Alcan Aluminum	−16.3	39.00
First Interstate Bancorp	−14.8	34.00
Bankers Trust	−13.7	44.00
Phillips Petroleum	−13.6	33.00
Median	**−18.5%**	

At times, price declines lured us outside Windsor's usual stomping grounds, provided they met other low p/e criteria. Selling at 20 times expected 1985 earnings, for example, Home Depot hardly seemed typical Windsor fare. The inventor of the "Do-It-Yourself Warehouse" store, the company revolutionized the home center industry. Though its super-large, no-frills, low-price stores attracted a flock of imitators, Home Depot was alone in being profitable.

In 1985, Home Depot expanded rapidly from 22 to 50-plus stores. Preopening costs and expanding overhead cut into profits. Unnerved investors abandoned ship, causing the sinking stock price to flag our attention. Upon examination, the company seemed to be managing its expansion well. We were normally dubious about "trees growing up to heaven," but at 10 times 1986 prospective recovery earnings, down 60 percent from its high, there was more fear than greed in this 25 percent grower. *Outcome: After about nine months, we enjoyed a 63 percent return on Home Depot, beginning in the second quarter of 1986.*

SEEK COMPANIES ON THE SQUASH

Dramatic actions taken by companies, as opposed to broad challenges posed by difficult industrial or economic climates, can trigger unwarranted selling pressure. Investors seldom have much ardor for shares issued by companies that are in the midst of refashioning themselves. This was not a judgment Windsor shared in 1989 when we started a new position in Owens Corning Fiberglass, the world's largest maker of fiberglass.

Threatened with a takeover in 1986, Owens Corning defended itself by borrowing heavily to buy its stock back from shareholders. Then it reissued "stub" shares that represented a fraction of shareholders' original stake. We accumulated our position in these "stub" shares. The extent of restructuring showed clearly on the balance sheet, where shareholders' equity went from positive to negative—meaning that the book value of shareholders' stake in Owens Corning was less than zero. Largely an accounting issue subservient to the fact that market value represented shareholders' actual stake, negative shareholders' equity nevertheless spooked most investors.

Unlike other companies that restructured in this fashion, Owens Corning had a clear success story. Part of the success stemmed from increased attention to earnings levers such as costs, productivity, and capacity utilization. We also believed the underlying fiberglass business was sound. New products and good service were visible in the company's rising market share in all its major markets. Customers included the bluest of multinational blue-chip companies engaged in developing new applications for fiberglass.

Because investors were jittery about the course of restructuring, the stock changed hands for about 5½ times trailing earnings estimates and less than 5 times toward estimates. We pegged earnings growth from operations in a range of 8 to 10 percent, plus equivalent growth as the company paid down its hefty debt load and applied interest payments to earnings. There was no dividend, but we expected Owens Corning to restore a dividend once shareholders' equity regained a normal footing. Where other investors saw an unfamiliar restructuring, we thought we saw a quality company in a good, sound business, with excellent growth prospects. *Outcome: Beginning in the first quarter of 1991, Windsor began to realize solid gains. In 1993, we sold Owens Corning shares for twice Windsor's cost.*

Beazer, PLC was a UK-based homebuilder and construction materials company laboring under a good deal of selling pressure in late 1991. Despite its British origin, the company rang up 60 percent of its shrinking operating profits in the United States. An expensive acquisition strategy had caught up with Beazer amid a construction recession. As a consequence, Beazer tottered on the verge of violating bank covenants. A plan to sell off the British operation in a public offering sent investors scrambling toward the exits. In this anxious climate, Windsor paid $4 a share, down from a high of $13.75 just a few months earlier.

In their haste to exit Beazer stock, investors failed to see the attraction of what would be left after the restructuring. Eventually, though, they saw the light. Beazer stock advanced 50 percent in the first two months that we owned it.

Look for Companies Moving Up the Quality Ladder

The case for investing in Gulf Oil in late 1978 revolved around a better recognition of the essential domestication of the company. We expected Gulf to get 85 percent of its 1978 earnings from the United States and Canada, versus 30 percent in 1973. Meanwhile, one of the most aggressive exploration programs in the oil industry was poised to begin paying off, paving the way for above-average future growth. The company faced a specter of uranium litigation, but a commonsense interpretation of the facts convinced us that Gulf would prevail. In any event, this concern weighed down the market's valuation of Gulf, resulting in a hefty 8.0 percent yield to make the wait for returns livable. The p/e on 1978 earnings was about 5.8 times, and we expected it to more than double. ***Outcome:*** *We sold these shares early in a silly season for oil stocks that was predicated on earnest expectations that the price of oil would reach $60 a barrel. Our Gulf stake posted returns ranging from 42 percent in November 1979 to 86 percent the following August.*

Late in 1975, National Distillers & Chemicals, though known primarily for its bourbons, was also a leading producer of several types of plastics and chemicals. We expected earnings to drop in 1975 and then rebound in 1976, aided by a recovery in chemical volume and a cyclical upturn in the brass manufacturing division, Bridgeport Brass. National Distillers (later, Quantum Chemical Corp.) was a candidate for a p/e multiple expansion as it became a higher-quality chemical company. With a yield of 7.3 percent, National Distillers would almost double, using our target multiple of 9.5 times 1976 earnings. We toasted a 60 percent gain in June 1976, after owning the shares for about 12 months.

SEEK BACKDOOR ACCESS TO INVESTMENT OPPORTUNITIES

Windsor's largest single energy purchase by far, in early 1985, was Shell Transport & Trading. This company was a surrogate for Royal Dutch Petroleum, which we owned already. Thanks to this arrangement, we were able to enlarge our stake in Royal Dutch beyond the usual cap. Royal Dutch owned 60 percent of the Shell Group, and Shell Transport owned 40 percent of the very same company. The only difference was the country of domicile. Royal Dutch headquarters was in Holland; Shell Transport was based in the United Kingdom.

The interlocking relationship between Shell and Shell Transport enabled Windsor to stake out a larger position in the same company than regulators ordinarily allowed. In this case, we bulked up beyond the usual limits on a particularly undervalued company that seemed tailor-made for institutional acceptance, barring a disaster scenario in respect to oil prices. We thought that, at four times earnings, with a noticeable yield and tremendous cash flow coursing through its veins, Shell Transport was too attractive not to gain more adherents in the marketplace.

Outcome: After owning Shell Transport for less than two years, Windsor garnered a 53 percent gain.

Amid robust demand for oil stocks in 1980, we kept alert to any price opportunities that might reassert our representation in the energy area, where we were purposefully underrepresented versus the S&P 500. In that spirit, we lifted our stake in a company called Northwest Industries. In effect, we were "backdooring" a participation in the oil field equipment sweepstakes, which then constituted about 4 percent of the S&P 500 but cost an arm and a leg to gain representation. Northwest Industries was a broadly based conglomerate with interests ranging all over the industrial map. It would rely for nearly half of its 1980 earnings on Lone Star Steel—in our opinion, the premier company, both in cost and profit, supplying drill pipe and casing for the domestic oil industry.

This represented a direct participation in the new economics encouraging the search for oil and gas in this country, not only in respect to the increasing number of wells drilled but also to the greater depth of those wells. Natural gas discovered below 15,000 feet was completely unregulated as to price, and could garner robust returns upon discovery. Northwest Industries sold for a little over five times its somewhat depressed 1980 earnings; its yield was 6.8 percent, and was likely to increase soon by 10 percent. This struck us as a more sensible way to participate in these sweepstakes rather than paying double-digit multiples and receiving virtually no yield. *Outcome: We began to liquidate this stake a year later. Windsor pocketed gains ranging from 68 percent in May 1981 to 125 percent in February 1982.*

FIND MISCATEGORIZED COMPANIES

Bayer AG was one of the Big Three German chemical companies in late 1990, when we added it to the Windsor Fund. Its product mix was quite attractive for such a cheap stock. About a third of earnings came from pharmaceuticals and other health care products, 8 percent came from agricultural chemicals, and 13 percent came from photographic or specialty chemicals. In other words, fully half of Bayer's earnings were not especially tied to the economy.

Nevertheless, the stock had declined 35 percent, just like any other chemical stock with products more exposed to business cycles. Even the cyclical part of Bayer's mix had in it a number of attractive specialties and lacked a great deal of basic commodity chemical content. Thanks to this product mix, we expected Bayer's earnings to outperform in an increasingly complex environment for global chemical companies. It was a fine, well-run company, and we bought it for a little over 6 times earnings. Lucky for us, investors saw it in a more pedestrian light. *Outcome: Late in 1993, Windsor began to reap above-market gains.*

SEEK CRITICAL MASS

This we learned the hard way.

Every category has its losers, of course, and US Industries provided us with a reminder that conglomerates are not exempt. Headed by a very talkative CEO named I. John Billera, which always made me think of someone testifying before Congress, US Industries was a highly aggressive, acquisition oriented company. It consisted of some 100 separate companies spread among six different industries. Besides external growth fostered by a bewildering pace of acquisitions, the company had grown internally in excess of 24 percent a year for five consecutive years. In retrospect, maybe some companies are just growing too fast to get a handle on, and for that reason alone we should have stayed clear of US Industries. But we didn't.

While unable to analyze each component company in USI completely, we nevertheless exercised our judgments on various industry fundamentals. The outlooks for apparel and services, for example, were considerably better than for the economy as a whole. Likewise, we saw eventually continuing growth in building materials, construction, and furnishings, when their environments improve—possibly in 1971.

In our estimation, the stock price was laboring due to investor uncertainty over the meaningfulness of reported earnings per share. They had been restated once already for a change in accounting rules and faced an additional adjustment in 1971.

Could USI properly evaluate so many companies at the rate it was buying them? Their answer, which satisfied us at the time, has been echoed in every merger and acquisitions boom since. Where nowadays investors talk about acquisitions "accretive to earnings in the first year," USI claimed it bought only businesses capable of 15 percent average annual earnings growth, with an added twist. Rather than take the risk that growth stumble, USI paid sellers on an installment basis. If growth slowed, the ultimate price tag was subject to adjustments. Typically, USI distributed stock or cash at eight times current earnings with a contingency payment based on future year's earnings. This appeared to create a substantial incentive for management to stay on, rather than cash in their gains and retire. Of course, if the stock declined, USI had to issue just that much more stock to satisfy the obligation, which became dilutive under the grind of circumstances.

In the end, the outcome was less congenial than our prediction, not least because the bombastic CEO could not give a consistent story to investors. Ultimately, USI fell short in one key aspect: its businesses lacked critical mass. Absent the ability to dominate markets, products and services cannot command premium prices. Except for a promising bump in price before 1970 was out, USI backslid and never recovered any forward momentum. In 1972 we began exiting the stock in dribs and drabs. In the final analysis, Windsor lost about half of its investment.

We always followed a practice in Windsor of having our large holdings working for us. In short, US Industries did not fulfill our expectations on the fundamental side. Although it was "dirt cheap" in the going marketplace, so were a lot of other stocks that were either accomplishing already or poised to.

CREATE OPPORTUNITIES FOR "FREE PLUS"

Situations spawned a free plus whenever companies we owned flourished beyond all expectations. An unexpected boom in personal computing ignited the stock of an ordinary little electronics retailer named Tandy. We did not anticipate Atlantic Richfield's rewarding oil field strike on Alaska's North Slope, another free plus. Mergers and acquisitions also bestow a free plus on investors. The challenge is to foster opportunities for a free plus, and low p/e investing is the most reliable method I know. If you own a stock where the negatives are largely known, then good news that comes as a surprise can have outsized effects. This is the mirror opposite of the situation that growth investors embrace, where a hint of bad news can take the pizzazz right out of a stock.

PLAY TO YOUR STRENGTHS

Without a team of professional securities analysts to comb bargain basements, emphasize your inherent strengths. They usually reside in a heightened measure of awareness about a company or an industry that you know firsthand.

Individual investors often have special insights into the companies and industries that employ them. I don't mean illicit inside information; I mean general knowledge about the best and worst companies in the industry, and why they line up that way.

Besides the quantitative aspects of industry fundamentals, you might have some notions about the qualitative aspects, such as prominent differences between company cultures and strategies. Some differences get exaggerated during their evaluation because people give undue and exaggerated weight to their own expertise, but at least you can put your life experience to work to improve your investment odds. Be wary, however, of investing exclusively in the company that writes your paycheck. You may like your employer's prospects, but if business goes awry, you don't want to see your nestegg vanish along with your salary.

SHOP AROUND THE NEIGHBORHOOD

Restricting investment to the industry in which you work obviously hampers diversification. A good place to seek investment ideas is in shopping malls. It never hurts to visit local retailers or to listen to what's hot with your teenage children; sometimes a winner turns up. One note of caution, however: Don't call your stockbroker just because a local retailer has a lot of traffic or a new gadget is selling out.

Execution separates good retailers from indifferent performers. You can't easily assess execution from the aisles. You might experience a retail moment in time relative to value, perceived value, or style, or whatever, but even that is not all you need to judge prospects for a stock. Having shopped the stock market extensively for retailers, I've learned the importance of execution—sometimes, the hard way.

A good buzz never hurts a business, but it won't substitute for good execution. A successful company has buyers with fashion judgment; timing; delivery; friendly prices; and good housekeeping. That's still the way the bottom line gets black ink. Breadth and depth of assortment enable a retailer to tease potential buyers with a fascinating array of styles, colors, and sizes, but customers whose sizes aren't there are left in a lurch. On the other hand, maybe you'll stumble on another Pier One, a retailer that produced bountiful returns for Windsor.

Pier One Imports was the nation's leading specialty retailer of decorative home furnishings and related items. The merchandise featured wicker and rattan furniture, baskets, pillows, floor coverings, and a line of "gypsy" clothing. About 80 percent of the goods it sold were imported from China, India, Taiwan, and other developing nations. The individual suppliers were, in many cases, rural, cottage-industry factors whose relationship with Pier One dated back 25 years.

As far as we could tell, Pier One faced no national competition. Over the years, the company had experienced its ups and downs. New management arrived in 1985 and livened up advertising, upgraded the merchandise offering, and sought out more attractive new stores. The results included better per-store volumes, higher grosses, and a well-organized expansion program that was able to underwrite a 15 percent growth in the store base.

We had had Pier One in our sights for some time. Along with other flourishing specialty retailers, however, it had a p/e ratio that was too rich for our blood. Then the chain was knocked for a loop in October 1987, when the market plummeted 500 points, or about 20 percent, in a single day.

Investors running for cover in the aftermath of Black Monday did not stop to notice that Pier One's earnings per share were en route to a 47 percent increase for fiscal 1988. On top of that, we foresaw another 25 percent advance in 1989. Our purchase price was a little under 8 times 1989 earnings—a very compelling ratio, given the prospects for sustained growth of about 20 percent. **Outcome:** *We doubled our money in six months.*

EXPAND YOUR HORIZONS

Local retailers constitute a narrow band of investment opportunities, at best. Think about places to eat, or the store where you buy office supplies, or the car in your garage. Investors encounter public companies every day; your search for low p/e stocks can start there. I've often been a fan of eating establishments big enough for a New York

Stock Exchange listing. From time to time, Windsor reaped attractive gains from the likes of McDonald's, Ponderosa Steak Houses, and Long John Silver. Windsor owned each of them more than once. Sometimes we made money, sometimes we didn't.

DEVELOP A CURBSTONE OPINION

Investing is not a very complicated business; people just make it complicated. You have to learn to go from the general to the particular in a logical, sequential, rational manner.

Curbstone opinions entail informed observations about the general condition of a company, an industry, or aspects of the economy that are likely to affect the first two. Ask and get answers to these questions:

- What is the company's reputation?
- Is its business likely to grow?
- Is it a leader in its industry?
- What is the growth outlook for the industry?
- Has management demonstrated sound strategic leadership?

Any service that systematically updates stocks can help. I'd go through new editions of *Value Line* every week. I don't read, much less follow, the valuations or predictions. I studied the numbers. This supplied a means of looking at every stock every three months, noticing price changes and p/e relationships that, in conjunction with other news, piqued my interest.

If you want to sleep well at night, do your own homework. Don't be hasty. Time spent nosing around usually comes in handy eventually. In any event, if the stock is as terrific as you believe, catching it a quarter point higher is less hazardous in the long run than firing before you aim properly.

Rewarding opportunities always populate bargain basements, but disappointments lurk there too. That's the nature of low p/e investing. Grabbing merchandise that meets the least criteria usually invites disappointment. But if you do the work and answer the right questions, you can dine out on the down-and-out.

9

~

CARE AND MAINTENANCE OF A
LOW P/E PORTFOLIO

PICKING STOCKS CONSTITUTES the easy part of low p/e investing. Dwelling successfully in woebegone regions of the market is a different story. Until results surface, few investors can muster the courage to buy down-and-out stocks that evoke blank stares more often than envy. Once results become visible, of course, the opportunities usually have passed.

This may sound like an odd introduction to building and maintaining a low p/e stock portfolio. But state-of-mind is central to the issue. Windsor's success flowed ultimately from our willingness to step outside the crowd's embrace and be exposed to the risk of embarrassment.

The psychological side of low p/e investing seldom gets the respect it deserves, yet it governs the outcome. If you take a poll on the subject, investors will routinely claim they have sufficient courage to make an investment, no matter how unpopular. Such claims are typical of human nature, but they don't often bear scrutiny. Anyone can recognize a bargain in retrospect and then take credit later for spotting it. When shares of a stock change hands for 30 times earnings, who doesn't recall the day when shares fetched only 12 times earnings? But where were the buyers then? Most were cowering in fear of the latest news reports or piling onto the speediest growth-stock bandwagon, even if its wheels were about to fall off.

Investors typically bristle at the notion that the crowd governs their behavior. Countless self-proclaimed contrarians declare that General Electric is a buy at 40 times earnings because it is such a good company.

Hang around long enough and you'll hear variations on that assertion repeatedly. The truth is, General Electric *is* a very good company—a *great* company, in fact. And the price could go to 80 times earnings. But with very few exceptions, markets don't work that way. You can't up the ante forever. Eventually, even great stocks run out of gas. So if you bet that GE will go to 80 times earnings, you're betting against the odds. At Windsor, we tried to keep the odds in our favor.

INFLECTION POINTS ABOUND

All investing trends seem to go to excess eventually. In the Sixties, the go-go era swept investors in and judgment out. In the early Seventies, the Nifty Fifty ruled supreme. In 1980, some experts foresaw a $60 barrel of oil, transforming oil companies to gold.

These fads clattered to their inevitable conclusions when expectations encountered reality. Fans bolted for the nearest exits, and sobriety returned to the marketplace. History books record similar extravaganzas stretching back centuries, frequently with special attention to the celebrated tulip-mania that drove tulip bulb prices sky-high in 17th-century Holland.

Excesses invariably give rise to inflection points. Signaling the end of trends gone too far, inflection points alter the investment landscape. They hand low p/e investors the chance to capture extraordinary gains afterward, once out-of-favor stocks regain the market's attention. It happens over and over again. The ability of the stock market to overvalue a good thing runs amok.

Inflections occur over extended periods, as in the drawn-out end to spiraling oil costs. Or they can occur in a single day, as in the 20.7 percent market decline by the S&P 500 in October 19th 1987. On more than one occasion, a pronounced, neck-out stand against the marketplace caused Windsor to underperform until a more discerning market corrected excesses.

The first period was the quality growth stock, "Nifty-Fifty" era in 1971, 1972, and 1973, when our cumulative total underperformance was almost 26 percentage points. However, as a result of keeping our head, our principles, and our perspective, in the ensuing three years (1974 through 1976), Windsor bested the S&P by a more-than-compensatory 63 percentage points.

Refusal to partake in groupthink caused us to underperform the market by 9.8 percentage points in 1980 but cascaded to Windsor's benefit in 1981. We recovered our footing and surpassed the S&P 500 by better than 21.7 percentage points. We'd pinned our reputation to a rout of that sort.

Another challenge occurred during a new-issue craze, a technology extravaganza that peaked in mid-1983. Windsor held about even with the market through that excess and actually finished 1983, including the postinflection period in the last half, nearly 8 points better than the S&P. The year following had a gangbusters pace: a 13.3 percent positive comparison for Windsor.

Owing chiefly to the relentless din of experts who fan popular delusions (with help from the media), the timing and the magnitude of inflection points take most investors by surprise. But some signals are unmistakable. The marketplace always becomes momentum-laden as inflection points draw near, rife with warnings that starry-eyed investors dismiss.

Notwithstanding pundits who claim otherwise, no one can predict inflection points with certainty. The most famous such claimant, Roger Babson, indeed predicted the Great Crash in 1929 in his investment newsletter. Less widely recalled is that Babson had been predicting the crash continually since 1926.

In fairness to Babson, a pioneer in investment management, warning signs often cry for attention long before an inflection point erupts. When investors far and wide agree, and the media trumpet that opinion, watch out. These are foothills of inflection points. As the Dow Jones Industrial Average languished near 700 in 1979, a classic *Business Week** cover story raised a dispiriting question then circulating on Wall Street: Were equities dead? Apparently not.

BEWARE THE DRUMBEAT OF POPULAR OPINION

Managing a low p/e portfolio entails the ability to read prevailing wisdom. It's not hard to find. Prevailing wisdom makes itself known every

---

* "The Death of Equities: How Inflation Is Destroying the Stock Market," *Business Week*, August 13, 1979, Industrial Edition 2598.

day, in newspapers and on Main Street. It's what most people think. As bull markets progress, prevailing wisdom becomes a drumbeat that drowns out the argument for a low p/e strategy. Ironically, the merits of low p/e ratios are most compelling amid the clamor for hot stocks and hot sectors, but that is when investors are least likely to listen.

Just before the United States and our allies unleashed Desert Storm, crude oil was selling for $28 a barrel. I thought it was way overpriced because that whole fandango would be resolved, resulting in plenty of oil production. As rhetoric heated up, the price climbed to $32. The consensus was that as soon as forces disembarked on the Saudi Arabian peninsula, in preparation for the attack on Iraq, the price of oil would zoom upward. So conventional wisdom declared. Well, as everyone knows, we attacked Iraq on the ground and in the air. And the following day, the price of oil slid to $22. Oil stocks suffered accordingly.

As trends become frenzies, the crowd demands allegiance that is hard to resist. If you don't think so, try this exercise: At the next presentation you attend, be the first person to applaud. Or, when next you hear a rousing concert, initiate the standing ovation. These are hard things for most people to do. Yet take it from me: Buying stocks on the squash is even harder.

My inclination to argue with a signpost has stood me well. The loneliness of the long-distance runner furnishes an apt image, even when I am right all along. When situations deteriorate, loneliness is more pronounced. Low p/e investors seldom enjoy the luxury of confirmation of their judgment. If you happen to manage a fund with $10 billion, no shortage of critics will question your judgment, as letters from irate shareholders attest.

If critics lack the fortitude for low p/e investing, so be it. Their carping was the price we paid for Windsor's superior results. To me, it was an acceptable tradeoff, in exchange for an investment style with long-term odds in our favor. By following a contrarian course, Windsor's faithful shareholders got the better part of the deal.

A warning: Do not bask in the warmth of just being different. There is a thin line between being contrarian and being just plain stubborn. I revel in opportunities to buy stocks, but I will also concede that at times the crowd is right. Eventually, you have to be right on fundamentals to be rewarded.

Windsor did not achieve superior results by going against the grain at every chance. Stubborn, knee-jerk contrarians follow a recipe for catastrophe. Savvy contrarians keep their minds open, leavened by a sense of history and a sense of humor.

Almost anything in the investment field can go too far, including a contrarian theme. Its saving grace lies in an interpretive nature, which depends ultimately on the eye of the beholder. At times, the value-yield approach has gained a disturbing following, at some risk to steady practitioners. But these investors comprise a broad and diverse group. Although some disciplines apply, a successful approach relies on judgment. Ready-made contrarian formulas supply prescriptions for failure.

WINDSOR'S BLUEPRINT: MEASURED PARTICIPATION

Windsor flourished by adhering to a rigorous, systematic, and contrarian portfolio strategy. But our strategy was also flexible. It hinged on "Measured Participation," an approach devised soon after I began managing Windsor. It displaced a conventional portfolio strategy that had boxed Windsor into its predicament.

Measured Participation gave us a new way to view a portfolio, outside conventional industry classifications. It encouraged fresh thinking about diversification and portfolio management. Instead of thinking primarily in terms of industry representation, Measured Participation established four broad investment categories:

1. Highly recognized growth.
2. Less recognized growth.
3. Moderate growth.
4. Cyclical growth.

Windsor participated in each of these categories, irrespective of industry concentrations. When the best values were available in, say, the moderate growth area, we concentrated our investments there. If financial service providers offered the best values in the moderate growth area, we concentrated in financial services. This structure enabled us to flout the constraints that usually condemn mutual funds to ho-hum performance.

Windsor's success relied on the freedom to stick our necks out. We were not compelled to ensure that Windsor was represented across every industry. Other money managers ordinarily fortified portfolios against downturns by diversifying along industry lines. If one industry lagged, another buoyed performance.

Some degree of diversification bolsters investment performance. No prudent investor puts all the eggs in a single basket. But too much diversification hobbles performance. Why own, for instance, forest products companies if the market has embraced them and you can reap exceptional returns by selling them? Worse, some portfolio managers whose portfolios are underweighted in a hot sector chase high prices, just to secure sufficient representation. As I see it, these money managers bought stock they should have been selling.

In Windsor's novel scheme, one difference was dramatically visible. Venerable blue-chip growth stocks occupied the lowest rung in importance—not the highest, as was typical for most money managers. This was the natural consequence of the popularity these household-name stocks usually enjoyed. While other funds had to own shares of all 50 of the largest S&P 500 stocks, we seldom owned more than a handful, and sometimes none at all.

Meanwhile, dull, ugly stocks found prominence at Windsor, owing to their frequent unpopularity. Insofar as they were capable of expanding their price–earnings multiples, they fit our profile.

No period highlighted our fundamental advantage more than the early Seventies, which began with highly recognized growth stocks in high gear, and ended with their rout.

Don't Chase Highly Recognized Growth Stocks

Stocks of any era's great growth companies fill the ranks of highly recognized growth stocks. Almost without exception, they remain great growth companies for extended periods of time. Consumers recognize their names: General Electric, Gillette, Coca-Cola, Pfizer, and Procter & Gamble are typical. Their financial performance, particularly their earnings, features outstanding longevity and assuredness. Their businesses are sound and global, and they usually dominate their markets.

Everyone wants to own highly recognized growth stocks. They're ordinarily quite safe, and they seldom embarrass shareholders. That's not a very good case for buying them at all times, as is starkly illustrated by the tale of the so-called Nifty Fifty. They were the market's most celebrated class of highly recognized growth stocks. Week after week, in 1971, 1972, and 1973, these stocks had a hypnotic hold on investors.

Sell-side research firms pitched them as "one-decision" stocks, meaning buy them and hold them forever. Behind this strategy lay the coupling of unlimited earnings growth with a limited supply of stock. Thus, investors widely believed that prices would go up forever. Shareholders counted on ever-escalating dividends and ever-escalating stock prices. But what this scenario really required was an unending supply of new investors who were more gullible than their predecessors.

I watched in amazement as investors clamored for Nifty Fifty stocks at the expense of dozens, if not hundreds, of sturdy growth stocks of lesser renown. As a student of market fancies, I expected this kind of phenomenon to surface from time to time. This fad's tenacity surprised me. While a handful of price–earnings ratios raced skyward, our low p/e goods languished. I never expected low p/e stocks to get respect in an adrenaline market, but this was ridiculous. Windsor posted a 25 percent loss in 1973.

NIGHTS ARE DARKEST JUST BEFORE DAWN

Those were bleak days. My report to shareholders in November 1973 reflected the dismal course of events and, even more forcefully, my resilient faith in Windsor's low p/e strategy:

> . . . [We] view the current devastation in the marketplace, not as a reason for alarm, but rather as one of opportunity. We believe we will look back on this recent period of excessively low evaluations of innovative, accomplishing companies as one not unlike the early 1950s, when stocks of good companies also could be acquired at prices of only four or five times earnings—prices that provided the opportunity for truly remarkable appreciation in ensuing years.
>
> It is my view, as Windsor Fund's portfolio manager, that there is a period of outstanding potential appreciation on the horizon. As a shareholder with a substantial portion of my family's resources invested in the Fund—and one who has personally and financially lived and breathed each good day and each bad day with the Fund since mid-1964—I hope you await the inevitable eye-catching appreciation of our Fund with the same solid confidence and eager anticipation as I do.

The Nifty Fifty fever broke in 1974, but the market did not come to its senses immediately. Investors abandoned the highly recognized growth segment and everything else in sight, including our merchandise. As the spectacular run ended and bloated p/e ratios fell earthward, the Nifty Fifty supplied a harsh object lesson in the hazards of too much faith in formidable growth stocks. At some point, even they cost too much. Some stocks took 7 years to recoup their losses; others waited 20 years.

In the Nifty Fifty days, we quarreled with the lofty prices and p/e ratios. But I had no irreconcilable aversion to highly recognized growth fare. Windsor owned several of them when opportunities arose, including IBM, McDonald's, Home Depot, Xerox, and Intel. Because the market tends to bestow relatively high p/e ratios on highly recognized growth stocks, however, they rarely represented more than 8 or 9 percent of Windsor's assets.

Lessons are only useful to the extent investors remember them. Memory in the stock market is notoriously short, as history has shown repeatedly. With all due respect for academic proponents of efficient markets, in my experience markets are continuously foolish, thanks to investors who, despite George Santayana's famous admonition, forget the past.

Investors usually invite catastrophe themselves, like two hunters who hired a plane to fly them to a moose hunting region in the Canadian wilderness. Upon reaching their destination, the pilot agreed to return to fetch them after two days. He warned them, however, that the plane could carry only one moose for each hunter. More weight than that would strain the engine, and the plane might not make it all the way home.

Two days later, the pilot returned. Despite his warning, each of the hunters had killed two moose. Too much weight, said the pilot. "But last year you said the same thing," one hunter declared. "Remember? We each paid an extra $1,000 and you took off with all four moose." Reluctantly, the pilot agreed. The plane took off, but after an hour gas was low. The engine sputtered, and the pilot was forced to crash land. The two hunters, dazed but unhurt, climbed out of the wreckage. "Do you know where we are?" one asked. "Not sure," said the other, "but it sure looks like where we crashed last year."

No more actual evidence is needed than events in 1998 and 1999, when investors again embraced a new generation of highly recognized growth stocks. In many respects, it looked to me like Yogi Berra's classic "*déjà vu* all over again," but with even more risk. This time, the dominant crop of highly recognized growth stocks included a less formidable phalanx. Caught up in Internet-related fervor, investors conferred highly recognized growth status prematurely on technology companies that lacked reassuring prospects. Their processes were new, and some of their technologies were embryonic. Also, competition had not yet taken its inevitable toll.

Look at a basket of stocks called the NASDAQ 100, which notched an 85 percent gain in 1998. It seemed outlandish to me that the total value of the stocks issued by these companies exceeded $2 trillion at year-end. But even more stunningly, less than 5 percent of more than 2,000 NASDAQ-traded stocks commanded 60 percent of its market capital and 100 percent of attention in the marketplace, especially from the media.

If this observation sounds awesome, consider another. Just five companies represented almost 40 percent of all the equity investment in the NASDAQ 100. That amounted to one fourth of the NASDAQ composite index investment and nearly 10 percent of the S&P 500. Even compared with the besotted Nifty Fifty era, never had so many paid so much for so few.*

WEIGH THE VIRTUES OF LESS RECOGNIZED GROWTH

While chasing big growth stocks, eager investors became Windsor's benefactors. Their inattention to less recognized growth stocks usually left us plenty of candidates for our low p/e portfolio. These companies exhibit earnings growth comparable to or better than the big growth stocks, but lack of size and visibility consigns them to the backbench.

One classic less recognized growth stock, Edison Brothers, was an old-line, family-run specialty retailer out of St. Louis. In 1974, its business centered on the so-called women's "dumb shoe" base, featuring several popular brand names. Efforts to diversify caused the company to fumble before reforming itself as a strong competitor in shopping malls. Earnings progressed, but a market obsessed with big growth companies took no notice. While scoping out the less-recognized growth segment, we discovered the stock and bought shares. In 1975, the market

---

* Apologies to Winston Churchill for twisting his famous tribute to Royal Air Force pilots in World War II.

embraced Edison Brothers and Windsor garnered a 137 percent gain. (Demonstrating the fragility of drawing perpetual straight lines upward and the hazards of specialty retailing, this company filed for bankruptcy in the 1990s.)

In 1982, less recognized growth stocks represented about 22 percent of the Windsor Fund. This was after starting the Seventies as a 5 percent stake. At the peak of the market's clamor for these stocks, appreciation outpaced our sales programs. As a result, one third of the Windsor Fund's assets resided in the less recognized growth group. After settling below 25 percent, less recognized growth stocks remained more or less at that level until my retirement. That's a good representation for this group in any portfolio.

Less recognized growth stocks of more recent vintage than Edison Brothers always inhabit the bargain basement. The Big Board lists hundreds living in the shadow of the high-flying Dow Jones industrials or the top NASDAQ listings.

Before plunging into this category, however, *caveat emptor*. Less recognized growth stocks may fall out of favor for reasons more substantial than investors' overreaction. One in five fails fundamentally every year—not always to the point of going broke, but the growth rates are lost and, consequently, the p/e ratios slip. They descend into the ranks of ordinary companies. Top names notwithstanding, an amazing number of technology companies were trading no higher in 1999 than 15 or 20 years earlier. Others were worse off.

I would be the first to concede that there is a larger degree of risk in this area than otherwise exists in the portfolio, but I have always been ready with a meaningful portion of the total portfolio to take an intelligent risk when the reward was more than commensurate. This opportunity is characterized in the following fashion:

- Projectable growth rates of 12–20 percent.
- Single digit multiples of 6–9 times earnings.
- Dominance or major participation in definable growth areas.
- Easy industries to understand.
- Unblemished record of double-digit historical earnings growth.
- Outstanding returns on equity, therein signifying management accomplishment, not to mention the internal capacity to finance growth.

- Significant capitalizations and net income totals therein qualifying companies for institutional consideration.
- Ideally, although hardly essential, some Wall Street coverage, so those that need their hand held will have a wet nurse.
- A 2–3.5 percent yield in most cases.

MODERATE GROWERS ARE SOLID CITIZENS

Moderate growth, the third heading under Measured Participation, fills a wide band that Wall Street's smart set frequently treats with disdain. These solid citizens encompass phone companies, electric utilities, banks, and even blue chips hemmed in by mature markets. They have always intrigued me, with their low p/e ratios and earnings that rarely grew faster than 8 percent a year. Absent superior growth rates, p/e expansion from depressed levels supplied robust gains.

Growth prospects aside, moderate growers tend to hold their price levels in difficult markets, thanks in part to above-average yields. In flush times for dividends, electric utilities and telephone companies paid yields in excess of 7 percent. (Even in April 1999, yields were not so shabby: 2.6 percent at Bank of America, 4.0 percent at First Union, 7.5 percent at Camden Property Trust; 8.2 percent at Brandywine Realty Trust, and 3.4 percent at Ford Motor Co.) All told, moderate growers supplied hefty yields, appreciation as reliable as investors can find, and dry powder when inflection points spawned more breathtaking opportunities.

CYCLICALS WILL RISE AGAIN

Stocks that comprised Windsor's cyclical participation grew earnings at average to above-average rates when business cycles were favorable. As industries and companies fell in and out of favor, p/e ratios charted regular ups and downs. We distinguished basic commodity cyclicals, such as oil and aluminum producers, from consumer cyclicals, such as autos, airlines, and home builders.

Timing is critical in cyclicals. They usually follow the same pattern. As earnings pick up, investors flock to them. When earnings begin to peak, investors abandon them. Ideally, Windsor bought cyclical stocks six to nine months before earnings swung upward, then sold into rising demand. The trick was to anticipate increases in pricing. We had to start with knowledge of an industry's capacity, and then make some judgments about sources and timing of demand increases.

In 1981, Newmont Mining's appeal rested principally on the case for a rebound in copper prices from depressed levels. This seemed to require nothing more than a normalization of demand, or an end to the inventory liquidation occasioned by very high interest rates. But the case also looked solid beyond. On any kind of realistic basis, world capacity would grow at a slower rate than the 3 percent growth in consumption. Newmont's position in copper was, importantly, domestic and relatively low in cost. Thanks to the company's overall diversity (which included gold, oil and gas, and coal), earnings, even at prevailing copper prices, put the stock on a cheap basis going in. ***Outcome:*** *We captured a quick run-up in Newmont's price almost immediately. Then the price slid by 40 percent, dipping 15 percent below our initial purchase price. The fundamentals remained intact, so we bought shares again a year later. In late 1983, Newmont shares reaped gains in the neighborhood of 61 percent. As always, we sold into strength.*

THE MARKET DOESN'T CAPITALIZE PEAK CYCLICAL EARNINGS

This critical concept warrants repetition. The market exercises surprising intelligence in at least one respect: Peak cyclical earnings never command peak p/e ratios. In other words, p/e ratios do not expand as if cyclical stocks were growth stocks. As pricing strengthens, a burst of enthusiasm precedes the upsurge in earnings. Seasoned investors recognize that the p/e ratio will start to retreat before peak earnings are reached.

That's why investors shouldn't be too greedy on the upside. The way to avoid this pitfall is to start with some notion of normal earnings—the earnings at a fortuitous point in the cycle. At Windsor, every investment in a cyclical stock entailed an estimate of normal earnings. We were not always right. At times, we underestimated and sold earlier than necessary. But this was a small price to pay, compared to riding the stock down the wrong side of the price slope.

ALL CYCLICALS MAY NOT BE SO CYCLICAL

To add a twist to the cyclical category, some stocks become progressively less cyclical. Thanks to tighter and more cost-conscious management, and a less cyclical economy, swings in the automobile industry should be less pronounced. The combination of eye-catching product mix and friendly prices makes for steadier earnings than before. You might wonder whether an exceptional string of record years is above normal, or merely the new baseline. A merger might add a business that softens the swings, or a new product may accomplish the same thing. A prolonged period of low or reasonable interest rates will normally extend the home-building cycle.

On average, cyclicals represented slightly more than 30 percent of the Windsor Fund—an appropriate level, absent confidence that cyclicals are due for a major move.

DON'T SWEAT MARKET WEIGHTING

We believed in concentrating assets where they were likely to produce the most bang. When Windsor managed $11 billion, we owned 60 stocks, and the 10 largest accounted for almost 40 percent of the whole Fund. When one fourth of Windsor was invested in oil stocks, three oil stocks accounted for the majority of our stake.

We never sought to own market weighting. We concentrated assets in undervalued areas. Windsor doubled up on some industry categories or jettisoned others altogether, as market climates warranted. Oil and oil services represented around 12 percent of the S&P 500, but, at various times, oil stocks comprised as much as one fourth or as little as 1 percent of Windsor. In disrepute, we grabbed them. In favor, we sold them.

Characteristically, Windsor owned only four or five of the S&P's 50 largest companies in terms of market value. They typically made up about 50 percent of the market weighting of our performance standard. One or two times, we owned none of the 50 largest S&P stocks. At one time, Windsor's largest S&P representation, BankAmerica, was sixty-seventh in the S&P 500's ranking by market value.

Concentration to this extent meant we might end up owning 8 or 9 percent of the outstanding shares of some of our major positions. This carried some extra risk, especially if fundamentals fell short and we had to eventually sell such large stakes.

Within the bounds of Measured Participation, emphasis shifted all the time. In 1990 and 1991, for example, Windsor highlighted moderate growers. Banks, thrifts, and insurance companies were suffering from a litany of problems, including hefty exposure to nonperforming commercial real estate loans, so financial services climbed to 35 percent of Windsor's assets. The S&P weighting was about 10 percent. In the early Eighties, food stocks consumed more than 8 percent of Windsor's assets, four times their presence in the S&P 500.

Flouting market weighting in the less recognized growth segment brought championship gains. Maybe I didn't spend enough time playing with trucks as a youngster, but, in the late Seventies, Windsor loaded up on transportation companies far in excess of their presence in the S&P 500.

TOP-DOWN OR BOTTOM-UP?

It is easy to get mired in a debate about top-down investing versus bottom-up investing. As one might suspect, top-down investing starts with a macroeconomic overview, and then adds some judgment about which stocks are apt to be favorably affected. Bottom-up investing starts, in effect, by weighing the individual merits of a list of stocks. Experts waste a lot of time arguing about which approach is better.

As advocates of Measured Participation, we attacked stock picking from both directions. Broad economic themes, at times, highlighted oil stocks or bank stocks; then we would burrow down to determine the fundamentals of each investment candidate. On other occasions, a particularly pummeled stock wandered onto our radar scope when its p/e ratio came into range.

The debate over top-down versus bottom-up investing has always seemed a little fuzzy to me. I just keep an eye on the economy and ask, where is a sector that's overdue for recognition? Case in point: Amsted Industries.

A favorable outlook for the economy in 1973 implied that more goods would be traveling from place to place to accommodate rising demand. This augured well for the rail freight business, we thought. Hence, we took a position in Amsted, which had fallen on hard times since posting record profits in 1967. Circumstances forced it to slash the dividend, an action that was not lost upon us at Windsor. In a normal year, Amsted's earnings were concentrated in the railroad equipment side. However, in its fiscal 1971, its rail business stumbled. Most investors fled, giving little thought to the interesting fact that Amsted's construction business kicked in enough income to lift 1972 earnings above the previous mark. A solid construction business and resurgent rail earnings added up, in our view, to an attractive company with increased earnings plus a higher p/e. All told, our prediction of a 35 percent gain had a nice sound to it. **Outcome:** *Amsted supplied many happy returns, beginning in 1975 when trimming our stake netted returns in excess of 50 percent. We took a breather afterwards, and ultimately collected returns in excess of 120 percent in 1976.*

Call it top-down or bottom up, but regulatory upheaval drew us to the slew of newly formed regional Bell operating companies in 1983. Initially, the markets had doubts about the suitability of these newly created phone companies. We didn't. Besides sound fundamentals—earnings growth of 6 to 7 percent a year, and yields approaching 9 percent—we saw total returns in excess of 15 percent available for 6 times earnings.

Not ones to hem and haw, we bought the hell out of that group before and after the breakup. At one point, telephones represented around 16 percent of the Windsor Fund. In this, as in other opportunities, Windsor was quick and hard-hitting. We were not always right. But without the resolve to storm the Bastille when we believed we were right, we'd have sacrificed much of Windsor's upside to guard the downside. In telephones, we were absolutely right. We banked handsome gains in a couple of years.

LEARN WHAT MAKES AN INDUSTRY TICK

Windsor chalked up its most eye-catching gains after anticipating correctly major inflection points. The ability to see these shifts coming and gear up for their aftermath requires both top-down and bottom-up analysis. A wise investor studies the industry, its products, and its economic structure. Industry trade magazines supply very valuable information long before it finds its way into the general consciousness. Prudent investors always stay abreast of developments, which is why casual investors usually get wind of change *after* the stock price adjusts.

To the extent possible, go out and kick an industry's tires. Try consumer goods yourself. Visit a distributor, or tour the plant where the industrial products are manufactured. Ask questions as if you were going to get half an hour of the CEO's time. That may not happen, but most public companies have investor relations arms that can provide answers to these basic questions:

- Are an industry's prices headed up, or are they headed down?
- What about costs?
- Who are the market leaders?
- Do any competitors dominate the market?
- Can industry capacity meet demand?
- Are new plants under construction?
- What will be the effect on profitability?

Top-down investors keep tabs on inflation. When quiescent, it's usually a friend. But when it swoops in with double digit increases, which happened twice during my tour at Windsor, inflation becomes a bogeyman that can distort all of your painstaking, bottom-up calculations. Double-digit inflation devastates fixed-income markets and, in consequence, ravages equity markets. A whole new standard emerges. It's somewhat different each time, and you must cope, despite constant flux and lack of predictability.

Growth of the economy is pretty much paired with inflation. It supplies the yardstick that reveals whether the industries in your portfolio actually measure up. In other words, the companies you own should at least match overarching economic growth if you plan to beat the market. Your growth, of course, determines your expectations for growth in earnings and concomitant growth in the p/e ratio.

I always watch three areas of the economy for signs of excess: (1) capital expenditures, (2) inventories, and (3) consumer credit.

BUILD FACT SHEETS

Answers to critical questions form the backdrop for building a low p/e portfolio. It's a lot to remember. At Windsor, we used concise fact sheets to condense and summarize our outlook for the stocks we owned. They enabled us to know where our portfolio and each investment stood at any interval.

At some risk of contradicting myself, I have insisted that investing is simple, but people make it complicated. I do not mean, however, that portfolio management is a snap. Managing a personal portfolio may not be a 24-hour job, as running Windsor was. But it beats me that some investors try to make a go of it without crunching numbers. Besides native intelligence and good judgment, pencil and paper—or their modern proxies, computer spread sheets—are critical tools. The major effort is expended on keeping track of returns via elaborate computer software. Some additional effort directed toward understanding industries and companies would boost the returns.

Fact sheets supplied a systematic approach to exercising our low p/e sympathies. Each fact sheet recorded these pertinent facts on all the stocks Windsor owned, grouped by industry:

- Shares owned.
- Average cost.
- Current price.
- Historical and projected earnings per share.
- Historical and projected growth rate.
- Historical and projected price–earnings ratio.
- Yield.
- Return on equity.
- Price projection based on earnings expectation and resulting p/e ratio.
- Appreciation potential.

Shares owned, current price, historical earnings, growth rates, and p/e ratios, yield, and return on equity were matters of record available from any number of sources published on paper and, nowadays, on-line. Average cost simply reflected the number of shares Windsor owned, divided by Windsor's total investment.

REASONS TO SELL

We built fact sheets, monitored terminal relationships, and then lived and breathed these price targets. Ultimately, Windsor sold shares for either of two reasons:

1. Fundamentals deteriorated.
2. The price approached our expectations.

The most obvious sale was the stock on which we made a mistake. If the best thing we could say about a stick was that "It probably won't go down," that stock became a candidate for sale. Each stock we owned needed a clearly visualized potential for growth.

A failure of fundamentals became obvious on two different yardsticks: estimates of earnings, and five-year growth rates. If we lost confidence in these fundamentals, we slipped out expeditiously. Reversing course in a dramatic fashion would have cost us far more, usually, than moving shares without attracting much attention.

We trimmed our position in Ponderosa Steak Houses, for example, when fundamentals slid in 1980. The original purchase had been predicated on a belief that the company had sufficiently upgraded its management organization, control structure, and individual restaurants. Having survived a perilous earnings downturn several years earlier, Ponderosa's management seemed to have learned hard lessons. We figured the company would prosper in good times and in the next cyclical test period, whenever it materialized.

Ponderosa fell short of our expectations. Customer count declines passed the point of acceptability, in our view, particularly in the context of a softening average ticket due to heavy promotional activity and high advertising expenditures. Some relief was experienced on the cost-of-food side, and operating expenses were well controlled; still, we expected earnings would decline sharply to less than half the 1979 level. This simply was not acceptable versus our expectations, even allowing for the difficult economic environment. Meanwhile, the stock, although about 31 percent below our cost, had recovered some 25 to 30 percent from its lows. We decided to cut our position importantly at that point and to move the proceeds to more fertile ground. Our other large restaurant holdings were passing the test more positively.

Unfortunately, given Windsor's type of investments, we did experience disappointments. But each day forced us to look ourselves in the mirror and adjust whether we were persevering with companies for which we had not paid a lot, even if some didn't measure up. Our task, which was never easy, was to try to discern those that were not fulfilling our expectations currently and would not do so on the near horizon. The need to recycle disappointments into new investments that were more likely to perform always put an additional burden on our creative juices.

STICK TO A FIRM SELLING STRATEGY

Fortunately, Windsor's winners outnumbered its losers, as the record shows. But successful stocks don't tell you when it's time to sell them. Beyond picking good low p/e stocks, Windsor's performance rested equally, if not more, on a firm selling strategy.

So long as fundamentals remained intact, we were not averse to holding stocks for three, four, or five years. But that didn't prevent us from taking profits right away. There were times we owned shares for a month or less.

The toughest investment decision is the decision to sell. You can be right as rain about a stock's potential, but if you hold on too long, you may end up with nothing. An awful lot of people keep a stock too long because it gives them warm fuzzies—particularly when a contrarian stance has been vindicated. If they sell it, they lose bragging rights.

Many investors can't bear to part company with a stock on the way up, lest they miss the best gain by not holding on. They persuade themselves that a day after they sell, they will have short-changed themselves by not capturing the penultimate dollar. My attitude is: I'm not that smart.

Falling in love with stocks in a portfolio is very easy to do and, I might add, very perilous. Every stock Windsor owned was for sale. In this business, if you can't get to the other side of your enthusiasm, you'd better be extremely lucky or else you are doomed. When you feel like bragging about a stock, it's probably time to sell.

Windsor calculated the appreciation potential for every stock, based on earnings expectations and projected p/e expansion. As a general tactic, we bought into weakness and sold into strength. Instead of groping for the last dollar, we gladly left some upside on the table for buyers as they awakened to our fundamental case. Catching market tops was not our game. This was preferable to getting caught in a subsequent downdraft, which is never a pretty picture. If others wanted to play the greater fool, that was their pleasure and we were always glad to accommodate them.

Typical investors establish price targets and begin selling as stocks approach those targets. This isn't novel. Because Windsor owned stocks on average for about three years—a span of about one market cycle—we needed a selling strategy that would adjust to new market cycles.

Toward that end, we tailored the selling strategy to Windsor's average appreciation potential. Our expectations for a stock always reflected overall expectation for the portfolio, which in turn reflected market climates. Everything was relative. We did not let absolute numbers beguile or dazzle us. Appreciation potential merely indicated the market's evaluation of a stock at two different points in time. As time progressed and markets changed, prospects for Windsor's overall appreciation shifted. In consequence, we adjusted expectations for the individual stocks in the portfolio.

YOU DON'T HAVE TO BUY AND HOLD FOREVER

When Gino's came into our view as an investment in late 1970, this fast food franchise launched by three former Baltimore Colts had shown extraordinary accomplishment. In its relatively brief life, it posted 45 percent annual growth in earnings per share for four straight years. Physical expansion by the company, which owned and operated all of its outlets (no franchisees), was proceeding at a rapid clip. There were plans in place for a lucrative entry into Southern California. We estimated that Gino's would continue to increase sales in excess of 25 percent annually, reflecting a more substantial base and a more competitive climate. Though high in its p/e range by our usual standards, some slippage in Gino's price combined with a torrid growth rate convinced us to pay approximately 24 times a share. As befits our philosophy, we always sit uncomfortably and somewhat apprehensively with high multiple companies. Obviously, Gino's was a mild step down Windsor's quality ladder, which gave us pause at even a hint of slipping fundamentals.

Outcome: A month after we bought the shares, indications of slower growth dimmed our confidence in the company's offensive capabilities. Before other investors put aside their enthusiasm, we punted—and pocketed a quick if ill deserved gain of almost 20 percent. Almost immediately, the stock stumbled, making us look even smarter.

We purchased and sold Gulf Oil in the second quarter of 1984, in a somewhat uncharacteristic short-term and entrepreneurial move. We made a judgment, at $65 a share (even after having sold it somewhat embarrassingly in the $40s a few months earlier), that a Standard Oil of California purchase at $80 would happen. Despite some Federal Trade

Commission (FTC) and Congressional consternation, this was a good judgment and we banked a short-term 24 percent profit. This was not our usual stock-in-trade, but the risk–reward ratio seemed intelligent and Windsor shareholders benefited as a result.

CIRCUMSTANCES THAT CALL FOR CASH OR BONDS

Ordinarily, we recycled sales proceeds into stocks with brighter prospects. In overpriced markets, however, Windsor periodically went to as much as 20 percent in cash. (A higher percentage wasn't prudent for an equity fund, in my judgment.) We stockpiled cash when the market got nutty and we couldn't find stocks to buy that made sense. Cash was a reasonably good anchor to windward. We also fudged a bit, when interest rates warranted, by owning intermediate-term U.S. Treasury securities when they had a good carry (current return plus a moderate opportunity for price appreciation).

In 1983, at the end of the second quarter, we invested $110 million in the new $11\frac{7}{8}$ percent 10-year U.S. Government bonds. In our judgment, fixed-income markets were as attractive as, or even more attractive than, an overextended part of the equity market. Interest rates in excess of 12 percent, versus a prospective 6 percent inflation rate, were resulting in a 6 percent real return for the investor. This gain was too good to be completely unrepresented in Windsor relative to equities. Accordingly, we attempted to be short-term optimists with this temporary investment, pending adjustment in the stock market.

Purists may label this either attempted opportunism or uncharacteristic flexibility. To do our job for the shareholders, however, we made judgments and backed them as called for. Windsor was not a closet indexer, a passive investor, or a random walker. Even our directors sometimes agreed or disagreed with the positions we took. We expected no less; differences of opinion were, after all, what made up the marketplace that we always tried to capitalize on. We did ask, however, for some understanding of our attempts to separate ourselves from the hurly-burly in order to create out-of-the-ordinary results. It should be recalled that our maximum progress usually occurred after an inflection point. (Absent a pronounced inflection point, our results for 1983 seemed even more extraordinary.) This is a key in attempting to understand how and why we sometimes defended unconventional positions and occasionally took refuge in cash.

Where there is panic, there is also opportunity. So, we did some prospecting in the junk bond market in the late eighties. Fixed-income returns were in the vicinity of 10 percent, so we thought we should take a look at downtrodden, quasi-equity instruments promising 20 percent (or better) yield to maturity. By and large, we found the market to be pretty efficient. Healthier companies were suffering far less carnage than those in which genuine doubt clouded any prospects for easing the debt burden. However, the market seemed to have gone overboard in assessing the undoubted risks of retailer R. H. Macy's situation. We responded with an investment in bonds with a 14½ percent coupon. Held to maturity, that amounted to a 27-percent-plus yield on our purchase price.

We examined the situation with our usual diligence. R.H. Macy was a product of a 1986 leveraged buyout (LBO), which in turn bought the Bullocks and I. Magnin chains following dismemberment of retail rival Federated Department Stores in 1988. The resulting entity was highly leveraged with negative equity as well as enormous sums in real estate and credit company debt. On top of this, management was caught leaning the wrong way at Christmas 1990. Heavy inventories were being carried into a slowing market that was further aggravated by Federated's desperation selling during its death throes.

The market feared that Macy's would follow Federated into bankruptcy, but we identified important differences. Macy's management team and strong franchise remained intact from the pre-LBO era, when Macy's was one of the most successful retailers in America. Investment in capital spending, and even new stores, had been kept up as bank debt was being paid down. The cash flow from operations managed to cover all required interest. Management responded appropriately to the Christmas disaster (and the subsequent slow retail environment) by trimming inventories and tightening costs and controls. On the equally important financial side, Macy's equity holders, including General Electric, had deep pockets. Access to capital enabled Macy's to take advantage of the junk panic. The announced sale of its credit card operation to GE Capital and the infusion of fresh equity from investors enabled Macy's to retire a considerable amount of junior debt. Effectively, Macy's accomplished a necessary restructuring of its overburden of debt, enhancing the stability of the company and the status of our senior subordinated debt. *Outcome: As expected, Macy's survived and we collected a 45 percent return after 10 months.*

The Times They Are A-Changin'

Much has changed in the world since I became a money manager, but the underlying nature of the investment challenge is the same. Low p/e stocks still offer opportunities to investors who dare to embrace them. But a crowd mentality still drives investing behavior. The key differences today are the flood of information available and the cadres of daytraders who stare mindlessly into their screens with scant perception of what companies do and a less-than-basic knowledge of fundamentals.

Conventional wisdom suggests that, for investors, more information these days is a blessing and more competition is a curse. I'd say the opposite is true. Coping with so much information runs the risk of distracting attention from the few variables that really matter. Because sound evaluations call for assembling information in a logical and careful manner, my odds improve, thanks to proliferating numbers of traders motivated by tips and superficial knowledge. By failing to perform rigorous, fundamental analyses of companies, industries, or economic trends, these investors become prospectors who only chase gold where everyone else is already looking. Mutual fund investors who think they can make money by chasing the hottest funds are panning in the same overworked streams.

No one is more grateful than I am for wide-eyed investors who chase tantalizing visions of overnight fortunes. We were, are, and probably always will be a nation of prospectors. Time and again, investors view the stock market as a vast, endless mother lode, with gold enough for all comers. But gold rushes finish ugly for a reason. Although every prospector counts on finding a valuable nugget, most return home empty-handed.

Sufficiently removed from Wall Street's hullabaloo, Windsor applied our low p/e sometimes boring principles in consistent fashion. We weren't fancy, just prudent and consistent. We always took note of prevailing opinion, but we never let it sway our investment decisions. All things considered, if I started again in January 2000, I'd follow the identical course.

PART THREE

~

A MARKET
JOURNAL

"Buy on the cannons and sell on the trumpets."
French proverb

WINDSOR'S SUCCESS CONCEALED *no secrets. We relied on relentless application of low p/e sympathies, abetted by attention to fundamentals and a liberal dose of common sense. As market climates shifted, these traits surfaced again and again. Take a look at the record; the accompanying journal chronicles Windsor's performance for the years 1970 through 1993, grouped around four major inflection points: It shows how we combed the bargain basement for quality merchandise and then sold it as other investors caught on. In patient, thoughtful markets, we usually maintained a respectable edge. In overwrought, adrenaline periods, Windsor sometimes lost ground. In the aftermath of inflections, our careful positioning in out-of-favor segments paid off. The results speak for themselves in the following narrative. (For a calendar-year-by-calendar-year comparison of Windsor versus the S&P 500 during my entire tenure as portfolio manager, see Appendix A.)*

Many circumstances and yardsticks have changed. Companies cited have grown, merged, or, in some cases, closed their doors. Dividend yields are not so lavish nowadays, and erstwhile p/e ratios seem almost quaint. Brief security analyses are not intended as current recommendations, but as testimony to the thought processes that shaped Windsor's fortunes. Are they still valid? I think so. The relationship of total return to the p/e ratio still governs my investment decisions, and the returns meet my high standards.

If a lesson emerges besides the merits of low p/e ratios, it should be that successful, long-term investment strategies need not rest on a few very risky glamour stocks. The record will show that we painted our canvas using a broad palette. At various times, Windsor owned representatives of all but one or two industries, and many were revisited more than once. Some payoffs were of the championship variety; others were nothing to be proud of. Now and then, we hit home runs, but our scoring relied chiefly on base hits. To go home winners, that's all investors need.

10

~

THE SILLY SEASON

1970–1976

THE LATE 1990S harked back to the early 1970s, the Nifty Fifty era. In both periods, investors emphasized a handful of glamour growth stocks at the expense of the wider market. Prices of fashionable stocks reached such high levels that, to my way of thinking, earnings could not live up to them. Hypnotized by rising market levels, investors lost sight of fundamentals. This behavior usually precedes inflection points. At the 1999 Barron's *roundtable, I borrowed a phrase from the 1992 presidential election to drive home my point that market levels deceive investors. I warned: "It's the valuation, stupid!" The market cap of Amazon.com, for example, exceeded retail sales of all bookstores in the world!*

Revlon's founder, Charles Revson, once said that women do not buy perfume, they buy hope. Investors have similar mentality in periods when just a few stocks command their attention. In January 1999, in the NASDAQ 100, the top seven stocks accounted for about half of the index's entire capitalization—or over $1 trillion of market capital. As p/e ratios ballooned in 1998, Microsoft gained 115 percent; Intel, a laggard by these standards, added 69 percent. Other increases were: Cisco, 150 percent; MCI Worldcom, 137 percent; Dell, 249 percent; Oracle, 93 percent; and Sun Microsystems, 115 percent. Having lived through a similar climate, I find such moves clearly unsustainable. Compare this scene with the early Seventies and how Windsor coped. It was the worst of times, but it became a cradle for the best of times.

1970: CONGLOMERATES AND CHINESE PAPER*

Windsor looked pretty good after posting better results than the S&P 500 each year since 1965, my first full year in charge. We weathered the crazy adrenaline markets of the late Sixties, which was more than could be said for many of the hot go-go funds that garnered more attention and, for three or four years, loftier returns. After streaking to fame and fortune, many crashed and burned. Others just faded away as investors grew skeptical about performance expectations. You can't sell hopes and dreams in a down market, and, in calendar year 1969, the Dow Jones Industrial Average slid 15 percent, to 800.36. As 1970 unfolded, the market grew even more distressed. On May 26, the Dow slid to 631.16, off 37 percent since flirting with 1,000 four years earlier.

While other fund managers wailed and donned hair shirts, Windsor plunged into the carnage with gusto. Though down slightly in 1969, Windsor still bested the market by almost five percentage points and outdid struggling go-go funds by ten to twenty percentage points. With a portfolio of solid, low p/e companies that held their own in difficult times, we were able to get our money back as needed when the market provided more promising investments.

In this climate, conglomerates all but begged for our attention. These companies had ridden to fame in the late Sixties, largely by marketing the whole as greater than the sum of its parts. Several of them nearly became household names: ITT Corporation, Litton Industries, Gulf + Western, and Ling Tempco Vought, to name a few of the best known. Most of them were driven by entrepreneurs with a vision—precursors, perhaps, of the best known corporate raiders two decades later. Their methods were similar, but their personalities were often distinct. Harold Geneen of ITT was the ultimate numbers man. Whether a business made cars or fishhooks, the bottom line told him the story that mattered. Charlie Bluhdorn, Gulf + Western's progenitor, was a flamboyant dealmaker. Jimmy Ling, the mastermind behind Ling Tempco Vought, seemed to build his company the way most people play Monopoly™: go round and round the board, and when you land on something you like that's not owned, buy it. If it's owned, buy it anyway.

Financial strategies hinged on a fairly simple concept: Boost the price–earnings ratio as high as investors will accept, then purchase

---

* Except where noted, dates refer to Windsor's fiscal years, beginning November 1.

earnings with a lower valuation, using shares of stock that came to be known as "Chinese paper." As new earnings get pumped up because of higher p/e levels, the whole becomes more valuable than its parts—and so on and so on. Eventually, of course, the limit was reached, as happens every time investors get carried away. Some earnings failed to live up to expectations. In other companies, synergies failed to materialize. Investors grew suspicious of lofty price earnings created, essentially, by promotional efforts. And then the market's downdraft delivered a *coup de grâce*. From peak to trough, ITT, Gulf + Western, and others plunged dramatically.

In bolting for greener pastures, investors overreacted and prices plunged too far. Collections of sound businesses fell to bargain basement prices.

Seizing an opportunity created by hasty investors driven by crowd psychology instead of sound analysis, Windsor began buying conglomerates in the summer of 1970. Representation grew to approximately 9 percent of Windsor's assets in 1971, and doubled in 1972. Not unlike the utilities and the banks in those days, there were good conglomerates and there were unsuccessful conglomerates. We believed we had established positions in accomplishers that had stood the test of time while enduring considerable adversity. We found them to be good practitioners of the most telling conglomerate virtue: the ability to funnel cash flow into the more rewarding areas of the product mix.

Tenacious Momentum

Almost without exception, the companies we owned continued to increase their earnings through a difficult economic period that culminated in record high earnings in 1972. In our perspective, they stood to produce attention-getting earnings again in 1973, yet languished at less than ten times 1972 earnings. According to our prognosis, which did not anticipate the remarkable tenacity of big growth stocks through most of 1973, discerning investors would focus on these dramatically undervalued situations with every increase in confidence in economic recovery. Prolonged dalliances in these circumstances taught us a big lesson: overvaluations and other seemingly obvious abuses can continue longer than expected. In other words, momentum rules until the inflection point arrives.

Eponymously named for its founder, J.B. Fuqua, Fuqua Industries was a fairly typical conglomerate. Projecting a much more favorable climate in

1971 and 1972 for Fuqua's eclectic mix of yacht and snowmobile manu-facturing, color film processing, radio and TV stations, and movie the-aters, we added it to Windsor's portfolio in late 1970. Windsor was taking a partial step down the quality spectrum, but Fuqua constituted an at-tempt to take advantage of the market's trepidation over all conglomerates, good and bad. The company's balance sheet was not as strong as we might have liked, but we felt any shortcoming was already in the stock price. *Outcome: In February 1971, Fuqua shares fetched an 89 percent gain, which was a prelude. In July, shares returned 125 percent.*

An investment in Gulf + Western corroborated our view that virtually everything is worth purchasing at some price. In 1970, Gulf + Western declined to that price. As was well known at the time, this company had maintained one of the most frantic acquisition paces in the conglomerate field, under the celebrated stewardship of Charles Bluhdorn. When we became interested, stock that had sold less than two years earlier for $60 a share was changing hands for $15 a share. Amid this steep decline, the company entered a consolidation phase in hopes of digesting the conse-quences of a pell-mell acquisition spree. We took note of the book value, thoroughly tested current operating earnings and cash flow, and counted on improved operating earnings in 1971, buttressed by a recovery in the earning power of Paramount Pictures and some finance subsidiaries.*

Moreover, we envisioned that several avenues of potential market un-derstanding would boost a dismal p/e ratio to a more robust level. Not unlike other conglomerates, Gulf + Western was spotlighting some of its better parts for special stock market appreciation by selling off mi-nority interests—a venerable practice billed nowadays with fancy monikers like spin-offs and equity carveouts. Another channel of po-tential understanding, other than just the basic cheapness of the equity, featured use of excess cash flow to repurchase stock—a rare event in those days, although it has become commonplace lately. Another matter was of no small interest to us. We calculated that by dedicating half of its cash flow to repurchasing shares, Gulf + Western could retire all of its common stock inside of five years. *Outcome: In January and Febru-ary 1972, returns exceeded 80 percent—roughly four times the Dow's progress in the same period of time. Much later, in early 1976, after the usual ebb and*

---

* After a series of transactions, these subsidiaries emerged as a public company called Associates First Capital.

flow in our stake, we recorded capital gains of 130 percent. In that period of time, the Dow advanced by less than 40 percent.

It never ceases to amaze me how much shorter the market's memory seems to be, compared to my own. Success requires more than memory, but, over the years, our willingness to act on a long-term conviction has rewarded Windsor shareholders. Investors can't assess risks, much less take intelligent risks, without some perspective; otherwise, they're at the mercy of the winds of fashion. This lesson is too easy to forget, even for those of us who preach it. Just nine months after the Dow scraped bottom in May 1969, amid widespread fears that the sky was falling, it seemed as if most investors had no memory of a market that wouldn't pay spiraling prices for stocks. At least a portion of Windsor's critical edge amounted to nothing more mysterious than remembering lessons of the past and how they tend to repeat themselves. You cannot become a captive of historical parallel, but you must be a student of history.

1971: A WALK ON THE WILD SIDE

Windsor entered 1971 astride a bull. In just six months, the market surged some 40 percent from its depressed low of May 1970. In that very short period of time, investors' appetites followed the classic evolution from emphasis on quality to interest in stocks with a more speculative taint. We could usually feel that shift occurring; the prices of stocks we wouldn't buy at one level would start changing hands at higher levels. This chiefly came about because the equity marketplace was increasingly populated by new cadres of institutional investors who were in hot competition with each other and thus were susceptible to buying panics and selling panics. To the degree our contrarian posture was advantageous, we set out to maximize the benefit of our conviction, a task made increasingly easier by a market that seemed to run well ahead of its fundamental underpinnings, losing sight of underlying value in the process.

Perhaps the best word to describe this period and, for that matter, all of 1971, is "paradoxical." On the plus side, we enjoyed a handsome increase in dividend income and some respectable capital gains, but only a modest increase in our net asset value. Despite these gains, however, Windsor's percentage increase in net asset value at the end of our fiscal year 1971 was below the S&P 500 for the first time on my watch. The margin was five percentage points. Generally, it seemed that where our fundamental model of expectation was realized or exceeded, the market did not respond with the deserved reward. Conversely, where we experienced earnings shortfalls in low-multiple stocks, the penalty too often was out of character with the shortfall.

The market's recovery in 1970–1971, like the whole history of sharp market recoveries, followed a pattern: Earnings recoveries tend to lag behind sustained market upturns by about six months. Early in 1971, with nine months of recovery on the books and three or four more needed to demonstrate real staying power, it seemed realistic to predict improved earnings starting toward year-end. With that view, however, came a question: Would the market be patient enough, through one or more quarters of lackluster results, to add to gains or, at least, hold on to them? I believed that the odds heavily favored an intervening retreat. Windsor's record reflects this assessment very clearly; securities sales outpaced purchases by as much as three-to-one.

As the market progressed, Windsor slipped further—a new experience for me. Explaining this lack of performance, I could only reiterate my aversion to foolish risks with shareholders' money, even when adrenaline was running pretty high once again in the marketplace. Then, as in years that followed, our strength always seemed to come from keeping our heads when others seemed determined to lose theirs. As 1971 developed, we stepped to the sidelines as adroitly as possible and saved our risk taking for more opportune moments. This approach, combined with lackluster performance in the "solid citizenry" area, left us a good bit behind the ebullient market parade.

Such is life in the low p/e domain. We seldom distinguished ourselves just before turning points in the market. We exercised our skills by anticipating life after turning points, rather than by trying to keep up with the madness that preceded them.

A Delicate Balance

The investment decision-making process cannot be analyzed acutely, but it worked for Windsor in a direction that usually resulted in companies' being well bought. I always tried to balance risk aversion with some measure of creativity. That goal found expression in the shares of White Motor Company, a manufacturer of heavy-duty trucks. White Motor was obviously a speculative purchase: In 1970, it lost, on an operating basis, some $14 million and had a write-off of approximately $15 million, despite an entrenched market position that had essentially withstood the test of industry and company difficulties. When we bought the stock early in 1971, we were not predicting an imminent change in this climate. However, from the vantage point of knowing the ultimate market—namely, motor truckers—I concluded that 1972 looked promising, not only because of increased industry volume but also because of the positive replacement cycle.

White's principal problem was in the somewhat chaotic farm equipment field, where essentially the whole 1970 loss was experienced. Management took steps to correct retail and inventory excesses, and, in 1971, it looked to me like the farm equipment business would break even. In total, and if my expectations for 1972 were to prove correct, earnings seemed capable of climbing to somewhere between $2.50 and $3.00 a share—just half the previous peak level. *Outcome: In August and September 1971, Windsor garnered gains in excess of 43 percent. In that quick span of time, the Dow Jones Industrial Average actually slid a few points.*

1972: IF IT'S GOOD ENOUGH FOR MORGAN . . .

For Windsor, 1972 was a year of living dangerously. We flouted the market's appetite for a handful of growth stocks (the Nifty Fifty), and went our own way. Against the backdrop of measured participation, our band of less recognized growth stocks, modest growers, and cyclicals was anything but sexy. To some observers, Windsor seemed out of sync with the times, just as we had looked somewhat laggard in the adrenaline days of the go-go era. To my way of thinking, however, we weren't out of sync with the market; the market was out of sync with reality. Saying that now doesn't do the experience justice. Everyone admits now, in retrospect, that the Nifty Fifty phenomenon was fated to implode. But at that time, ordinarily sober investors bought the argument that unlimited earnings growth and a limited supply of shares spelled perpetual capital gains.

The silly season was at hand. Because Windsor was suffering, that season seemed to last forever. The champion of this school of investing, Morgan Guaranty, blithely bought outstanding growth companies irrespective of price. In those days, you could literally hear other investors declare, "If it's good enough for Morgan, it's good enough for me."

Early in 1972, as the growth stock fetish of the marketplace continued to feed on itself, price levels seemed very extended. Windsor manifested this concern; our sales of securities in January outpaced new purchases by more than two to one. Unfortunately, our opportunity to withdraw very profitably from this hyped segment of the market was limited. The only worshiped growth stock we owned was IBM, which we viewed as the most sensibly priced—in fact, the only sensibly priced—big-name growth stock we could put our hands on.

Despite our best efforts, Windsor's performance continued quite poor statistically through mid-1972. The marketplace stubbornly refused to acknowledge continuing confirming fundamentals in the great majority of our equities. Actually, we had the pleasure, albeit somewhat aided by the economy, of marking up several of our 1972 earnings estimates. Meanwhile, nothing could shake my opinion that the market could not, for too much longer, pass up, with as much unanimity, our undervalued holdings.

As Nifty Fifty hijinks progressed, disappointments mounted and hard lessons were learned. One of the casualties was a company called Brockway Glass. We initiated this stake in October 1971, to gain participation in the glass container field. Reversal of the purchase, at approximately our purchase price, came in January. We recognized early that product pricing in this ordinarily gentlemanly industry was not fulfilling our model. Reality dashed our expectations of a healthy earnings increase in 1972; instead, we had no improvement over 1971. We imposed on ourselves an obligation not only of value, but also of a conduit through which the marketplace could recognize that value. In the case of Brockway Glass, we lost that conduit.

We could not twiddle our thumbs while awaiting the inevitable inflection point, so we continued our hunt for companies with sound fundamentals and low p/e ratios, especially in the decidedly unpopular cyclical segment.

IBM for Sale

For the first time in my term at Windsor, we sold shares of IBM, the only true highly recognized growth stock we owned, and, hence, our only opportunity to capitalize on the market's clamor for growth stocks. It was not without some soul searching that we started to sell some of our IBM as it edged toward 38 times prospective earnings of $10.75 a share.

It should be recalled, though, that when both 38 times and $10.75 of earnings were not looked upon by Wall Street as realistic, we kept purchasing IBM in an effort to maintain a maximum position. Thanks to this foresight, plus market appreciation, this holding increased to more than 6 percent of the Windsor Fund which, in the face of extraordinary demand, we trimmed back to 4 percent. Although at that middle stage of the Nifty Fifty phenomenon IBM still changed hands at a reasonable level relative to the pronounced overvaluation of most growth stocks, sane observers like ourselves reasoned that it would undoubtedly share in a redetermination when growth mania approached its realistic and ugly conclusion.

November 14, 1972, marked a memorable day. For the first time, the Dow Jones Industrial Average closed above 1,000.

"The Dow Jones Industrial Average closed above the 1,000 mark for the first time in history," *The Wall Street Journal* reported on November 17, trumpeting progress that the Dow would retrace within weeks. "The Dow finally put it all together," went the *Journal*'s account, "the peace rally,* the re-election of President Nixon, the surging economy, booming corporate profits and lessening fears about inflation and taxes and other uncertainties of 1973."

Observers noted the influence of just two stocks, IBM and AT&T, whose favorable growth expectations had fueled the rise. "With such kingpin issues leading the forward surge, the market fed on its own momentum."[†]

1973: TANDY IS DANDY

Enthusiasm launched 1973 on a giddy note. Notwithstanding its new record, the market needed all the help it could get. Watergate, rampant inflation, serious shortages in natural resources, increasing disaffection toward the war in Vietnam, and rising interest rates made 1973, from an investing standpoint, a difficult obstacle course. Before January was out, the Dow had slipped back under 1,000. It remained south of this

---

* This refers to the market rally in expectation of an end to the divisive Vietnam conflict.
† Vartanig G. Vartan, "Dow Finishes Above 1,000," *The Wall Street Journal*, November 17, 1972, p. 1.

attention-getting benchmark until March 1976, sinking as low as 577 in December 1974.

When trouble is brewing, skittish investors cast an eye toward sectors that aren't going away. Being skittish, most snap up the usual suspects with reassuring names and no blemishes: big food companies, energy companies, and utilities. Wall Street research follows this pattern—more often than not, investors are led to the safe havens that the researchers have already identified. We also hunted for companies that had solid footing but were not so obvious as the tried and true.

Farm products, particularly harvestable grains, are an important segment of the U.S. economy. We reasoned that beyond the elements of favorable climate and fertile land, the industry relied on dependable and efficient farm machinery. John Deere & Company exemplified the qualities we sought.

Written off by many investors as too cyclical, this company was the outstanding farm machinery manufacturer—not only in this country but probably in the world. Though unloved by equity investors, Deere was poised to capitalize on carefully laid plans to satisfy a growing demand for farm equipment. Moreover, its products were increasingly migrating from farms to suburbia. Earnings had been and would remain cyclical, but, in my judgment, the cyclicality was less important than conventional wisdom had indicated. Besides its farm equipment business, Deere's growing participation in construction and home consumer products represented a quarter of its sales. This quality company in a growing field seemed capable of fetching 12 times earnings in the market, suggesting an appreciation potential of 29 percent.

Happily, Deere exceeded our expectations. We began to trim the stake after only a few months, in September 1973. When those shares changed hands, we pocketed a return in excess of 40 percent. Subsequent sales, in November and December 1975, garnered from 22 percent to 32 percent, once more against the backdrop of a thoroughly depressing industrial average.

Beyond the Blue Horizon

A handful of highly recognized growth stocks still drained the market of its energy. A "blue funk" engulfed all stocks, but none more so than cadres of less recognized growth stocks. The devastation created extraordinary appreciation opportunities in companies necessarily of higher-than-ordinary risk. To the extent prudent judgment would allow, we shifted our investors' assets into these promising areas.

Among these stocks, none deserves mention more than plucky little Tandy, the most prodigious single source of gains that Windsor owned during my tenure. I usually thought of myself as a contact hitter, usually capable of getting on base and maybe even stealing a base or two. Thanks to outstanding research by Chuck Freeman, who became portfolio manager after I retired, we both thought Tandy was going to be a winner. We were not expecting a grand slam, however.

When we discovered Tandy, it was one of America's leading and most successful practitioners of the specialty retailing concept that was just surfacing. We initiated this spectacular stake by purchasing 50,000 shares in May 1973. By year-end, Windsor owned 165,000 shares.

The company was the brainchild of Charles Tandy, a maverick Texan retailer. *Fortune* magazine described him as "a marathon talker with a highly informal management style, and he was known to rouse executives from their beds with telephone calls in the small hours when a new merchandising idea came to him."* However idiosyncratic, his style succeeded. "In a mere fifteen years he had transformed a sickly group of stores called Radio Shack into an awesomely profitable, worldwide chain of 7,000 retail outlets."

When Windsor noticed Charles Tandy's retailing concept, management's strategy was to seek out and then aggressively expand promising specialty formats that had good growth potential and opportunities for leadership. We had a dramatic example in Radio Shack. Once a failing regional chain hawking low-end electronics goods, it accounted for almost three quarters of Tandy's profits in 1973. After acquiring Radio Shack in the early 1960s, Tandy nursed it into one of the largest national retailers of consumer electronics goods. Subsequently, Tandy developed and achieved commendable success with a group of retail chains appealing to hobbyists and do-it-yourselfers in home tiling, needlework, and other handicrafts. There was also an increasingly profitable leather goods operation. Tandy's only flaw, so far as we could tell, was nonmembership in the blue-chip category. Judged by any other standards, it looked highly

---

* Irwin Ross, "Charles Tandy's Ghost Can Rest Easy," *Fortune* magazine, November 19, 1979, p. 114.

promising to us, if somewhat more venturesome than our usual fare. (It had no dividend to buffer us if our analysis proved wrong.) Earnings had progressed in 13 consecutive years and were compounded at 16 percent over the four prior years. We pegged long-term growth prospects at 12 to 15 percent, and 15 times earnings was a sustainable multiple. Nevertheless, Tandy's shares were changing hands significantly below the high it had etched two years earlier.

On our model of earnings expectations and prospective p/e, we figured Tandy for appreciation potential of 80 percent. This analysis never contemplated an onslaught of personal computing and the whole coterie of silicon chip-driven consumer electronics. Tandy's early leadership in the personal computing revolution dramatically highlights what I call a "free plus," or favorable developments above and beyond any scenario we had contemplated. Spurred by attention to a primitive computer with far less memory than a floppy disk today, consumers flocked to stores selling the primitive TRS80 computers, and investors flocked to the stock.

Free Plus Jackpot

With Tandy, one free plus seemed to follow another. I've never stopped to calculate the overall extent to which this little company enriched Windsor shareholders. But in the course of owning Tandy (let alone two lucrative spin-offs, Tandycrafts and Tandy Brands) and selling and repurchasing and selling, Windsor had a stunning series of gains: 157 percent in November 1975; 348 percent in January 1976; and a breathtaking 520 percent in February 1976.

It was good to be on the right side of this clamor, and better yet, to get out at the right time. We sold our last Tandy shares around 1980. A decade and a half later, we could have bought them back for the same price.

We got no help from Tandy in 1973, however. The market's performance went from bad to worse. Instead of a free plus, the economy handed us Watergate and a Middle East conflict that spawned an oil crisis. This constant turmoil all but barred thoughtful investors from taking time to study and ferret out undervalued situations. Instead, they tended to invest in a superficial, simplistic, knee-jerk fashion. Circumstances offered scarce hope that other money managers might come around to our way of thinking. All they could do was react to rapid changes in market prices and put out fires.

Patience Is a Virtue

Toward year-end, the slide accelerated. The swiftness of the devastation was unique in my 20 years of market observation. The Dow Jones Industrial Average started November above 948, and ended it below 823, a 13 percent decline. I had never before been exposed to a market that was so oblivious to earnings support, which previously had kept good companies from being blitzed in down markets.

A "sell at any price" mania seemed to inordinately depress our total portfolio and deprived us of our usually good downside performance in bear markets. On paper, one fourth of Windsor's net asset value eroded in 1973—hardly the kind of job that Windsor shareholders deserved. When Windsor took such a humbling bath in 1962, Wellington hired a new manager. Maybe I was deaf to grumbling, but I never sensed that my job was in jeopardy. With characteristic confidence that the market would have to embrace our sound companies sooner or later—hopefully, sooner—I invoked the reassuring words of Benjamin Franklin in our annual report:

> *Be honest; toil constantly; be patient. Have courage and self-reliance. Be ambitious and industrious. Have perseverance, ability and judgment. Cultivate foresight and imagination.*

1974: BACK TO REALITY

At long last, the highly recognized growth stocks came under considerable selling pressure. If sustained, the pressure promised to burst the usefulness of these bloated creations almost irrespective of their intrinsic worth. We hoped it would finally flush out the camp followers and other shorter-term investors who had prostituted the area for some time. For all but these ill-advised gamblers, a goodbye to the Nifty Fifty promised better days (1) by removing the intimidating shadow of the growth stocks from the rest of the marketplace and (2) by bringing more deserving sectors to the foreground.

Windsor was well positioned for such a turn, and we looked forward to a more equitable and broader rotation to market segments in which we had a substantial stake—commodities in short supply, banks, and entrepreneurial less recognized growth areas. With the numbing spell of the

Nifty Fifty removed from the marketplace, merits of other attractive areas became more obvious. The evolution finally began to have some meaningful impact on our performance. For 1973, we were some 10 percentage points inferior to the S&P 500, but, early in 1974, we recaptured 90 percent of the deficit. More than anything else, this superior performance was reflective of how big growth and oils stocks, which made up nearly half of the S&P 500, were receiving their comeuppance. Being purposely underinvested in these two areas, we benefited accordingly.

However, because I am a price-sensitive gradualist, it seemed to me that we were honor-bound to start gaining representation in both of these disgraced areas, given more reasonable evaluations. In addition to our highly recognized growth entries, we added Amerada Hess convertible preferred and Pennzoil to Windsor's portfolio.

The new challenge in the marketplace, early in 1974, rested on determining buy points on several other good growth stocks that were being hammered repeatedly. Almost routinely, in the aftermath of excessive overvaluation, there is a compensatory penalty on the downside.

Long on Shortages

As Windsor embarked on the second quarter of 1974, we continued to do reasonably well in the performance derby. Our performance gave strong evidence of attention-getting earnings increments by the commodity suppliers that constituted almost a quarter of the Windsor Fund. Our "shortage" interests were concentrated chiefly in aluminum, copper, chemicals, cement, zinc, and sugar—all likely beneficiaries of price increases. Besides the inflation problem and the Watergate imbroglio threatening the Nixon presidency, the market was grappling with a very dramatic and unprojected upward reversal of short-term interest rates. It was difficult to imagine these imponderables clearing up all at once, but changes at least hinted that the future direction would be positive. Agricultural commodity prices had declined sharply from their earlier highs, offering some hope for more stable food costs. Meanwhile, the quantum jump in world petroleum prices seemed to have stabilized, with good prospects ahead for a decline.

With markets as unpredictable as they were, Windsor's performance turned somewhat negative toward late Spring. Moderate growers came under widespread selling pressure after Consolidated Edison wiped out its dividend. It was an overreaction, of course, and we held fast to our principles. However, the downdraft affected not only the electric and telephone utilities; investors' concerns also unduly pummeled the banks. This did not bode well. The positive fundamentals we projected in these areas were very much on track, but the marketplace appeared to be saying that the problems stretched far beyond the scope of anything we could foresee. A stubborn market refused to reward our copper and aluminum area (about 10 percent of Windsor), even in the wake of price increases.

Nevertheless, we judged this a good time to have all of Windsor's assets working for shareholders. The level of stock prices represented, in our estimation, the best common stock buying opportunity in 20 years. We were not alone in this assessment, but we were in the minority. Fearing further tumult, most money managers were heavily committed to cash or cash equivalents, when they should have been taking advantage of exceptional opportunities.

No Place to Hide

Performance in the summer of 1974 allowed us to hang in with a pretty good year-to-date result, despite our fully invested position. With the obvious exception of cash, there were no real havens from the carnage of this market. The area that continued to feel the most pressure was the highly recognized growth segment in which we had minimal representation; but the inevitable bloodletting in this area had progressively influenced the whole marketplace. Panic was obviously rampant, and illiquidity was the order of the day. Judgments were not being made on a rational basis. Follow-the-leader and reaction-after-the-fact were propelling momentum in the marketplace. One could legitimately ask: "Where does it all end?" I was then as inadequate as most anybody in providing the answer. However, one always has the ability to look at one's portfolio with seeming facts in hand, and remain confident accordingly.

Despite the bleakness of a landscape strewn with commodity shortages and President Nixon's resignation on August 4, consumers were beginning to realize that the world was not coming to an end. We saw no reasons for consumers to reduce spending below 92 percent of disposable income (the historical level). They were to be aided and abetted by a somewhat better real disposable income trend in 1975.

Against this dynamic backdrop, Windsor was valued at a ludicrous 5.2 times earnings with a yield of 6.7 percent. We continued to be gratified

How Measured Participation Changed Windsor 1971–1982

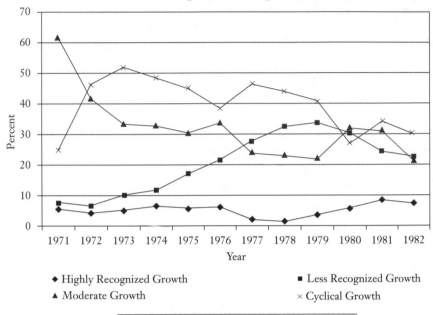

◆ Highly Recognized Growth   ■ Less Recognized Growth
▲ Moderate Growth   × Cyclical Growth

by the significant dividend increases on a number of large components in our portfolio. In July and August alone, dividend increases made up about 21 percent of the Windsor portfolio, ranging from a 4.7 percent increase by General Telephone to a doubling by Reynolds Metals. The median dividend increase for 13 companies—a list that included AT&T, Motorola, Kennecott Copper, Consolidated Freightways, and Safeway Stores—was 16 percent.

Increases like these were not only attention-getting, they were real. Shareholders were receiving pronounced increases in their dividend returns on their investment. Some testimony to the quality of the portfolio was also apparent, not only in the increased earnings, but also in the financial solidity that encouraged the directors of these companies to pass along some of the earnings to the shareholders. The other side of the 5.2 price–earnings ratio on this well-rounded portfolio was an earnings yield of nearly 20 percent. One could despair and say that few of these facts bore much relevance in an emotionally depressed marketplace. However, when other investors finally realized that the sky was not going to fall, the measures of financial strength that distinguished Windsor companies ultimately gave our shareholders a significant advantage.

Performance continued decent, if not outstanding, as Windsor entered the final stretch of 1974. We maintained our edge versus the averages and competitive funds, despite our fully invested position. This tactic was justified by the remarkable values in the marketplace and by our desire to be responsive on the upside when the inevitable rally arrived. The economic horizon added to our confidence. Steps initiated by President Gerald Ford to whip inflation were beginning to work, and investors were starting to notice. A significant rally from previous lows was finally triggered.

Windsor was still due for disappointment in late October 1974, however, when the traditional growth stocks snapped back to life. It seemed to us that underinvested participants were scurrying to get back into the market by spending their accumulations of cash, in knee-jerk fashion, by focusing on the same narrow roster of highly marketable equities. November started out less cruel. Rhyme, reason, and rationality seemed to gain strength in the marketplace, along with broader participation and selectivity related to fundamentals. We welcomed this climate and looked forward to benefiting the Windsor Fund shareholders accordingly.

Browning-Ferris was small, garden variety, less recognized growth company that had, in our judgment, excellent growth rates and very moderate multiples. It was, in effect, a garbage carter, or, euphemistically, a solid waste disposal company. However pedestrian and unpalatable this business, it nevertheless is prominent in our society and performs a critical utilitarian service. Before a fall from grace, Browning-Ferris had been acquired by Wellington's growth-driven portfolios at much higher prices than prevailed in November 1974. Nevertheless, it remained, in our judgment, the best operator in a tough field that demanded not only significant capital but increasing technology as well. The company's record showed annual earnings growth of some 17 percent over the previous four years, and a demonstrated ability to sustain annual growth of 15 percent. This growth rate, in combination with a yield of approximately 3 percent, made it a very worthwhile holding at 5.7 times fiscal 1975 economic prospective earnings. **Outcome:** *We essentially doubled our money (about 40 percent better than the market) in a little over two years, although we would have done better in a competitor, Waste Management.*

The event that bothered me the most, relative to our 1975 outlook, was the complete cave-in of auto sales. It did not affect us directly; we had eliminated our auto stocks. However, it reached its tentacles out to a number of supplying industries, and domestic sales needed a robust recovery if our sanguine 1975 outlook was to be fulfilled.

Overlaid on the auto disappointment, a shortage syndrome seemed to afflict everything: gasoline, paper, photographic film, sugar, and even diet soft drinks that used sugar substitutes. At some point, even toilet paper was in short supply. As these deprivations, real or manipulated, ended, "quick and dirty" inventory shrinkage got underway and had a moderating effect on pricing. We predicted it would pretty well run its course by the end of the first quarter of 1975, but this judgment hinged on maintenance of a consumer purchasing thrust, including a recovery in the pace of auto sales. If both were to happen, we thought then, it still seemed likely that economic activity in 1975 would not vary much from 1974, although the first and second quarter comparisons faced pressure.

After five years of toiling against the pesky resilience of a single overpriced market sector, Windsor ended 1974 beaten but unbowed. As committed as ever to a low p/e philosophy, we were about to find out how right we were.

1975: WINDSOR TRIUMPHANT

Two decades after hitchhiking to New York in a vain search for a job, my career was making indisputable headway. Bruised but unbeaten by the Nifty Fifty, Windsor emerged afterward as a leading player in the mutual funds industry. Moreover, our resolute combination of measured participation and low p/e was holding up as a formula for negotiating very difficult markets. Although 1974 did not disgorge the bounties we had expected amid a crumbling Nifty Fifty, we approached 1975 with continuing confidence and undimmed optimism. We had a dynamic collection of solid, high-yield, and moderate growth stocks.

The new year started out by continuing the negative toll on failing high p/e growth stocks. In contrast, there was better recognition of solid values and some recovery in areas requiring more imagination, such as secondary growth stocks. One caveat in competitive comparisons had applied to both 1974 and 1975: Our principal adversary was the S&P 500. If we measured up well there (excluding the silly season of 1972 and 1973, when the growth stock prices' actions were fueled by unnatural forces), we would do well in the competitive group. We did get ten percentage points back in 1974, but if the silly season judgment was at all accurate, we expected to recover enough to post a superior five-year performance record.

The bedrock of the portfolio resided in solid citizenry: moderate growth companies and cyclical growth companies. The latter consti-tuted half of the Windsor portfolio. In 1975, we sought to recover from the ashes of 1973 and 1974, both in the stock market and in the overall economy. We saw no reason to veer from a continuing interest in com-panies that had relatively assured prospects. Without being able to gauge the impact of the Pension Reform Act, which imposed a more rational and prudent framework on managers of pension assets, we looked for-ward to its influence on investment practices. We expected a stock mar-ket recovery to manifest itself in emphasis on good finances, significant size, large market share, and relative ease of understanding.

We felt strongly that this recovery would move beyond the market's fetish with the Nifty Fifty growth stocks. It had already started to in-clude solid moderate and cyclical growers that additionally carried at-tractive yields. Our list had significant representation: Safeway Stores, American Telephone & Telegraph, CBS, John Deere, Kennecott, quality banks, Union Carbide, and Monsanto, among other holdings. Admit-tedly, most of these had less appreciation potential than our triple or quadruple potential of more creative and riskier equities. However, lower targets were not inappropriate for more assured results, and it seemed as though this dominant, quality arena at reasonable multiples had even greater exploitation potential. As a result, our early 1975 thrust was vis-ible in this area.

As the first quarter progressed, we inched very close to recouping the 16.8 percent loss Windsor had suffered in 1974. The good advance was a reflection of: (1) a fully invested position; (2) very handsome gains in the opportunistic, less recognized growth areas; and (3) a far better shake in some of our better value merchandise, perhaps best exempli-fied by the banks.

A rapid recovery in the marketplace was somewhat out of character with near-term confirmation by the economy itself. However, early in 1975, we also recognized that the market had plunged too far downward. Contrary to conventional wisdom, it would at some point be as silly on the upside as it had been ludicrous on the downside.

Sweet Success

Capitalizing on our optimism about commodities and farm-related products, we gave careful attention to the fundamentals of A. E. Staley Manufacturing, one of two domestic producers of high-fructose corn syrup, a sugar substitute. With the price of sugar burgeoning, corn syrup looked a lot tastier to industrial sugar users—producers of soft drinks, baked goods, and a host of other food products. Even after the price of sugar declined sharply toward a more normal level, fructose remained a very economical alternative. Further declines in the price of sugar threatened fructose prices somewhat, but a growing acceptance of fructose promised to stimulate consumption and sustain profits. In an effort to satisfy demand, Staley was expanding capacity, and earnings were climbing at a significant pace. We envisioned record 1974 earnings of about $6 a share to balloon to more than $15 in 1975. It seemed only realistic to view this as a high-water mark for some years to follow, pending new capacity and increased soybean processing, but we were drawn to the creation of a whole new industry, with Staley in the forefront. Purchased at approximately 3½ times the year's earnings, this excellent industry participant was predicted to sell at 10 times established earnings, giving us a very worthwhile appreciation potential. ***Outcome:*** *Sweeteners, led by Staley, proved rewarding and durable. We logged about a 50 percent profit in an indifferent market.*

Near the midway point in 1975, it seemed prudent to concede that the easy money from an undervalued market had been made. At higher than 800 on the Dow, after a sharp 38 percent recovery from the December bottom, we expected slower going. In keeping with this seemingly realistic attitude, we continued to take our foot off the accelerator a bit on the purchase side. We were not afraid of the level of the marketplace; rather, we were aware of the frenzied pace of recovery and the probable future opportunity to buy into single-issue, group, or even market weakness, using our moderate cash position (7.5 percent of Windsor's assets). In addition to the gradual profit realized from some specific areas where we had been successful and held significant positions, we rechanneled proceeds into solid, less risky, total return situations.

Meanwhile, we continued profit taking among out ample winners: CBS, Union Carbide, and Safeway Stores. We actually enjoyed more than a little market success and/or recovery during the period when the marketplace recaptured some of its imagination, not only in the friendly less recognized area, but also in conglomerates like Gulf + Western, Walter Kidde, and White Consolidated.

The most significant sale involved Jim Walter Corp., an entrepreneurial, more-than-average-risk Windsor Fund investment that contributed to excellent results. We had initially bought shares of homebuilder Jim Walter Corp. in the summer of 1972, and we added to it the following spring. Its shares enjoyed a 50 percent run-up, double the market's progress in the same span of time. Our outsize position, both in respect to the shares outstanding of the company, as well as in Windsor, was being sold steadily into an ebullient marketplace, as investors awakened to building recovery prospects and the company's promising coal business. In traditional Windsor fashion, we used this strength and market enthusiasm to capitalize on our successful analysis.

Along with the bouquets we were heaping on ourselves as we outdistanced the market and our competitors, there was a less satisfying experience with Eaton Corporation. It was hardly a disaster; it performed no worse than the market since we had purchased it in mid-1973. But the accomplishments of the company, a prime participant in heavy-duty truck transmissions and axles, and other industrial areas, did not fully live up to our earnings targets through 1973 and 1974. Given the testy economy in mid-1975, and facing an extremely difficult heavy-duty truck environment (probably for the rest of 1975 and on into 1976) and shrinking backlogs in the forklift manufacturing business, Eaton's earnings made a poor comparison with record results in 1974. We preferred the sidelines during a period of extreme test but, as always, reserved the right to reenter the fray some 6 to 12 months later.

Our affection for unloved energy-related equities highlighted Texas Eastern Transmission, a pipeline transmission company with a major participation in British North Sea petroleum discoveries. This stock had been enthusiastically evaluated in the marketplace a few years earlier, when it was selling for over $60 in 1972 and 1973. Since that time, earnings had continued to progress at a 7 percent annual rate. (The Federal Trade Commission was quite realistic in allowing an adequate pipeline return for the transmission companies, despite declining throughput.) In addition, the North Sea realization became quite prominent in the earnings stream in 1976 and beyond, and we looked for an addition, over a three- or four-year period, of $1.00–$1.50 of earnings from this source.

Superimposed on a gently rising earnings scale from the rest of the company, an acceleration of earnings growth to 10 percent or better per year seemed relatively well assured for a number of years. With a yield of almost 6 percent going in and an improvement in prospect in the latter part of the year, coupled with a market evaluation of only a little over seven times earnings, we envisioned a handsome appreciation as North Sea oil rekindled the market's enthusiasm for oil service stocks. Our returns on this investment, while short of stellar, outperformed the market by a wide margin. In November 1977, shares we sold enjoyed a gain of nearly 58 percent. Over roughly the same stretch, the Dow slipped under 850, a 15 percent decline.

We remained competitive in an environment that had recovered some imagination and willingness to give a fairer shake to companies that were a bit off the beaten path. The big growth stocks began to be measured more on their individual merits, rather than as a group in the marketplace. This more realistic market gave Windsor a better climate in which its virtues could be appreciated.

Cashing In

We continued to go easy on the accelerator; sales outpaced new purchases by more than two to one. We were not blue about market opportunities, but we were somewhat wary of the pace of advance. In keeping with this perspective, we challenged ourselves with alternative opportunities while continuing to realize profits on very successful investments.

In a market that was scratching its way back to former levels, Windsor's hefty realization continued in sales of Jim Walter (+40 percent), CBS (+35 percent), Monsanto (+60 percent), Colonial Penn Group (+100 percent), and Safeway Stores (+40 percent). In addition, we started to take profits on very successful investments in Tandy (+150 percent) and Amsted Industries (+74 percent). Tandy represented probably our single, most successful, significant-size investment, as reflected in an average cost of $16 per share on 300,000 shares purchased from the summer of 1973 through the end of 1974. As a result of a tripling from our purchase price, not to mention a fivefold advance from the 1974 low, we started to capitalize on this very successful merchandiser of consumer electronics, as our appreciation targets were being approached.

With our portfolio showing a prospective earnings gain of better than 10 percent in mid-1975, relative to an overall corporate decline of 15 to 20 percent and an estimated increase of 20 percent in 1976, we found it difficult to be bearish. While admitting that the signs of inflation were a bit discouraging, we were satisfied that it would turn out to be somewhat aberrational and that a 6 percent or so inflation target for the Consumer Price Index (CPI) was not unrealistic. Little did we know that double-digit inflation lay ahead of us. What seemed particularly cogent, in August 1975, was the fact that Windsor Fund was selling at only a smidgen over 7 times 1975 earnings and 6 times our early line on 1976.

Dividend increases in 1975 also underscored Windsor's good health. Over 40 percent of our holdings raised dividends; only one company trimmed its dividend.

1976: THE JOY OF STOCKS

After outperforming some 90 competitors, Windsor entered 1976 with the wind at its back. Among funds larger than $100 million, our 54.5 percent advance was almost five percentage points better than our closest competitor, and 17.4 percentage points better than the S&P 500.

Windsor's boxcar returns earned boasting rights and compensated us for the ragged years when we bucked the all-encompassing growth stock hysteria that engulfed the marketplace, to the detriment of Windsor's relative performance. Our five-year track record placed us just behind the competitive group average and a bit lower than the S&P 500. Neither comparison glittered, but in a series of unnatural years, we had clearly held our own and, more importantly, stood well positioned to vault to the front of the pack in 1976. Meantime, our 10-year score, the one that ultimately matters, had us leading by a wide margin. In that span, Windsor's 80.3 percent increase outdistanced the nearest competitor by more than 5 percentage points and the No. 3 competitor by 20 percentage points. Moreover, Windsor's gain amounted to twice the competitive group average.

Days of the Roundtable

I joined the annual *Barron's* Roundtable for the first time in January 1976, a month of impressive market vigor. The Dow vaulted to 975 from 858, a 14 percent gain. It's difficult to say when, in the course of the market's steady progress, delight turns to concern and then to fear. After the somewhat "heady wine" of January and early February, however, we were not particularly nervous about the level of the market or, particularly, Windsor companies, which were selling at 7½ times 1976 earnings. We wondered, though, as always, about the sharp pace of the advance, propelled chiefly by the liquidity seekers' renewed interest in common stocks. A digestion of some sort loomed, we thought, once the source of thrust ran its course.

A more important part of our strategy was to continue what we had always done fairly well: recycle the proceeds from both realization and mistakes into "behind-the-market," undervalued, common stocks. In early 1976, good yield and reasonable price–earnings ratios directed our attention to domestic oil stocks. A new energy bill virtually assured an upward path for pricing that promised to boost bottom lines. Other investors despaired somewhat over the politicizing of domestic crude oil and natural gas pricing. To us, the prices represented honest value and an excellent four-year track for earnings, not to mention the total oil prominence in the S&P 500 (some 15 percent of the total). If the market's enthusiasm persisted, we were prepared to cycle oil stocks back into cash, an outcome that eventually came to pass and yielded substantial benefits—sooner than expected—for Windsor shareholders. Within two months, we started to realize some excellent value appreciation from a friendly cost basis.

Meanwhile, the market's appetite for Windsor's formerly beleaguered stocks continued to grow. We were pleased to accommodate the marketplace. Tandy, of course, stood out; other stocks were close behind as a great bit of Windsor's value phalanx earned attention. Imagination, creativity, and a disposition to do a little further work encouraged a ferreting out of an increasing number of our "goodies." Telling profit taking was visible also in Deere & Co., General Telephone & Electric, White Consolidated, and U.S. Shoe Corp.

RCA, however, was eliminated at a respectable profit of 15 percent, essentially that of the market since acquisition. However, two very important struts of our original analysis were not, at least over the near term, coming true. First, the market for color TV sets failed to share in the recovery in consumer purchasing thrust that had been evidenced in other areas, although it seemed as though this would eventually happen. Second, and more important, the very strong second-ratings position of NBC to the network industry leader, CBS, had deteriorated very sharply. This might not have shown up in earnings for a few quarters, but it removed a very necessary qualitative component of the analysis. It not only promised to scar the bottom line, it also impinged on the multiple targets we had been using. Interestingly, and somewhat discouragingly, the stock appreciated significantly after its elimination from the Windsor portfolio. So be it. We must act on our model of expectation and let the chips fall where they may.

Scrub and Purge Time

Ever cognizant of "scrub and purge time," we jettisoned our disappointments. Whether cashing in or bailing out, we continued to convert market enthusiasm into proceeds, both to replenish cash and to reinvest in overlooked moderate growth companies that combined excellent yields with decent growth rates and reasonable price–earnings ratios. Toward this end, we bolstered our domestic oil exposure to almost 10 percent of the Windsor portfolio—or 14 percent if the segment included diversified natural gas stocks, which were using their cash flow in oil and natural gas drilling and exploration.

We remained optimistic with respect to the business outlook's, near and intermediate term, although a small red flag was popping up alongside the indifferent May retail sales. However, we took this sign to be an aberration. Although we were not skilled in predicting the path of the market, we nevertheless thought that the averages were pointed in an upward direction. Perhaps even more importantly, we were in a period in which value portfolios were getting their due. In that kind of climate, we were immensely optimistic about Windsor companies' sporting a weighted average price–earnings ratio of only a little over seven times earnings.

Meantime, Windsor's rebounding performance ranked second among 106 competing funds. Performance aside, this struck me as an amazing total of funds for an allegedly moribund industry. Superior performance was additionally gratifying because the conventional wisdom (usually right, in this case) held that superlative performers in one year seldom distinguish themselves in the ensuing year.

We continued to draw down or, more correctly, take profits in the cyclical growth area, as the marketplace grew increasingly enamored of "smokestack" America. We were accommodating in both the aluminum and chemical segments where outstanding appreciations resulted and, of course, yield support and the yield components of total return diminished accordingly. We maintained a significant exposure in this area, though with only 38 percent representation (down from 45 percent at fiscal year-end and 48 percent in August 1975). These group delineations were never perfect (i.e., in the eye of the beholder), but the remaining representation in this area, while somewhat diminished in the basic commodity area (most particularly, chemicals), still had a rather considerable participation in the producers' durables or capital expenditure area. This was a fertile area for appreciation in our judgment as we visualized the outlook for 1977. The momentum showed up principally in our conglomerates: Studebaker-Worthington, Gulf + Western, Walter Kidde, and White Consolidated.

So Goes Glory

It's wise to take bows quickly in this business. For calendar years 1970 through 1976, Windsor posted a stunning 83.2 percent advance versus 57 percent by the S&P 500. In 1976 alone, Windsor's 46.4 percent return outstripped the S&P 500, which chalked up a 26.8 percent advance. But uncertainty always looms. Lots of fluctuation within a narrow range characterized the market for most of 1976.

It was our perspective and conviction that, with the Dow at 932, the market rested on rather good support legs, as manifested by growing earnings, dividends, and easing interest rates. However, the digestion going on in early Fall seemed to reflect apprehension focused most prominently on (1) the increasing possibility that the economic expansion was aborting, and (2) an increasing likelihood that Jimmy Carter would win the Presidential election. We avoided any attempt to project the outcome on the political scene into intermediate or long-term investment scenarios, but it seemed fairly clear to us that the pause in business activity should be no more than a pause. A more favorable outlook would have to wait until consumers regained enough confidence to spend their increasing cash reserves and until business leaders tapped their mother lode to increase capital expenditures.

To us, the evidence seemed strong, both historically and in the existing market climate: More positive trends were going to develop over the near term. Accordingly, we viewed 1977 earnings prospects positively, and acknowledged the further likelihood that an absence of financial excesses would provide a favorable 1978 backdrop of potential increase as well. On the strength of these optimistic assessments, we looked forward to the development of a more favorable, imaginative, and probing market climate that would suit Windsor very well.

11

~

FOUR YARDS AND A
CLOUD OF DUST

1977–1981

INTEREST RATES, OIL prices, and successive commodity shortages commanded the market's attention as the next inflection point approached. Less recognized growth stocks were the heroes in the early months post Nifty Fifty; this time, we relied on a much wider assortment of companies and industries. Banks, conglomerates, consumer durables, multiline insurance, and electric utilities all heaped rewards on Windsor's shareholders.

1977: A CLEAN SLATE

Our portfolio structure soon showed some relatively sharp changes. To make room for cyclical auto stocks, our sale of IBM halved our highly recognized growth segment. Eliminating AT&T caused our moderate growth segment to decline. We also added to our less recognized growth component; we still regarded it as the area of greatest price opportunity. It seemed that the market had come almost full circle in its quest for yield and its deemphasis of growth. That quest had been just as intense and single-minded in the opposite direction in the early 1970s. Our sale of IBM notwithstanding, we continued to search for misunderstood companies in the highly recognized growth area.

A very significant switch was undertaken when Windsor funneled proceeds from IBM and AT&T into a like amount of General Motors and

Ford. As a matter of course, Windsor usually owned only seven or eight of the top 50 stocks in the S&P 500, which made up about half of that index's total value. We had nothing against the top 50, but they usually seemed overfollowed, overresearched, and, all too often, overowned and consequently overvalued. At the same time, we recognized that prejudices could slip into these equities. We were inclined to hedge our bets to a moderate degree in this market-dominating concentration.

For example, we became aggressive purchasers of domestic oil stocks in the latter part of 1975 and early 1976, and we still held significant holdings in Shell Oil, Atlantic Richfield, and Standard Oil of Indiana, all of which ranked in the top 50 of the S&P 500. In addition, for a number of years, we had held positions of approximately 6 percent in both AT&T and IBM. We regarded each stock as undervalued in its own particular spectrum; AT&T was one of the solid citizenry, and IBM stood tall in the highly recognized growth segment. Each was an excellent performer over the intermediate term, not only relative to the market, but, particularly in IBM's case, relative to its brethren.

In each case, however, we were faced with a diminution in intermediate-term earnings. AT&T had already enjoyed a quantum jump in earnings stemming from better regulatory climate. IBM's pricing became very aggressive, and, inexplicably, rental and service revenue growth became prosaic. Without pretending to have all the answers, we were forced to question the validity of our aggressive 14 percent projected growth rate for IBM, at a time when appreciation potential in the total portfolio was virtually twice that of Big Blue.

Four-Wheeled Sympathy

When we directed these proceeds toward the auto industry, General Motors and Ford were selling at approximately six and four times earnings, respectively, and yielding more than 9 percent and 7 percent as well. The marketplace was clearly saying that these earnings and dividend levels were abnormally inflated by extraordinarily good car sales in both 1976 and 1977. We disagreed with prevailing wisdom. New, more gasoline-efficient packages made built-in obsolescence respectable after decades of largely cosmetic design changes. This engendered an excellent replacement market for carmakers. Along with fuel efficiency came other comfort, safety, and conservation-minded design improvements. We failed to predict the stultifying combination of high interest rates and recession that dampened car buyers' appetites. Although our faith in four wheelers ultimately paid off handsomely, this early round ended in a draw.

Competitive performance had continued decent in the second fiscal quarter. Windsor's 4.4 percent advance was almost 3 percentage points superior to the S&P 500 and 3 full percentage points superior to that of the competitive group average. Moderate growers contributed to this above-average result. In addition, the less recognized growth spectrum weighed in with truly spectacular help from Pizza Hut, with its impending Pepsico merger. In effect, the imagination segment came through with a couple of big winners and several of the championship genre.

This was, ideally, how a portfolio should be orchestrated. The risk segment showed the spectacular gains, but a solid performance came from the plow horses as well. The challenge of portfolio management is not hard to fathom; one never quite knows the source of near-term performance. With sufficient diversification and some skill in assessing potential undervaluation over even a short period of time, the shareholder should benefit.

We were not without some disappointments. However, even disappointments can be absorbed if the positive side measures up. We were encouraged by how we continued to crank out a reasonably satisfactory result even when the market was depressed and, theoretically, our riskier merchandise could have suffered accordingly. The fact that it did not suffer augured well for the future, particularly if and when the market turned a little more optimistic.

Ennui pervaded the equity marketplace toward midsummer, although we continued to feel positive about the opportunities for undervalued securities. We conceded all the well-known negatives, but it seemed to us that the positives—high-magnitude increases in dividends; an economy growing, albeit slowly, without excesses; and an Administration with some cognizance of business needs—outweighed the perceived negatives.

Value Reaffirmed

Our first tentative cut on 1978 earnings underscored Windsor's value strategy. We noted a price–earnings ratio of 6.1 times 1978 earnings, which, on average, seemed altogether too low an evaluation versus an estimated 9½ percent growth rate and a current yield of 4.9 percent, or about 5.5 percent projected into 1978. We showed a portfolio earnings gain of almost 19 percent for 1977, and, prospectively, more than 11 percent in the new year. This was an accomplishing portfolio by virtually any standard, and considerable appreciation was in store for such a low price–earnings ratio. We continued to move gently toward a larger participation in the less recognized growth segment, and we made an accompanying shift from the moderate growth portion, mainly AT&T, into cyclical growth, mainly autos. This did not reflect a particularly strong move back into smokestack America; this area had suffered a severe price comeuppance, particularly in steel, chemical, copper, paper, and some machinery areas.

Big Oil

The portfolio had one new holding: an almost 1 percent position of Exxon, the world's largest oil company, and, with its 3.8 percent weighting in 1977, the third largest representative in the S&P 500. We were very conscious of companies with large S&P weightings, and we attempted to challenge ourselves regularly with potential undervaluation here. We seldom hedged, and an Exxon stake was not hedging. Instead, we were conscious of the very large S&P weighting relative to the impending Alaskan North Slope oil happiness, which Exxon delivered along with admirable representation in almost all of the world's new production areas. By our calculations, these attributes would foster an 8 percent (or better) annual increase in earnings, not to mention a formidable 5.9 percent yield. Singly, these were desirable traits; together, they were qualities that a risk-averse marketplace would not overlook for long. Our targeted 88 percent price increase, relative to 116 percent for the whole Windsor portfolio, was not compelling in and of itself. However, two other factors were at play: (1) the relative risk, and (2) the fact that the appreciation potential, though below Windsor's average, was superior in our judgment not only vs. the marketplace, but it was also some 20 percentage points better than the stocks we were selling. That had to be the ultimate yardstick in attempting to maximize portfolio gain. *Outcome: Exxon met our medium-term, defensive expectations for a large oil company. It outperformed the market by about 2 percentage points. An ample yield widened the margin.*

We were wrong in our judgment—admittedly fragile and somewhat out of character with any imagined expertise—that the market would bottom out around the 900 level. Instead, in August 1977, we found ourselves near 850 and still looking for a bottom. It seemed that we were at a value point, as evidenced, in part, by a 6 percent yield on prospective 1978 earnings for the Dow.

Reflecting the difficult market background, Windsor's performance slipped by 3.6 percent in the last three months of fiscal 1977. However, we added to our relative advantage for the year. Once again, the Fund was the best performer within the competitive group by a fair margin. We were particularly pleased that we performed relatively well in this down period, despite our increased representation in the less recognized growth area, which was intended particularly to aid our upside dynamics.

Windsor's gradual buildup of the less recognized growth category continued, although this reflected the good relative performance during the quarter more than it reflected transactions. The other significant change in portfolio mix during the quarter was the increase in the cyclical growth area. As usual, the market applied a broad brush on the downside. We tried again to take advantage of this lack of discrimination to increase our representation in basic industries that were still intact and were looking for increases in 1978 earnings. Our nose for value led us far afield. We snapped up fertilizer producers on the one hand and, on the other, aluminum and glass container manufacturers hampered by capacity restraints. We looked forward to improved operating rates and pricing.

Meanwhile, we dined out on Pizza Hut. The sale to Pepsico netted a 100 percent gain. As Pizza Hut's surprising value illustrated, if you are right in your judgments, the market will find a way to reward you even in a period of retreat by professional investors.

1978: OPTIMISTS' CLUB

The market labored into 1978 and was discouraging to most of its participants. However, at the risk of sounding like Pollyanna, we chose to look at the positive side: expanding earnings, growing dividends, reasonable pricing, and continuing linkage to the real world meant mergers and acquisitions. While institutional investors demurred, corporations snapped up assets at bargain prices, relieving weary shareholders of their burden at premiums to the depressed market.

Windsor was valued at 5.6 times earnings, or an earnings yield of 17.9 percent. (Earnings yield is the flip side of p/e. Instead of price divided by earnings, it's earnings divided by price.) Our shareholders received an estimated growth rate of 9.7 percent and a current yield of 5.5 percent for a total return of over 15 percent. This, of course, meant that even if the p/e stalled, we were in a position to deliver a 15 percent annual return to our shareholders well into the future. If the p/e expanded, as I thought it would, the return to the shareholders boggled the mind relative to the average common shareholder's rewards. Even in an onerous climate, Windsor more than held its own over the 5-, 10-, and 15-year spans, with annual returns of 7.7 percent, 7.4 percent, and 10.4 percent, respectively—nothing to be ashamed of in a market that had essentially done nothing during these periods.

Strategically, we added to the less recognized growth portion with proceeds coming from highly recognized and moderate growth areas. Important in this build was a renewed fascination with domestic oil stocks. Atlantic Richfield, along with Sohio, possessed the best dynamics of the domestic oils relative to the near-, intermediate-, and long-term capitalization on the Alaskan North Slope.

Among stock transactions in early 1978, further sale of IBM stood out. We had been using IBM as a source of funds at our convenience, to a point where it had almost been eliminated from the portfolio for the first time during my management of the Windsor Fund. Leading up to 1978, it had been a highly serviceable, quality-laden, highly predictable, high-quality equity investment that had done spectacularly well relative to its brethren—namely, highly recognized growth companies.

In this process, IBM evolved from being dramatically undervalued in that overvalued area to now being, if anything, a little on the high side relative to other highly recognized growth stocks. Taken together, four years after the Nifty Fifty crumbled, highly recognized growth stocks still did not pass through the Windsor filter, though Kmart and McDonald's came close. Adding to my concern about IBM, I noted very moderate growth, in the single-digit range, for the very important rental and service revenues. This was probably the best single indicator of IBM's ultimate growth, and it meant that Big Blue had been "eating its tail" for several years by selling equipment outright.

Good performance persisted, both absolutely and relatively. Windsor's 12.8 percent advance outpaced our nearest competitors by nearly four percentage points, and the S&P by slightly more. Significant performers included Ford, large bank holdings, broadcasters, some conglomerates, recently purchased insurance stocks, aluminums, specialty retailers, and several less recognized growth stocks.

A Burst of Adrenaline

The market caught fire in the latter part of April 1978, after a long period of ennui. It was difficult—impossible, really—to pinpoint the inflection point ahead of time. But I happened to be in Europe in mid-April, rubbing elbows with investment communities in London, Zurich, and Frankfurt. Almost everyone conceded the obvious appeal of our market if one could only gain confidence in the stability of the dollar. Whether the subsequent thrust came from Europe or some other source, I still don't know. But when the fuse was lit, apparently the excessively liquid position of institutional investors who were trying to mastermind the marketplace drove them to some kind of participation. This seemed particularly true after a monster move on Thursday, April 13; Friday, April 14; and Monday, April 17. In just three trading days, the Dow Industrials raced up by nearly 6 percent. Afterward, the ticklish and obviously challenging question was: How far would this move run in the other direction when, inevitably, the pendulum retraced its progress? Notably, the economic, fiscal, and monetary background had not changed so much, although psychological struts such as Federal Reserve Chairman G. William Miller's resolve and the Carter Administration's renewed consciousness were undoubtedly factors.

Given the new joy in the marketplace, we eased off the purchase side a bit, exercising our inclination to accommodate a more ebullient marketplace. Naturally, we would have liked to recycle the proceeds into areas that were behind the market, but only on our standards. We managed to do both. We realized good prices and also did reasonably well at reinvesting a meaningful portion of the proceeds. In addition, we became something of a conduit for "camp followers" as our cash flow grew more robust in a matter of weeks. No avalanche was occurring, but a Spring thaw that had begun.

New Horizons

We welcomed the opportunity to broaden our horizon. Besides traditional investments, we set out to introduce some new names to the Windsor Fund. Some, at the time, seemed a bit more stuffy or stodgy than the less recognized growth fare, but as the market grew more excited, we grew more cautious.

An investment in Aetna Life and Casualty added a new dimension: multiline insurance companies. I hesitate, in retrospect, to pick the trigger point for taking a stand in this area. The marshaling and assessing process had been continuous during the period when our exposure was restricted to Colonial Penn, a more niche-oriented insurer. When Aetna hiked its dividend twice in less than a year, boosting it by 83 percent, we saw increasing confirmation of the viability of the new level of record earnings in 1977. Not only did this create a formidable 6.4 percent yield for Aetna (in combination with a growth rate of 10 percent at only a little over four times earnings), it also put pressure on competitors to measure up.

We saw no reasons to declare the insurance underwriting cycle dead, nor to demand better performance than had been rung up in 1977. Both Aetna and Travelers had very significant accident and life earnings, and the predictable engine of investment income seemed capable of chugging on at a double-digit rate. This added up to a formidable growth participation at a very nominal p/e ratio, not to mention the generation of future dividend increases. If, as we expected, 1977 marked the peak of the underwriting cycle, we still looked forward to more double-digit dividend increases. *Outcome: In early 1982, a 71 percent return insured satisfaction for Windsor shareholders.*

Phantom Menace

A sharp recovery proved more durable than some observers had feared, but it served up some fluctuations after mid-April lows. This was not only a comeback in the tried and true highly recognized growth stocks after more than a four-year slumber, but it also delivered a considerable shot of adrenaline to more speculative companies. The emphasis on these companies focused significantly on major institutional investors that found themselves with too much cash. They recommitted in familiar, traditional, highly marketable areas like the established growth companies and perhaps the smaller, more imaginative institutions in some of the very marketable, more speculative companies.

It is fair to ask where we were during the big upward move by a familiar slew of growth companies, since we had pronounced ourselves capable of assessing the whole spectrum of investment opportunity at any point in time. The only apology I felt was due concerned Boeing, which gained 129 percent.* We had had a positive and astute perspective within Windsor, and I should not have missed it. Also, I suppose, we missed SmithKline Corp., based almost in our own backyard outside Philadelphia, and that was regrettable. In my defense, it was somewhat of a freak in respect to a single drug that could have accounted for half of the earnings in 1979.

In terms of Measured Participation, Windsor experienced an increase in the moderate growth segment, at the expense of cash. Meanwhile, we eased up on the less recognized growth stocks by harvesting some of the high double-digit growers. In their place, Windsor added companies with more modest growth rates—Atlantic Richfield, Owens Corning, U. S. Shoe, and, to a lesser degree, Aetna and Travelers. Our analysis gave cause for some apprehension about the surge upward; the suggestion of growing speculation by individual investors was most manifest in the Atlantic City gambling stocks, which were experiencing a boom.

Third-quarter purchases were somewhat right of center for Windsor. In other words, they were more in our traditional conservative mode. We altered this stance to a considerable degree as the Seventies progressed, not because we changed so much, but because considerable market opportunities opened up, particularly in the less recognized growth stocks. They were all low p/e and, with one exception, Owens Corning, they all had significant yields.

A Narrow Edge

The final fiscal quarter of 1978 began on a mixed note. We lagged slightly behind the S&P 500, which had declined 2.7 percent. Somewhat better year-to-date and trailing 12-month comparisons looked a little better, but the "edge" was not up to our usual targets.

Disappointment centered around the fact that our delusions of grandeur did not build to the sky. Having exercised enough foresight to take significant profits, particularly in the less recognized growth segment, we redeployed the proceeds in a combination of solid citizenry with high yields and low p/e ratios—the usual Windsor fare plus some liquidity. During the last two weeks of October 1978, the market took back some gains. However, instead of retracing 5 to 7 percent, rather typical of

---

* A decade later, we caught the airplane maker's similar takeoff.

a sawtooth advance, it actually gobbled twice that span. The Dow fell 110 points, to 792.

Despite our carefully laid plans, we gave more ground than we should have. Our performance versus the competition was acceptable, but against the S&P it was not so hot. During that savage two-week period, we gave up about four points of performance differential. As if it had not been sufficiently underscored before, we learned once again that we did not seem to do well in a chaotic market. Our merchandise always has needed gestation, pause, and contemplation—hardly the characteristics of a "putting-out-fires" period.

1979: SCARCE DWELL TIME

It is always a little difficult to summarize results, particularly over a short period of time. Suffice it to say that the market continued to be peppered by both encouraging and discouraging news relative to macro subjects as mundane as the economy, money supply, interest rates, the dollar, and international developments. As a result of various and sundry interpretations, it either surged or plummeted from week to week. Accordingly, there was not a great deal of trance or dwell time available for other institutional investors to develop an interest in our type of overlooked, misunderstood, and fall-in-a-crack type of company. In other words, people seemed to spend their time either putting out fires or figuring out what changes, if any, were warranted in money managers' preoccupation of the day: market timing.

To the degree that a lot of our companies needed a special, quiet hour to highlight their virtues, they continued lost. All this, of course, was an oversimplification, and perhaps a somewhat glib one at that, because some segments—chiefly, domestic oils—did particularly well. On the other hand, areas that grabbed either emotional headlines or special consternation because of where we were in the economic cycle suffered market overreactions.

We continued to seek constructive values available in the marketplace, and, at the same time, were less pessimistic than many of our peers about inflation and interest rates. We readily conceded that our strengths lay mainly in seeking out undervalued situations, so that's where we spent the vast majority of our time. In other words, we usually aspired to a relatively fully invested position and left the market timing to those with more than our share of skill.

Planes and Trains

Transportation stocks caught our eye. On the airline front, we grabbed a significant position in Delta Airlines. The price had changed very little since we sold a stake in 1967, when Delta was the largest holding in a much smaller Windsor Fund. Since that time, earnings, dividends, and book value had expanded by about three to six times, and the company continued to show its mettle versus the competition on virtually all fronts, including ultraconservative accounting, solidity of capitalization, and relative nonunion status. Very simply, it was an all-round quality operation. Although the industry faced unclear consequences of deregulation, Delta's financial strength supported an outstanding relative position, and the critical capacity-to-demand relationships were tight enough that all competitors had room to grow. Not unlike the rest of the company, the dividend was ludicrously conservative, and we anticipated quantum jumps as the company moved toward a 20 to 25 percent payout. **Outcome:** *In February 1981, shares of Delta landed a 55 percent gain.*

On the theory that it's difficult to have too much of a good thing, we added more chips to the transportation area. Santa Fe Industries was a very well-run and maintained railroad. Moreover, not unlike Union Pacific, it had a vast Western natural resource base ranging from petroleum and forest products to coal and uranium properties. The railroad was experiencing excellent traffic gains because of coal property additions, a new GM Oklahoma assembly plant, and natural growth, particularly in grain exports. This expansion, coupled with increased natural resource prices (particularly in petroleum products) and some physical increases, suggested to us a growth rate on the order of $8\frac{1}{2}$ percent. The dividend yield was nearly 7 percent and was due for improvement, so snapping up shares for five times earnings promised an excellent total return. Before the year was out, Santa Fe shares fetched 61 percent more than our cost.

A New Look at Big Growth

We increased the long-neglected, highly recognized growth area at the expense of the cyclical growth category. For some time, we found our high-growth opportunities almost exclusively in the less recognized growth area, but two highly recognized major growth companies came into view: Kmart and McDonald's.

We continued to positively view the value available in the marketplace, though we were somewhat conscious of the magnitude of an advance from the bottom. Accomplishing companies in the $100 million to $400 million capitalization range still attracted us. These were prime candidates in the "knock-off" merger and acquisition sweepstakes, which remained a market phenomenon.

The biggest sizzle came from sales of domestic oil stocks after a 33 percent appreciation. These were not box-car numbers, but they were good journeyman appreciations in big stocks in which we had made a significant bet in the previous year. We also rang up a 17 percent gain from shares of International Minerals, together with heady appreciation yet again in Edison Brothers, Martin Marietta, and White Consolidated. Other sales were smaller or "get your money back" appreciations, coupled with outright failure in Sambo's and a switching of part of the disappointing Johns-Manville position into a comparable, enlarged holding of Owens Corning.

We began to accumulate a meaningful position in Borg Warner, allowing Windsor shareholders to raise the question: "Why in hell are we buying another auto-related equity?"

Fortunately, this was also the market's perception of Borg Warner and the principal reason it was selling for 4.4 times 1979 earnings. Only about one-fourth of sales went to passenger car original equipment, a considerably smaller total than in years past. Other parts of the company manufactured air-conditioning equipment, a chemical component of high-impact plastics, pumps used commonly on energy fields (no sentimentality here), and a guard service, plus a potpourri of other transportation industry products built off of the original equipment base. In the course of evolving from management by the Ingersoll family to a group of professional managers, Borg Warner became a more effective and competitive company. One needed no more evidence than the increase in return on equity to more than 13 percent (from 8 or 9 percent in the old days). Needless to say, the company had an excellent yield that was scheduled for improvement. Despite an approximate one-third payout of earnings as dividends, the company had some excess internal generation of capital and an excellent balance sheet with latent borrowing power.

This opened the door to more acquisitions not unlike the very attractive purchase of Baker Industries in 1978. This appetite was also etched in the proposed acquisition of Firestone, which would have essentially tripled the sales of Borg Warner. The transaction was aborted, however, when Borg Warner, to its credit, refused to pay a price for Firestone that would have ruled out sufficient incremental earnings. *Outcome: Borg Warner shares notched a 37 percent price gain when we accommodated the market's appetite in fiscal 1980's third quarter. This advance outpaced the market by five percentage points.*

Cyclical Redux

Midway through calendar 1979, Windsor's most telling change in our broad portfolio classifications was revealed in cyclical growth. A two-percentage-point increase was more than accounted for by an approximate 4½-point increase in our aluminum position. This reflected our conviction that the economy was already in a recession that was likely to bottom out in the fourth quarter. According to this scenario, 1980 would be a year of moderate recovery and gradually ascending business activity.

In June, the consumer area corrected with a vengeance, particularly on the automobile side, which was impacted by the gasoline "problem." In contrast with prevailing wisdom, we did not think, as this emotionalism passed, that consumers would adopt a bomb shelter attitude. Instead, they would moderate their previous, somewhat optimistic behavior. This automotive inventory excess was significantly corrected on the production side in the third quarter and, to a lesser degree, in the fourth quarter, seemingly ensuring another decline in constant-dollar GNP in both these quarters. We only needed a decline in the third quarter to technically qualify for a recession after the 3.3 percent decline in the second quarter.

If these expectations materialized, we thought that 1980 in terms of physical output, was likely to be about the same as 1979 or a bit better. This outlook formed a favorable backdrop for some cyclically oriented basic industries—those that were operating near capacity with seeming price statesmanship and little new capacity coming on stream. The aluminum industry fit this description almost perfectly, prompting us to increase existing holdings of Kaiser Aluminum and to add two new large positions in Reynolds Metals and Alcoa. These three competitors' factors were selling for four times 1979 earnings and not much different on 1980 earnings, and were further buttressed by yields in and around 6 percent, outstanding cash flow, and improving capitalizations.

Despite our large oil sales and decreasing representation in this area, we switched some of the proceeds into Gulf Oil. Gulf was not only cheap (less than five times earnings) and high-yielding (almost 8 percent), but it was much more of a domestic company than popular perception recognized. The company was also completing a burdensome natural gas contract covering some 40 percent of its total deliveries. This contract was slated to run out during the 1985–1986 calendar period, boosting the company's earnings by at least $1.00 a share. In effect, Gulf supplied an excellent "anchor to windward" that combined excellent appreciation potential with obvious defensive characteristics. *Outcome: By late 1980, Windsor enjoyed an 88 percent gain on its investment in Gulf.*

Dazed and Confused

It was a little difficult to fully explain our shortfall in October 1979. We had demonstrated some degree of foresight by taking the top off of a lot of "happy" stocks and accumulating some liquidity—as much as 9 percent of assets at the end of September. This should have been enough to create a no-worse-than-average performance in the shellacking that resulted from the Fed's dramatic tightening on the weekend of October 7.

For the second October in a row, Windsor had been decently prepared but turned in a poor performance on the downside. We were a little perplexed and frustrated. This was particularly apparent in the financial arena where we had extraordinary sized holdings and were attempting to prove something out of the ordinary. I could understand why the S&Ls, with their near-term exposure to the rapid increase in short rates and the short-term orientation of their holders, would be fair game in a downdraft. However, it seemed that the banks, particularly ours—being somewhat right of center, importantly regional, and allegedly well held by investors—should have been more resistive on the downside. However, as conduits of and participants in the Fed action, the banks feared a margin squeeze. The difficulties remembered from last time cast a long shadow and seriously eroded the markets for these equities. In addition, several other areas of previous superior performance gave a good hunk of it back in the October devastation. An area in which we were pointedly and purposely underrepresented versus the S&P—namely, oil stocks—were outstanding performers during the quarter.

The Fed's moves in October 1979 virtually guaranteed the therapy of a recession for an engine that was already starting to miss. The real question that remained was whether the landing would be soft or more typical of most postwar recessions. I contended that it would be milder than usual, if for no other reason than that the traditional excesses were not as marked as in the past. Plenty of pundits said, however, that it would be as deep as and even more prolonged than the usual postwar recession.

Either assessment was fragile because we were in new uncharted territory with respect to the level of interest rates.* The carnage that had occurred in the equity market was every bit as pronounced in the bond market. The Salomon Brothers Bond Index declined by 8.9 percent in the month of October alone. The good that emerged from all this was not only the strong signal to international markets with respect to the dollar, but also the removal of the speculative froth from the commodity markets. Absent a halt, commodity markets threatened to lose their senses. A speculative binge launched from a gold and silver base was spreading rapid-fire into other commodity markets. This, of course, would have knocked the props out from under my soft-landing scenario, which had grain and industrial commodity markets behaving much better in this period than during the 1973–1974 experience. Even as sanity returned to most commodity markets, however, the international price of oil remained a problem. After a quantum jump to the vicinity of $40 a barrel, OPEC's price discipline eroded. Barring another Iranian crisis like the one that had led to hostage taking at the U.S. Embassy, I expected prices to simmer down and take the opportunism out of price jumps initiated by the more militant and grabby OPEC members.

Windsor accommodated investors' rising demand for oil and oil-related stocks. This group produced more than one-third of the Fund's advance of nearly 20 percent in 1979. We wasted no time in reaping the rewards for sticking our necks out by selling oil stocks when most

---

* The interest rate on 30-year Treasury bonds ended 1979 just over 12.5 percent on the way toward a peak of 15.2 percent on October 26, 1981.

investors were clamoring to own them. At their peak, oil stocks represented 19 percent of the Windsor Fund. By the time we ended our fiscal year, on October 31, oil stocks made up less than 5 percent. But perhaps we celebrated a bit early. As things turned out, oil stocks had a long way to go, at the expense of our other holdings. Meanwhile, 1979 was another year in which to enjoy being in the stock-picking business.

1980: LEANING AGAINST THE WIND

Calendar year 1980 capped a period of institutional groupthink, if not imprudence, fueled by oil-related stocks. The likes of Schlumberger, Halliburton, Standard Oil of Indiana, Shell, Union Oil, and Union Pacific doubled, on balance. The first two were genuine growth companies, but the others were rather ordinary by thinking people's standards, and they faced a future comeuppance. Also, those six were not the only big-company stocks that appreciated an extraordinary amount in 1979; they were just the most sensational. In and of themselves, they accounted for more than 10 percent of the S&P 500.

For basic "grubbers" like us, this was a very tough track to go up against. It's a wonder we did as well as we did, considering the rank discrimination against the other end of the spectrum—banks, insurance, finance, food stocks, and other so-called interest-sensitive areas—where Windsor had major concentrations.

Windsor labored badly, not only versus the S&P but versus the competitive group as well. The short explanation was *energy;* our below-average participation was limited to a maximum holding in Exxon and a very significant holding in Gulf. But for one exception, we were completely absent from the domestic scene as well as from the services area and so-called near oils. Missouri Pacific, an oil transporter, had moved sympathetically with Union Pacific, another in a long line of "energy half-breeds."

Encore Ennui

Put another way, the market had been savagely selective with asset plays led by the quite frenzied oils. Most of the rest of the marketplace stalled in a state of ennui because of interest-rate sympathy with either fixed-income securities or consumer stocks, or—you name it.

Unfortunately, Windsor experienced too little frenzy and too much ennui. In retrospect, considering Windsor's traditional contrarian approach, I suppose our poor showing was not entirely surprising. We never salivated for the last dollar in a major move (i.e., the oil stocks). Instead, we tried to take stocks from undervalued to fairly valued. We left "greater-fool" investing to others.

With an outlook that predicted a decline in corporate earnings of 5 to 10 percent, we banked once again on companies with more predictable earnings. Thus, we emphasized a strategy featuring sympathy for the moderate growers with requisite high dividend yields and low p/e ratios. Meanwhile, we trimmed Windsor's exposure in less predictable cyclical sectors, but not with enviable results right away. The asset plays and inflation hedges beyond the oils, which caught the market's fancy, belonged to the cyclical growth area.

It did not seem necessary to prove much more than we already were attempting to prove in the overlooked and neglected areas such as banks, retail, apparel, transportation, and autos, where we had out-of-the-ordinary positions. As a result, we had to look elsewhere for opportunities while peeling off those areas where we were participating already—chiefly, the oils and aluminum.

Stock prices started going our way a little during the second quarter, particularly because of unparalleled decline in short-term and, to a lesser extent, long-term interest rates. After an unparalleled increase in interest rates, it seemed only equitable, and even natural, that the retracement would also be record setting. We were wary of celebrating prematurely, however. Even with an increasingly negative outlook for the economy at that juncture, we sensed that the swift decline in rates might have been too much too soon. Still, it seemed clear that interest rates had finally peaked.

Windsor participated in this market move, thanks to above-average direct exposure to the interest-sensitive areas—chiefly banks, finance companies, and insurance companies. We also stood to benefit from lower interest rates in a secondary wave, through foods, retail, building, and perhaps apparel. The equities in these secondary sectors did well, but nowhere near as well as when short-term rates declined. At last, the market was starting to vindicate our strategy, which was founded on reasonably high earnings predictability and sustenance, low p/e ratios, high dividend yields, good earnings dynamics, and interest sensitivity. Nobody knew how far this would carry, but it was fun to see our little orchard start to bear some fruit.

Throttling Back

The Dow surged 200 points, to 966, between March and mid-August. The decline in long-term and short-term interest rates, the unusual amount of institutional liquidity, and an inclination to look through the valley of the recession all fostered this marked advance. We had been long-term fans of undervaluation of the equity marketplace argument, but an advance of this intensity and regularity, for better or worse, made us a little wary. At the same time, we were realistic enough to be aware of our inadequacies in making market judgments. We took our foot off the accelerator, but only until we accumulated around 8 percent in cash. Additionally, we ratcheted down a shade the riskiness of the equity corpus of Windsor Fund.

In weighing the case for cash, we had to consider the prospects for the imagination portion of Windsor's portfolio. Performance in the two previous declines had left us somewhat disappointed. With a lot of merchandise not on traditional trust investment and counseling approved lists, we were mindful of air pockets in adverse markets. On the other hand, we expected our bevy of moderate growers, some 28 percent of the portfolio, plus cash equivalents, to supply an important offset if the market lost ground.

What's New Is Old Again

Considering the degree to which energy and technology stocks ruled the waves in 1980, while the so-called interest sensitive area was "ugh" accordingly, it's a wonder Windsor's fourth fiscal quarter wasn't disastrous. Our more imaginative areas—transportation, merchandising, apparel, and aluminums—kept us in the race.

Quibblers questioned our absence from energy and technology, as well as our seeming death wish in the interest-sensitive areas. At that juncture, I thought the record should play out before invoking the terminal post mortem. Moreover, the technology reservation was never our favorite hunting ground, for three reasons: (1) constitutionally, it was too risky for us; (2) the total return relative to the price paid didn't pass through our filter; and (3) we held no discernible edge here, versus other people in the marketplace. We never masqueraded as having the expertise needed to distinguish ourselves from the hurly-burly in the technology areas.

On the oil front, we delineated ad nauseum the reasons we believed this declining asset industry, particularly the domestic oils, was rather long in the tooth. Actually, until the Iranian–Iraqi high jinks,* clearly defined inventory accumulation on virtually every front was having an impact on the international price of oil. Meanwhile, a combination of conservation and utilization of alternative energy sources aided and abetted the marked fuel-oil consumption decline patterns. Then the confrontation erupted and the number-two and number-three OPEC countries, Iran and Iraq, were knocked completely out of the box. We held that these two belligerents would be heard from again on the supply side because, inevitably, the shooting would eventually stop. Thus, we saw no reason to get too excited about the oils. As it turned out, we were right. After a short-lived spike, oil prices resumed a declining trend.

Nasty Sawtooth

An increase of three percentage points in long-term fixed interest rates blitzed the interest-sensitive front. In our portfolio, this group included banks, finance companies, and savings and loans, as borrowers grew timid. Telephone and electric utilities also suffered; high rates chilled yield-sensitive dividend coupon clippers. Other high-yielding stocks were also affected. We thought the Spring decline in long-term interest rates had gone too far, but we didn't think that the sawtooth would essentially take us back to the March interest rates highs and principal value lows.

Unfortunately, at least in the first blush, the equity marketplace generally penalized only the equities with a high enough yield to fluctuate in sympathy with fixed-income markets. This allowed the rest of the marketplace to have a life of its own. But at some point it had to become more obvious that an assured 14 percent or so return on long-term fixed income securities offered a very appealing alternative to all common stocks, not just those with high yields. The unfortunate or even unfair part of all this was that our interest-sensitive or high-yield common equities posted growth rates of 8 to 11 percent. These offered very formidable and competitive total return, not only against the fixed-income securities, but against any other securities that had recently outperformed this portion of the Windsor Fund.

---

* A prolonged war between Iran and Iraq broke out in September 1980.

By adding to our McDonald's stake, we committed nearly 4 percent of the Windsor Fund to the most undervalued of the highly recognized growth stocks. Despite negative real growth in existing locations for two years—chiefly a result of price increases in standard McDonald's fare—we believed the money machine was alive and well. However, there was a flip side. More than half of earnings arose from franchisees' rental revenues, which were based on dollar volume. This probably represented one of the best inflation hedges around. We thought this 18 percent grower, plus a nominal yield, was a veritable giveaway in the highly recognized growth spectrum; the discount to market multiple was approximately 25 percent. This was unparalleled in McDonald's history and it suggested that a great number of investors disagreed with us. Of course, taking the unpopular view was how we made our money. ***Outcome:*** *In 1981, when the S&P 500 slid by nearly 5 percent, McDonald's shares fetched a 43 percent return. We continued to sell down Windsor's stake in 1982 for gains as high as 50 percent, amid a 21 percent S&P advance.*

Other significant sales included an important disposal of our large Kmart holding. Our sale of Kmart, our only highly recognized growth stock other than McDonald's, reflected a decision to push those monies into McDonald's where the appreciation potential was larger and the testing in the crucible was more confirming. Put another way, our long-time philosophy called for concentrating the portfolio prudently, but as opportunistically as possible, in the companies that were measuring up and had the largest appreciation potential.

1981: The Pendulum Swings Our Way

Our stubborn resistance to groupthink in 1980 brought much better tidings in 1981. Performance in the early months of the new year was as great as it had been dismal in 1980. We were more than three percentage points ahead of the competitive group, and we almost caught up with the S&P for this 12-month period. This illustrated vividly how fickle the marketplace can be and how necessary it is to prepare one's portfolio for future markets, rather than chase a will-o'-the-wisp in existing ones, particularly as they grow less rational.

Not unlike the early Seventies' hijinks in the big growth stocks, it was only a matter of time before the energy and technology caper was hoisted upon its own petard. There was a good bit of institutional group-think and imprudence in chasing a number of these stocks to price points that simply didn't make sense by prudent investors' standards. One should be careful not to predict the complete fall of Rome, but in a marketplace full of camp followers, 1981 demonstrated yet again that it was no longer fashionable to brag about or savor one's holdings when they had been propelled by conventional wisdom. Not only was the oil area a classic depleting-asset industry that had been driven only by price, but the ever fascinating technology areas proved once again that they bore some allegiance to the business cycle.

After causing so much hardship in 1980, Windsor's contrarian outlook positioned us perfectly once events ignited the bank, retail, restaurant, and transportation segments that populated the Windsor Fund.

In a trend sense, for better or for worse, success seemed to beget success. While enjoying every moment of the turnaround, we were determined (1) not to overstay but (2) to still coax "easy money" from the industry participants. Predictably, we started to sell some banks that had not quite reached our traditional sell points but where we had an outsized position. This compelled us to move a little earlier than usual. Additionally, we exploited the opportunity to trade discovered banks for comparable but price-laggard banks.

Delta Airlines was a telling example of our doing well what we always tried to do: Select the outstanding company in a difficult industry or environment, and fight our way upstream as those qualities became more obvious to the market. Few industries had been so affected by change or so subject to severe financial setbacks as the airline industry. Delta, however, combined outstanding management, finances, and accounting, and persevered in the difficult deregulated environment with outstanding success. The Windsor shareholders benefited accordingly. This was the second time we had made championship money in Delta. **Outcome:** *Within the year, Delta's soaring sales price brought gains in excess of 75 percent.*

We continued to enjoy superior results in the second quarter. Contributors reflected the mirror image of 1980. Merchandising, restaurants, transportation, and, to a somewhat lesser degree but still quite positive, banks, foods, and insurance all delivered for us. In addition, some of our special situations were noteworthy. Most significant were our major positions in Northwest Industries, our side door into the oil field equipment sweepstakes, and Whirlpool, which participated in the housing boom.

The absence of technology and an energy weighting at about half of the market averages also supplied important assists.

Searing Turnabout

After enjoying a market frenzy, oil stocks skidded almost mercilessly. The reason for the searing turnabout was simply that the quantum jump in the price of oil triggered aggressive production by the Saudis. They opened the spigot too far and tripped off a decline in the price of oil, which slid $5 a barrel. This development, in tandem with deregulation of domestic oil prices, altered the stock market's perspective on the oils group. All of a sudden, new circumstances deprived oil producers of an ever upwardly spiraling price while the volume declined. As for the technology area, it was found wanting as a result of lagging economic activity.

As buying into weakness was one of our strengths, so we wasted no time. Widespread declines of 35 to 50 percent from the December highs attracted our price-sensitive eye to the oil arena. Our ardor for p/e ratios in the 5 to 6 times area cemented the analysis. We took proceeds from realizations in restaurants, merchandising, and transportation stocks, and snapped up nearly $80 million of oils, almost half of Windsor's purchases for the second quarter of 1981. As a result of the divergent paths, the plunge of oils in the marketplace, and our aggressive purchase activity, we narrowed our gap with the S&P weighting. Once again, we exercised the right to readdress a negative perspective when conditions, most notably price, changed markedly. We accepted the risk of moving too early, particularly because aggregate earnings in 1981 were not expected to exceed the 1980 figure.

As mid-1981 approached, we rounded off existing oil holdings and started a position in Texaco, probably the most woebegone of all the major oil companies. Four downward revisions of reserve positions in Louisiana had damaged investors' view of the company. We conceded that Texaco was probably not the best run oil company on the face of the earth, but thought nevertheless that (1) it was improving and (2) it had been overly discriminated against in the marketplace. Our purchases, at approximately four times the current year's earnings, were yielding almost 8 percent, thanks to a dividend increase. This beleaguered profile gave little recognition to the excellence of the company's balance sheet and to the ability to spend $2 billion annually to continue the quest for domestic hydrocarbons.

A Peculiar Foray

Uncharacteristically, we also became interested in the broad technological segment. This area was significant in the S&P 500 and, compared to others, we brought no extraordinary skills to the table. However, at a price and in a somewhat cowardly way, even we became intrigued. We soon had a new position in NCR, known formerly as National Cash Register.

NCR had been revitalized, redirected, and refinanced since the early Seventies. In those days, NCR had attempted, under considerable marketplace pressure, to convert from an electromechanical company into a 20th-century electronic data processing leader. Significant progress had been logged since then, but it gained only passing market recognition. We purchased shares at approximately 5.7 times 1981 earnings with even a modicum of yield at 3.8 percent. Admittedly, 1981 promised no bellringer increase over 1980, but we thought the quality of the earnings, the technological effort, and the balance sheet were all quite good. In combination with the 12½ percent prospective growth rate, this looked to us like an opportunity. *Outcome: When sold a little more than a year later, NCR shares fetched a 40 percent gain, about twice the Dow's advance in that period.*

Convinced at this juncture that the bond market lagged behind most other security markets, we justified an attempt to grab off 5 to 10 percent appreciation while waiting to use cash for future equity opportunities. This plan did not work out well in the short run, when an uptick in long-term rates to 13.6 percent trimmed bond prices. It seemed odd to me that critics valued so positively the equity marketplace and the dollar but shunned the bond market, despite considerable evidence that inflation was abating. Equity investors, still worried about double-digit inflation, had not yet accepted this opinion. Conventional thinking about fixed income caused them to miss a once-in-a-generation opportunity. By November 1982, long term bond yields were 10.5 percent.

Off the Charts

We put together a gratifying third quarter. Windsor moved 18 percentage points ahead of the S&P 500 and 14 points ahead of our competition for the first nine months of 1981. This edge was of such magnitude that we expressed doubts about ever seeing it duplicated again over such a short period of time.

The best groups we owned were oils, electric utilities, containers, and a large U.S. Shoe holding. Actually, we did not have "out" positions in the oils and electric utilities, but, somewhat unusual for us, we were close to an S&P weighting. The S&P equivalent in the oils was a recent phenom; we had been quite successful in catching near bottoms on a number of situations. In truth, we were a bit lucky in our timing of oil stock purchases. We were merely buying value that measured up to our standards when we enjoyed virtually instantaneous gratification from owning shares of Conoco, the subject of a celebrated takeover battle.

We had started buying Conoco in March 1981. By the end of May, we owned almost 500,000 shares at an average cost of about $52 a share. In May, responding to a tender offer by Canadian oil producer Dome Petroleum, we sold about 40 percent of Windsor's stake for $65 a share. Still satisfied by the fundamentals after the price slid back again to $52, we added to the position. Shortly thereafter, amid a takeover battle between bidders Dupont and Seagram's, we sold the shares for $81. Although we did not collect the final Seagram's price of $92 or the Dupont cash price of $98 a share, we did rather well for the shareholders on the whole transaction. Our profit was over $14 million during this rather brief holding period.

Following in Conoco's wake, the rest of our domestic holdings quickly blossomed when the Street's favorite game became conjecture about the next target. For example, two months after buying Pennzoil shares, we pocketed a 50 percent gain.

Sensing investors' shift away from less recognized growth as 1981 progressed, we reduced this position. The proceeds enlarged our stake in the unloved cyclical growth category. This buying opportunity followed a burst of enthusiasm for cyclicals, accompanied by ebullient 1982 earnings estimates. We had voiced skepticism. As expectations for these earnings faded, prices came into our region, most notably in the aluminums.

Our price opportunism reflected an approximate 100-point decline (about 11 percent) in the Dow Jones Industrial Average. This slide occurred when the equity market made some downward adjustment relative to the sad state of fixed-income securities. It seemed, to me at least, that success in ratcheting down inflation set the stage for a more positive tone in the bond market, both short and long. President Reagan's commitment to cutting taxes gave an additional boost to economic prospects. There was a considerable amount of groupthink and professional anguishing in bond circles, not unlike the periodic afflictions of the same character in equity markets. However, it seemed only a matter of time until markets recognized that the Fed meant business (a long-term positive), and that the real return on fixed-income securities was about 6 percent. This level of real return, which measured an investor's return over and above the level of inflation, was the highest it had ever been in my investment career.

On the sales side, we started to garner important gains in some of our favorite stomping grounds: banks, merchandising, and transportation, in addition to oils. The conglomerates pitched in, too. This was within our rather consistent pattern of selling into strength in areas where we had proven a great deal by our "four yards and a cloud of dust" standards. Success was etched more dramatically than usual, as the sheer appreciation magnitude of 53 percent attested.

We seldom showed such a tall percentage gain; our sales were ordinarily laced with a few failures and some breakeven. Indeed, the third quarter of 1981 had a few of each. Our task was always to hold these disappointments to a minimum and to deal with them early, in an effort to keep the portfolio, in a right-of-center way, as dynamic as possible. Notwithstanding these exceptional results, we remained on guard to maintain our value standards with an open mind.

12

~

THE RIGHT STUFF

1982–1988

THE FOOTHILLS OF the next inflection point began amid devastation in the oil stocks, declining interest rates, and the arrival of the Reagan Administration's tax cuts. This was the start of a seemingly inexhaustible boom, but, in October 1987, it was punctured by the sharpest one-day decline in the market's history. When the dust settled, Windsor took its edge over the S&P 500 into my third decade as portfolio manager.

1982: NEW DIMENSIONS

In 1982, the year that the Reagan bull market started, Windsor surpassed $1 billion in assets under management. But size did not distract us from our contrarian ways. We remained faithful to our most distinguishing characteristic: sympathy for out-of-favor, overlooked, misunderstood stocks. Coupled with our lean-against-the-wind approach, we stressed constancy toward our disciplined embracing of equities with low price–earnings ratios.

Our overarching macroeconomic assessments were visible in 1982. Formidable positions in the banks and in AT&T bore witness, along with significant profit taking in foods, restaurants, supermarkets, electric utilities, finance, insurance, apparel, and other retail. These companies possessed a combination of excellent total return relative to the p/e paid, and were attention-getting in the magnitude and assuredness of their earnings growth during a period of economic difficulty. Meanwhile, our bottom-up approach led us to our stable of "crack" companies—a group of companies with an approach to diversification that fell into a crack outside standard institutional coverage. "Crack" companies were valued quite inefficiently in the market.

In January 1982, the banks and the aluminums, both out-positions, were particularly burdensome. The aluminum reasoning was no mystery; operating conditions and results in the industry were miserable, to say the least. The Street was virtually unanimous on how unattractive the area was, and panic selling became the order of the day.

Recession Jitters

The bank weakness was a little harder to explain. Banks could not shake off their nagging fear of a prolonged recession—a fear we did not share. Fourth-quarter 1981 earnings had been quite satisfactory, and dividend increases continued to flow confirmingly. The trauma of monetary crosscurrents and possible loan losses in an onerous economy gave the banks pause. Instead, advances in 1981 left them a little out of breath. Some of the same shadows were also cast over our total portfolio. At some point in the inevitable evolution of the marketplace, the simple randomness of the market can take something back after having just produced a showcase period.

Our trades were consistent with our past enduring principles. At the same time, however, we were prepared to take prudent risks whenever the price reward seemed more than commensurate with those risks.

PPG Industries, an underappreciated company in which we had made money twice before, was purchased at 45 percent below its 1981 high, for less than five times our 1982 earnings numbers. The yield was 7.4 percent. This overlooked and underrated company had done a remarkable job in two pedestrian areas: coatings (paint) and glass, most particularly architectural glass in commercial and industrial buildings. An inorganic based and somewhat average chemical business, plus a small entry in the reinforced fiberglass area, rounded out the rest of the product line. PPG had a significant dependence on the sluggish automotive and building industries but nevertheless posted healthy earnings in 1981. This accomplishment freed the imagination to predict the bottom line that could be generated if and when the automotive and residential building markets recovered. With a prospective 10½ percent growth rate, this well financed and conservatively managed company generated very appealing appreciation potential. **Outcome:** *PPG produced better-than-market gains during 1983.*

A polarized market tended to crimp our search for new ideas in some of the regions we liked best: defensive, moderate-growth, consumer stocks. We headed instead for depressed energy and cyclical stocks. Dividend cuts by stumbling energy companies heightened the need for selectivity. We emphasized natural gas, oil service, and banks—all denizens of the market's no-fly zone.

Get Out When the Getting Is Good

Our narrow edge over the competition seemed rather disappointing after such a robust 1981. We obviously aspired to roundly outperform all standards in each year, and the traditional expectation of surrendering in the wake of outstanding years was not so valid in Windsor's case. We did not look a gift horse in the mouth too long. Instead, at early opportunities, we realized meaningful profits after proving something out of the ordinary.

Through the second quarter of 1982, where we were good we were very good. Previously dull areas all distinguished themselves. Ordinarily, successful concentrations with such an order-of-magnitude sustained superior performance because we would not give away this advantage on disappointing stakes.

We experienced the most difficulty during 1982 in our efforts to catch "falling knives." These were areas where we hoped our judgment on entry-price valuation points compensated us for prospects that were less than outstanding—chiefly, oil services, natural gas transmission, and diversified and domestic oils. Whether disappointing results underscored diminished skills or another case of market overreaction had to be endured, we could not say at the time.

Outcome: *As the S&P advanced by more than 22 percent in 1983, any "falling knives" landed safely. The oil well equipment and service index gained 26.5 percent. Our big winner was Halliburton, up 32 percent. Royal Dutch, Exxon, and Gulf Oil (our No. 2, No. 3, and No. 4 positions) gained, respectively, 28 percent, 30 percent, and 70 percent. Relative performance continued strong in 1984. While the S&P logged a slim gain of only 1.6 percent, Royal*

Dutch, Atlantic Richfield, and Exxon (our No. 1, No. 2, and No. 3 positions that year) advanced, respectively, by 14 percent, 11 percent, and 14 percent.

Off and Running

After mid-August, the market stunned everyone. From 777 on August 12, the Dow Jones Industrial Average raced beyond the 1,000 mark on October 11, a stupendous 44 percent advance in only two months. Sixteen years after flirting with 1,000 for the first time, in January 1966, the Dow finally crossed this level to stay.

Happily, Windsor participated. We edged past the S&P by 1½ percentage points in the final quarter of our fiscal year, which ended October 31, and we beat our peers by twice that margin. Windsor achieved this successful outcome despite three notable liabilities: (1) our large and growing cash position, (2) a larger stake in oil stock than the competitive group, and (3) our historic tendency to lag behind when the market experienced explosive bursts of investor enthusiasm.

The market's rapid gain triggered sales keyed to our price targets. This activity overwhelmed our ability to reinvest the proceeds in any kind of thoughtful, reasonably researched manner. We intended to put our cash back to work as opportunities arose and endured our scrutiny. Downdrafts helped. On a single day in late October, after the Dow had retreated 4 percent and slipped below 1,000 for the second time, we put a substantial chunk of cash back to work.

In terms of market sectors and individual stocks, the August rally was somewhat compressed. So-called "soft cyclicals" posted disproportionate performances. These consumer/moderate-growth/defensive stocks, together with a variety of household-name, blue-chip, shelf-goods stocks, had performed well since the beginning of 1981. Their earnings recovery, coupled with the market's embrace, produced very heady prices for some very prosaic moderate growers. This was symptomatic of a market fueled by (1) a heavy run from cash and (2) a lot of people playing catch-up at the same time.

In the short run, in periods like this, investors tend to turn to the tried and true or to whatever is acting well, while avoiding what is acting poorly. No sector exemplified this condition more than the energy stocks, which comprised almost a third of the Windsor portfolio.

Availing ourselves of a downtrodden part of the market's characteristic failure to identify worthy stocks, we applied ourselves to finding new opportunities in the oil patch. We bought the survivors on the same basis as the casualties. This was somewhat reminiscent of what we had been doing for some time with our bank holdings. We would buy well situated and well run regional banks at little or no p/e premium to the many troubled money center banks. As 1982 neared its conclusion, this strategy began bearing fruit above and beyond the stellar performance of banks in general. We began looking to our energy holdings for similar positive relative performance in 1983.

1983: ROTATION, ROTATION, ROTATION

Windsor began its 25th anniversary year in excellent form. Once more, our low p/e strategy chalked up healthy gain in some areas and kept us out of trouble in the market's havoc-strewn regions. We enjoyed good returns from our banks, notably those in the Southeast, while steering clear of Texas banks caught in the lingering oil blues. We also avoided the carnage visible in the likes of erstwhile market favorites: Warner Communications, Eastman Kodak, Pepsico, Texas Instruments, Digital Equipment, and others.

The marketplace, in the language of pundits, was quite "rotational" as the year began. Within its advance, the market scratched, searched, and probed for areas that were behind and deserving of focus. To the degree we embraced and emphasized situations that had been overlooked, unloved, and undiscovered, our concentrations flourished in a more thoughtful climate. Our efforts to stand in the path of corporate buyouts paid off twice. Each time, our purchase price was doubled.

There were plenty of earmarks of a market, at least in a number of segments that appeared overextended: the technology and other imaginative segments; the vast bulk of the consumer area, whether retail, hard goods, or consumer nondurables; and, at the speculative outreach, the airlines. The appetite for these equities appeared unrelenting, and it was etched not only in advances piled on advances, but also in total dollar volume of stock sales. Hardly a day passed without four or five new issues being announced. In several cases, the demand was so powerful that extra shares were added at the last moment. This, of course, did not constitute the kind of boring market that Windsor characteristically did well in. For all its excitement, though, the market itself did little more than churn for a three-month stretch.

In this climate, Windsor remained quite conservatively, or even defensively, postured. This hardly exemplified aggressive, dynamic investing, but it seemed to us the better part of valor. Instead of taking refuge in closet indexing with a portfolio that mimicked the S&P 500, we elected to represent our shareholders in areas where they stood prudent investors' chances of making a buck, without extending their necks in a market that, to us, seemed overwrought. It was not news to Windsor shareholders that we were out of sync with the higher p/e scheme of things. The two-edged state of affairs constituted some advantages and some disadvantages.

For better or worse, we recalled how things had looked six months earlier. Although we thought financial assets were quite undervalued then, we weren't so sure fundamentals had improved quite as dramatically as prices. While not overjoyed with our ensuing lack of success, we tried, as always, to align Windsor with tomorrow's markets. We proceeded to manage shareholders' money with confidence that we chalked up the most progress upon inflection points in the marketplace, when abrupt changes in emphasis shine the spotlight on our wares. This defensive wariness, however, did not overlook our sense that an economic recovery already underway would foster good profits in the next three years.

A Bit of Twitching

What saved us—and made it possible for our shareholders to fully participate in a frothy market—was the general market rotation of industry groups. We were both active and opportunistic in trying to emphasize undiscovered and undervalued areas. When a searching, probing, discerning market eventually discovers these, the shareholder is well served by our "before the action" emphasis. All in all, this position caused us to twitch a bit. But we stood ready at all times to close the loop, given new price opportunities either in selected areas or in the general market itself.

Our cash position was somewhat high, despite our best efforts to keep it from growing. We were determined, even if the general market continued to go up, to not go beyond the 20 percent cash level. In our judgment, that's all we prudently could attempt to prove in superimposing our judgment on the shareholder. After all, our shareholders selected a full plate of equities when purchasing Windsor Fund in the first place. We had never held ourselves out to be market pundits.

We stuck to our characteristic waiting game. Our investors, for the most part, had long time horizons and understood our strategy. Besides our obligation to give them a prudent participation in an up market, we owed them some sense of reality as to the risks being taken when things became frothy.

This expectation marked a change from the old days, when our performance was usually etched by doing only about as well as the market on the upside, yet going down significantly less when the market inevitably stumbled. During the opportunistic, post-Nifty Fifty markets from 1975 through 1982, our posture was more aggressive. However, we thought that financial assets were significantly undervalued, particularly since 1980. We tried to represent shareholders apropos of this conviction. The swift upward progression that had started in August shifted the odds, and we positioned ourselves less aggressively. Consistent with this view, virtually all of our second-quarter purchases were focused on electric utilities, oils, natural gas, insurance, and the banking area.

Fancy Footwork

Despite a heady market during the third quarter of 1983, Windsor managed to still show adroitness and price sensitivity in its choice of investments. Instead of straining to stay fully invested, we exercised our advantage by letting individual price opportunities come our way rather than chasing pell-mell in a frenzied market.

Our third-quarter purchases exploited prices that had tumbled from their bull market highs. Here is a sampling:

Third Quarter 1983	Average Purchase Price	1983 High
Manufacturers Hanover	$38.9	$51.00
Federal	24.6	30.25
Dart & Kraft	64.0	77.25
Aetna Life & Casualty	39.0	43.50
Cigna	41.3	51.50
Travelers	30.1	34.25
Amerada Hess	25.7	30.00
AT&T	64.5	70.25
Norfolk Southern	55.0	60.25

In 1983, a fairly quiescent fourth quarter extended Windsor's string of market-beating performances. For the calendar year, the final score was Windsor, up 30.1 percent; S&P 500, up 22.5 percent.

There wasn't much progress in the overall market, although quite a few companies paid a stiff price for not living up to Wall Street's earnings expectations. The market inflicted a penalty because so much anticipation had been built up in adrenaline stocks, both in and outside of the technology arena. This was more our kind of quarter, in the sense that we always tried to stay out of trouble. If some of our allegedly lackluster holdings were picked up, we normally did well.

Although the market suffered a moderate decline of almost 6 percent from its highs, we did not bite off much of Windsor's liquidity. Purchases for the quarter only modestly outpaced sales. We were in no frenzy to recommit, preferring once more to wait for natural and noticeable price opportunities to come our way. This patience was additionally buttressed by a conviction that the bond market was not without some appeal, particularly given an almost 12 percent certain return on intermediate-term government bonds. Actually, we reckoned that Windsor might add still more to its liquid assets while Congress dragged its feet over raising the federal debt limit.

This did not sound like very exciting investing for an equity fund, but at day's end the return the shareholder eats is not discriminating. At the time, I could not help but wonder whether, over the next several years, the total return in the stock market would be a great deal better than 12 percent. This comparison underscored the competitiveness of highly assured returns from the fixed-income market. Theoreticians undoubtedly would say that if a virtually guaranteed annual return of 12 percent is available, equity markets should serve up a return two or three points higher, to compensate for the greater risks taken.

Banking on Banks

A new sizzle was noticeable in our bank area: money-center banks. It marked a departure from our previous strategy, which had featured regional, more exclusively retail-oriented banks. Our bank strategy in 1983 was quite good. We were purposefully without representation in the Texas banks burdened with oil-related problems, and we had next to nothing invested in the New York banks that were laboring under the weight of troubled loans in Latin America. Our portfolio was not designed by chance. These two areas had been significant underperformers. (The bank index for 1982 was down about 7 percent.) Windsor nevertheless owned Virginia National, Central Bancshares of the South, First Union, Amsouth, and South Carolina National. All five advanced between 62 and 38 percent for 1982. It may have seemed that these relatively small banks didn't amount to much, but, in concert, they accounted for 3½ percent of Windsor's assets.

Our largest purchase was JP Morgan. These shares, together with shares of Bank of Boston, accounted for three-fourths of our purchases in the final quarter of 1983. JP Morgan was the premier money-center bank. It had a strong currency and trading function and, by far, the best capital position of the New York banks relative to assets. In addition, Morgan had inflicted on 1983 earnings a provision for loan losses and a concomitant stockpiling of bad loan reserves, as if there was going to be an international "accident." The other New York banks did not take these precautionary steps.

We did not foresee such an accident, though we could not deny the possibility that one might occur, given bankers' penchant for getting into trouble. We expected banks to muddle through. If an accident occurred, however, Morgan's earnings and balance sheet were sufficiently braced. Other banks were not so well provisioned.

As is so often the case when areas of the marketplace are under attack, investors can buy the best at little or no premium. There was some premium (about a p/e point) on 1983 earnings, but we believed that Morgan's earnings were stated much more conservatively. On the other hand, if the banks generally did indeed muddle through, earnings for Morgan would not suffer the prolonged impact of undue provision for loan losses. The stock was purchased at about 5.3 times 1984 earnings and at only about six times 1983 earnings. In our judgment, its 5½ percent yield was about to go north of 6 percent.

1984: LEAPS AND BOUNDS

We defended our investment performance laurels successfully. For all of 1984, Windsor posted an increase just shy of 20 percent, versus 6.2 percent for the S&P 500. A strong and growing reputation keeps new cash flowing in, and Windsor grew by leaps and bounds. Our track record supplied great advertising. Windsor had increased by 1,904 percent since

I became Windsor's portfolio manager. An 8.8 percent average annual growth rate by the S&P 500 seemed pale next to Windsor's 12.2 percent a year.

We credited performance to a handful of factors, starting with adroit positioning in AT&T and its spin-offs. While most investors tiptoed around wondering what to expect, we had shed a substantial stake in Ma Bell and snapped up shares of the new Bell operating companies. They woke up in 1984, and Windsor shareholders banked the results. Our substantial energy sector perked up also, as did the banks. Despite a testy environment, banks chalked up earnings and dividend increases that gave Windsor more than a few bell ringers. Consumer durables, chiefly autos, started to produce gains in the ebullient market that developed.

Windsor was fully invested by the second quarter; we were counting our intermediate-term government bonds as investment. We regained this position on our terms. We were buying value, at least as we perceived it. We scooped up compelling prices that were down by sharply prior highs.

Besides pushing General Motors to a maximum stake, we accumulated shares of Ford Motor Company at a lower price. These shares were almost dirt-cheap by any standards; we paid just 2½ times 1984 earnings for what soon became 2 percent of Windsor's portfolio. Ford had probably done a better bootstrap job than GM, considering the depth, particularly in quality, to which Ford had plunged. Ford was enjoying bottom-line success on a par with its archrival, and it had strengthened its balance sheet mightily. Ford had a superior position overseas, principally in Europe. The quality of Ford's products had significantly improved, and, not without some risk, its new models stepped out in styling as well.

Taste is a very individual judgment, and not everybody personally responded to Ford's styling. But the company certainly created a different profile and, more importantly, captured marketplace acceptance. It also had an excellent relative position in trucks, which represented about 40 percent of its domestic vehicle units. The dividend had been increased to yield something just short of 5 percent. However, the corporation had an almost infinite capacity to increase the dividend further, given (1) the conclusion of pending labor negotiations and (2) evidence of sustained earning power.

We recognized that car sales in the coming year were apt to resemble a normal year more than a peak year. Nevertheless, America's love affair with a set of wheels, although somewhat diminished, was still alive and well. Our favorable outlook featured the nonadvent of a gas price of $2 or $3 a gallon. OPEC's weak grip, combined with a good recovery in the U.S. economy and a greater sense of well-being in the country, all pointed toward stable oil prices. This rekindled the big-ticket purchase of an automobile, which still was very potent at the forward edge of more discretionary income. *Outcome: We were right about Ford. Starting in 1985, Windsor banked robust gains. For the year, Ford's stock rose 85 percent versus 33 percent for auto stocks in general and 28.5 percent for the S&P 500.*

Stepping Out

We continued to expand step-out positions in appliances, automotive, building and construction, and transportation. We leavened this exposure with more traditional additions (funded in some part by sales) to banks and electric utilities, as well as significant additions to the recently depressed insurance and oil segments. As per our philosophy, even when we gained a more normal representation in a broad area, we still tried to prove something by taking outsized positions in specific undervalued market sectors.

Our important additions to the multiline insurance area were on an extremely depressed base. The marketplace had all but given up on any improvement in the mortally wounded commercial property and casualty purveyors. We believed, and had been saying for some time, that insurers' suicidal pricing could not persist for long. Some major industry components had already suggested that renewals of existing businesses would not be undertaken unless price hikes of 15 to 20 percent were accepted. Turning a massive ship around always requires time and an extension of one's patience. We thought, however, that steps were being taken in 1984 that would, in 1985, rectify the horrendous losses in the property and casualty segment of the business.

The joy was that the insurance stocks had been beaten up unmercifully. The dividends with very high yields were safe, in our judgment, and the other components of the business were cranking along in good fashion. We thought we were planting some valuable seeds for the future, but we conceded a modicum of risk where Windsor did not already have some. *Outcome: Multiline insurance companies came through as predicted in 1985. An average price gain of 40 percent smoked 14.3 percent for the S&P 500 in the comparable period of time. Capping this performance, our stake in Cigna posted better than a 56 percent advance.*

Windsor shareholders were well served by a significant addition to our stake in Reynolds Metals. In a disappointing year for aluminum producer shipments and realizations (after a good 1983), Reynolds's earnings measured up very well. We noted, moreover, that customers' aluminum inventories were shrinking. In fact, 1984 end use had actually been very good—ahead by about 14 percent. With moderate gains in 1985, aided by a continuing good economy (including housing and autos), and with domestic producers perhaps aided also by a weaker dollar, we envisioned aluminum pricing returning to second quarter 1984 levels. Our purchase price was 4.4 times 1985 earnings. *Outcome: Reynolds, a big winner in 1983, held its own in 1985 and then rewarded Windsor in 1986. The stock price advanced 47 percent, nearly 30 percentage points more than the S&P 500 benchmark.*

1985: HOPE VS. FUNDAMENTALS

The market seemed propelled more by hope than by scintillating fundamentals in early 1985. Earnings continued to be somewhat disappointing, and attention-getting thrust seemed to be largely missing. Restarting the engine was difficult. Also, interest rates had not really come down from the levels of late 1984, so a market move threatened to become a self-fulfilling prophecy. Advisers who were not doing well could ill afford to sit on cash, once the train appeared to be pulling out without them on board.

We were uncharacteristically bereft of new passions. Our hiatus was etched against a panorama in which many of our value areas passed from quite undervalued to only somewhat undervalued. In other words, the market embraced, with some enthusiasm, a lot of our value merchandise. Owing either to our shortcomings or, more likely, to a paucity of new price opportunities, we could not uncover our usual allotment of reinvestment opportunities. Could the market be getting more efficient? We wondered.

Even when we emphasized the depressed energy area to a significant degree, these seeming values had vanished before we arrived. But areas like semiconductors, where pricing was chaotic and unit volumes were disappointing, suffered dismal fourth-, first-, and second-quarter results. The marketplace, in my fragile judgment, seemed not only to have looked through this deep valley, but also to have assumed lockstep success thereafter.

Meanwhile, an avalanche of new cash poured into the Fund. However much we basked in the warmth of the high compliments to our efforts over the years, additional cash created a challenge. A critic might have charged that we were being too rigorous in implementing our usual standards for investing. Instead, we could have taken a more blanket approach in fulfilling our obligation to provide shareholders with full-bore equity investment. However, our approach was both highly selective and price-sensitive, and these traits represented our edge relative to other institutional investors.

We had faced the same challenge before. Just two years earlier, in the summer of 1984, we had closed the loop by becoming fully invested.

After eight consecutive quarters, our record of beating the S&P and our competitive group ended in the third quarter of 1985. As much as anything else, we were done in by our growing supply of cash, which of course could not match the returns that stocks garner in an up market. Virtually all the groups and components of our stock portfolio were upward participants with the S&P 500.

A Shift in Emphasis

In this climate, Windsor's most significant shift in emphasis occurred in the banking sector, where steady realizations had reduced our overall position. The shift nearly lopped by half the banks' position in the portfolio. However, purchases outstripped sales in the third quarter of 1985. This reversal, in our judgment, reflected a change in relative attraction between the strong regionals on the sell side and the appeal of good money-center banks (usually New York-based) on the buy side. Put another way, stock prices recognized the relative assuredness, financial strength, predictability, and low exposure to foreign loans in the regional banks. Meanwhile, prices of money-center bank stocks reflected exposure to troubled loans emanating from Latin America. What had been overlooked was the excellent job that several of the money-center banks had accomplished in shoring up their balance sheets and reserving against bad loans. In effect, the excellent earnings progress of money-center banks had been realized despite onerous increases in provisions for bad debts. This combination rendered earnings of a much higher quality than was widely believed.

We initiated this strategy with purchases of Citibank and Bankers Trust. So began the eight-year Citicorp saga that followed a tortuous path that plunged to despair and eventually culminated in victory. Citi-corp and Bankers Trust were both aggressively and successfully mining incremental niches. In Citicorp's case, it was somewhat unusual for a money-center bank to expand its credit card operations not only under its in-house label, Diners Club, but also in conjunction with Visa and MasterCard. By changing the rules of engagement, Citicorp became a juggernaut with a critical mass of 10 million plastic-card holders. This base promised to generate earnings growth in retail banking of 30 per-cent a year or so, into the foreseeable future. This also was a very sensi-ble way to reach out its tentacles notionally, without having to pay the acquisition premiums that mergers commanded.

Oil Resurfaces

Toward year-end 1985, the market seemed a bit optimistic, if not pushy. The pushiness was apparent especially in that corporate earnings con-tinued on the lackluster side. Meanwhile, a bit of downward movement in interest rates encouraged the stock market.

Bank additions essentially shored up our Citicorp holding to some-thing over 3 percent of assets, as we continued to try to prove some-thing out of the ordinary with our concentrations. The market had been somewhat disappointed in the third-quarter earnings (up 13 percent), but it failed to recognize the substantial haircut Citi took with a quan-tum increase in reserves for bad debts. Citi's important sizzle was a price less than six times our estimate of 1986 earnings, a 50 percent discount to the average p/e ratio in the market. This discount reflected genuine apprehension about Latin American loans. Fears were aggravated, at least in Mexico's case, by the downward spiral in oil prices. The per-spective that the market overlooked was that Citi's earnings in 1985, and prospectively for 1986, were severely burdened by the loan loss pro-visions, which were twice as much as in 1984. Put another way, earnings were very conservatively stated.

To stem the cash inflow, we decided to close Windsor to new investors in 1985. Completely out of character with an industry that aims at gath-ering the most possible assets under one roof, we concluded nevertheless that pressure to put a torrent of fresh cash to work would cause perfor-mance to slide. We were in business to post superior returns, and depart-ing from convention was not new to us.

1986: RUNNING ON EMPTY

The first quarter of 1986 did not yield our most illustrious result, but that did not come as a great surprise. A runaway market was extracting a penalty for holding cash. We had been "somewhat from Missouri" relative to the pace of things, and that pace was clearly accelerating to an unsustainable rate. At what point the market would run out of steam, I could not predict. Meanwhile, Windsor was making a bit of a statement with 20 percent of our assets in cash.

The market seemed to have a life all its own. Even when it received a seemingly bad shot of news, it displayed great resiliency. Recovery from an interday disappointment sometimes had a high-to-low range of as much as 2½ percent. So-called "program purchases" and sales triggered by S&P 500 levels contributed to this volatility. Often, an economic indicator created a reaction.

In addition, the market's strength seemed, at least in some part, attributable to the dramatic decline in oil prices. Economic pundits seized on this development to show that inflation would not ratchet up. If anything, they hinted, it could go down somewhat. A sharp decline in interest rates was good for inflation and for economic growth—the best of both worlds. The only thing wrong with this Pollyanna-style scenario was that the fluctuations in oil prices might have turned out to be just that: fluctuations.

More Than Met the Eye

During the first portion of fiscal 1986, Windsor was a smidgen below the S&P and just shy of one point inferior to the competitive group average. This may have sounded poor, but, considering the stance we were taking (and assuming that the inflection point argument was valid), it was a decent performance in view of the animated state of the marketplace. We still had a significant cash position—some 22 percent of assets. Moreover, we held a large and nasty oil commitment.

A few of our concentrations—namely, the banks—did quite well in this climate. Even including relatively new stakes, most notably Citicorp, our banks were up almost twice as much as the S&P 500. Another area that measured up very well was the autos, particularly our very large Ford position, which had grown from 5 percent to 8 percent of assets, thanks to its remarkable appreciation. Other life preservers were savings and loans, NYNEX, and, believe it or not, our two very large oil positions, which accounted for 10 percent of assets until we trimmed them back to 9 percent. Our twin holdings, Royal Dutch and Shell Transport, together gained virtually twice as much as the S&P 500 in the first months of the year.

All in all, the start of 1986 deserved a B+. If our assessment of the risks in the marketplace was at all correct, we were due for an even better grade.

After July 4, new buying opportunities surfaced on a reasonably wide industry plane. Although the market was off quite sharply on July 7 (it rang in with a decline of 3 percent), the lowest register on the S&P in July was only slightly behind its high-water mark. Generally speaking, this was no prescription for bargains to emerge. But many individual securities, particularly in selected areas, suffered sharper declines from their individual highs than the fabric of the overall marketplace suggested. During July alone, we found a few of these opportunities off from their recent tops, including: Cigna Corporation, off 25 percent; Citicorp, off 18 percent; Aluminum Company of America (Alcoa), off 23 percent; and Travelers Corporation, off 23 percent.

Looking across the landscape of consumer stocks, which made up nearly one-third of the S&P 500, we were struck by how many of these areas appeared overvalued, such as food, beverage, retail, soap, photography, and media. The only area of considerable value, in our judgment, was the automotive one, which made up about 4 percent of the S&P. With a lack of more appealing alternatives, we extended our automotive participation to 13 percent (from 12 percent) with the well-timed addition of a Chrysler stake. A year later, Wall Street analysts added Chrysler to "buy" lists for the very reasons that had lured us. As new investors embraced Chrysler, we accommodated them.

The two aluminum companies, Alcoa and Alcan, added to our existing stake in an industry we thought was on the brink of an earnings breakout. Accordingly, we increased Windsor's position to almost 4 percent of assets with the addition of the two largest industry factors. Despite a lackluster economic backdrop, an upturn in financial performance supplied evidence that increased demand and limited worldwide capacity would precipitate a gradual price improvement. This, in combination with reduced production costs, suggested heady additions to 1987 earnings that would surprise the marketplace. **Outcome:** *Our expectations materialized. By early 1987, Windsor's aluminum stake captured capital gains in excess of 50 percent.*

Ebb and Flow

Windsor weighed in a mite better than the S&P 500 and the competitive group during the final quarter of 1986. October was terrible. Our shortfall was not attributable to being wrong on fundamentals. Instead, the ebb and flow of the fortunes of our concentrations inevitably hampered total performance from time to time. Naturally, we hoped fervently that the market would smarten up to some of our excellent values, resulting in good performance for calendar 1986. But, for better or for worse, that outcome was in the lap of the gods.

The one continuing and disquieting aspect of the marketplace was frenzied finance, as reflected in a "merger-a-week" pace. This was good in the sense that it kept managers on their toes with respect to enhancing shareholder values, but it also bothered me. Besides straining our system (for credit and otherwise), the trend often forced deficient managements to gut their companies and take on debt in order to retain their independence. In view of these pressures, any random fluctuation that came along, like a recession, threatened to aggravate the situation.

A stake in National City took me back to my Cleveland roots for the third time in Windsor's history. A statewide Ohio bank with $12 billion of assets, it had grown substantially since my departure a quarter-century earlier. National City had solidified its quality position in respect to all the important statistical bank yardsticks, including a willingness to responsibly represent shareholders by not paying fancy prices to acquire other banks.

1987: KA-BOOM!

At the start of 1987, the market still defied an inflection point. Performance continued to dazzle us. After advancing in each of the first five trading sessions, it passed the 2,000 milestone. "Carried aloft by the stock market's stunning New Year rally, the Dow Jones Industrial Average closed above 2,000 yesterday for the first time ever," *The Wall Street Journal* reported on January 9.* This struck us as a flight from reality.

Despite the market's ebullience, the economy continued blah. Our moderate growth expectation was not seemingly violated by ongoing trends.

---

*John Crudele, "Dow Tops 2,000 for the First Time," *The Wall Street Journal*, January 9, 1987, p. 1.

The dollar had been in a virtual free fall for several months. Among other consequences, this forced the Federal Reserve to be more circumspect in its management of short interest rates, particularly relative to our delicate negotiations with the likes of Japan and Germany. The Ivan Boesky episode was simmering, and attention was focused on illicit insider trading by Wall Street investment bankers. It continued to be second- and third-page investigative copy in *The Wall Street Journal*. More principals seemed to be involved at every turn, and the coverage seemed destined for the front page. Elsewhere in the news, the Iran blunder* plagued the Reagan Administration, which could not bury its decision or explain it even to our allies, much less to the moderate Arab countries. As details surfaced, the Administration was looking increasingly toothless. Meanwhile, Congress seemed to be making only moderate progress in ratcheting down the severity of the federal deficit. This medicine did not promote a pretty picture for the marketplace, a welcome price surge notwithstanding.

Defensive Posture

Windsor's strategy was somewhat defensive. First-quarter sales outstripped purchases by two-to-one. We were determined, despite some misgivings about another silly season in the marketplace, to keep Windsor's shareholders 80 percent invested in equities. As the first quarter ended, we were just shy of this goal. It was not appropriate for us to superimpose our concerned judgment any further. Our shareholders had chosen equities by choosing Windsor in the first place.

We had to scramble a bit to retain our standards while still staying sufficiently invested. This was etched in a new position, more adventuresome than usual, in BankAmerica. This once great bank had fallen on hard times and was in the throes of a tortuous turnaround. This stake alone accounted for one-fourth of the quarter's purchases. It reflected the need to exploit turnaround, special-situation investments that did not lend themselves to ordinary Windsor yardsticks.

BankAmerica, in somewhat of a survival mode, was selling off some of its more salable niches. These disposals included its interests in Charles Schwab & Co. and Bank d'Italia. It had stabilized losses from bad loans and had built sufficient reserves against existing bad loans. By siphoning off $2

---

* The ill-fated arms-for-hostages effort that haunted the Reagan Administration for the rest of its term.

billion, a sum equal to half the bank's interest income, these reserves had devastated earnings. (A more normal number for a bank this size would have been $300 to $400 million.) We believed, and had some supporting evidence, that these provisions were about to be ratcheted down significantly. In combination with a considerable purging of head count, we visualized, under a fortuitous combination of circumstances, earnings of $4 a share in 1989–1990. This, of course, would fetch a great deal more than $14 per share, the going market price. **Outcome:** *BankAmerica shares chalked up a 63 percent price gain in 1989, versus 22 percent for the S&P and 17 percent for the bank group. And that was just a prelude to calendar 1990, when BankAmerica posted a whopping 122.5 percent advance while the bank group gained 19 percent and the S&P lost 11 percent.*

Other additions in our defensive mode were more familiar Windsor fare. Windsor lifted stakes in IBM, aluminum, General Motors, insurance, and S&Ls. The sales side was almost exclusively made up of realizations. They were particularly concentrated in the oil arena, where we once had an outsize position, almost exclusively built up in earlier years when unloved domestic oils were on the squash. As was well known, OPEC had carved out, among the cartel members, a couple of deals that had considerably firmed up the price of oil. The world finally beat a path to our door and, unsurprisingly, we accommodated the marketplace a fair bit.

Yin and Yang

I could not recall another period in which Windsor's participation in both the good and the bad was as marked as in the second quarter of 1987. The differential for group industry performance was searing for the first four months of the calendar year. Overweighted areas such as autos (Ford, up 61 percent), aluminums, IBM, and oils were quite spectacular. So-called interest-sensitive participants such as S&Ls, banks, and the utilities were, on balance, little better than cash. Fortunately, participation in the auto segment represented about 18 percent of the portfolio, and the oversized aluminum position was our surrogate for basic, cyclical, commodity participants that benefited from a weaker dollar.

The oils, as a result of our significant profit taking, were a bit below market weighting. Still, they were about double the competitive group. Elsewhere, it was gratifying to see IBM finally measure up; our day-by-day purchases on the downside had seemed like a walk into the valley of death. From a bottom of $116 in mid-January, the stock surged, in a wonderful example of groupthink, to $167.

In April and very early May, Windsor was a fairly aggressive buyer. Once more, we took advantage of a down market, off about 9 percent from the high. As always, these moves were enhanced with additional price opportunities in selected areas. In a marketplace that finally seemed "long in the tooth" by our reckoning, financial intermediaries and Ford still struck us as excellent values.

The sales side was peppered with realization, in the oils, in aluminums, and even in newly purchased Chrysler. These embodied excellent gains, most notably in the oils about a year after almost everybody thought they were going down the tubes. At that point, the conventional wisdom had said it was virtually impossible for OPEC to get its act together. From those July lows, a representative list of domestic oil stocks doubled in price, and a number of Wall Street analysts were starting to recommend the stocks. In characteristic fashion, we were going the other way. From a 28 percent stake in 1986, we winnowed our position to around 10 percent, midway through 1987. The aluminums and Chrysler also dated from the summer of 1986, when a decline in July and August enabled us to boost our stake in these areas. During a year's interval, these equities advanced in price about 60 percent. With our appreciation goals met, we were starting to scale down our holdings in both.

As the summer advanced, Windsor's performance was miserable. Areas that we had touted—insurance, savings and loans, and utilities—trailed a 10½ percent advance by the S&P 500. This reflected sharp performance dichotomies in the marketplace. Basic cyclicals and some growth stocks were leading the market.

Something Is Bound to Happen

It is all well and good to cite underperformance. Eventually, one has to deal with what is going to happen. I did not know when, but I expected the market would inevitably hit an inflection point and bring some of the latest silly season to a screeching halt. Absent a crystal ball on which Monday, October 19, was clearly marked, I could not predict the events, or series of events, that would precipitate an inflection. However, in mid-1987, we were in a very fully valued marketplace that assumed everything positive that *might* happen *would* happen. This, of course, is not how the real world operates.

It would have been naïve to say that one outcome or the other was a certainty. One never knows how emotional markets will unfold. It seemed as though we had an awfully good hedge. A fair hunk of our portfolio—notably, the financial intermediaries—had been tested by the interest-sensitive syndrome and adjusted accordingly. The rest of the market had not been subjected to this test. We contended then, as always, that all common stocks are affected by interest rate moves. There was even a school of thought that said that high-growth stocks were more influenced than our typical total return holdings.

Critics observed that Windsor was chockfull of dull, below-average, nonaccomplishing companies. We thought otherwise. Our evidence? Windsor's weighted aggregate earnings for these stocks should increase 21 percent in 1987 and another 15 percent in 1988. We had pretty good sustenance, it seemed—everything else being equal—in a marketplace that was allegedly earnings-driven.

A number of overlooked companies were buying their own stock at very rewarding and sensible prices as opposed to, say, Merck and Coca-Cola. These buybacks made additional magic by enhancing earnings per share while also sopping up capital that some observers feared might start chasing overpriced assets.

Black Monday

The market finally hit the wall in the fourth quarter, with a short-term vengeance that even we had not expected. That spasm manifested itself most dramatically on October 19, "Black Monday." As measured by the S&P 500, the market went down 20½ percent; the Dow was down even more. This unprecedented plunge was, no doubt, aggravated on the downside by automated trading programs—"portfolio insurance" designed to stop losses. An inflection point had finally materialized. It was the consequence of attractive and very competitive interest rates; overexuberance in the equity marketplace by "momentum players"; and a response of increasing concern toward the Reagan Administration for its failure to cut a deal on the budgetary deficit, the ill-fated nomination of Robert Bork to the Supreme Court, and general all-around ineffectiveness on several fronts.

Our foresight had left Windsor defensively positioned. Asset values declined only 69 percent as much as the averages. This was a shade disappointing, however, in view of our large cash position. It suggested that our common stocks outperformed the market only a little on the downside. We had hoped for better.

Windsor's post-Crash strategy was simple. We were prepared to deploy our dry powder in a more reasonable market. During October's last 13 market days, we were net purchasers of $751 million in common stocks (15 percent of assets) with particular emphasis on Black Monday and the following day. We were quick to capitalize after experiencing the correction of 20 to 25 percent. For the S&P, the correction was on the order of 31 percent through the close of Monday, October 19. With the return to more reasonable levels, we felt honor-bound to put all of our cash and some of our bonds to work in stocks.

A bigger question could have been raised at that moment: "Was the outlook for 1988 damaged as a result of the market's collapse?" I didn't think so. Windsor's figure of 2 percent growth for the economy had increasingly become the consensus number, and possibly was on the high side. While this rate was worrisome, I stuck with it because I did not think that the man or woman in the street—the consumer—would adjust spending habits because of what was happening in a marketplace that was very important to those of us who were in the investment business. This presupposed that the stock market's machinations would vanish from the front page and the evening news, allowing life to go on. As a harbinger (one must continue always to look for these), auto sales in the last days of October (post October 19) were in line with our expectations.

By far the most telling evidence of new portfolio frontiers was a significant position taken in the airlines. We had not owned airlines stock for about 18 years, with the exception of a small Delta holding in 1979 and 1980. We chose a fairly broad exposure to what we called "the good guys" as our principal thrust. American was probably the best managed long-term entrant in the industry, but it bore the onus of being too aggressive in expanding its capacity. Delta was second on the qualitative ladder but it had suffered an unfortunate number of very un-Deltalike glitches in the summer. Northwest Airlines, reflecting some of the oligopolistic clout it enjoyed in Minneapolis, accounted for nearly two-thirds of the traffic originating in Detroit. Unfortunately, it fell somewhat short on the service side; its 1986 merger with Republic Airlines did not proceed smoothly. However, we thought that management and the unions were getting their arms around the problem and were on the way to a solution. We also utilized, to a lesser degree, USAir. Its acquisitions of regional carriers on the West Coast and in the East gave USAir an entry into the geographically dispersed, critical mass needed to be competitive in the new airline sweepstakes.

All these companies had excellent finances—for airlines—and had "quality survivor" written all over them. We thought they were very cheap (around four times prospective 1988 earnings) but they did not have very good yields, so we expected to absorb that penalty into our dividend stream. However, as always, we were prepared to take an intelligent risk in different-than-usual Windsor goods if the price opportunities were persuasive enough. These equities got crushed in the downdraft even before October 19. Our average price was 37 percent below the 1987 highs, and even these highs were not as ebullient as other parts of the market.

1988: THE AFTERMATH

After failing to gain much traction in the immediate aftermath of the Crash, Windsor finally had a more presentable month in January 1988. We rang in the new year with a seven-percentage-point edge over the S&P 500 and an 8½-point edge over our competitive group. It was about time for a bounceback, especially by the financial intermediaries that had served Windsor so poorly in 1987. In a marketplace that was up nominally in January, these stocks vaulted about 13 percent or so. Other parts of the portfolio also were stalwart: the autos, the long dormant airlines (plus Boeing), and the electric utilities. So, in effect, we won on virtually all fronts.

Return to Retail

For the first time in almost six years, we developed an interest in specialty retailers; very simply, we had been priced out of that market. We had had sympathy for this group in the past. In 1979, as much as 13.7 percent of Windsor constituted a stake in specialty retailers. We did not reenter their playing field, however; they reentered ours. The equalizer was the pummeling this area absorbed, not only because of the popularity of general retail, but also because of the aggressive market we were in. Commonplace was a searing haircut of 50 percent or more, chiefly as a result of the perception that the Grinch would steal Christmas in 1987, in the wake of Black Monday. We did not subscribe to the widespread expectation that consumers would cancel spending plans just because money managers were shedding alligator tears. In effect, it was a difficult and quite price-promotional Christmas. We expected that the quality participants would show up comparatively well and that Christmas *would* come again, maybe even as soon as 1988. Our retail sympathy further underscored our desire to strike out into new areas and give our shareholders a somewhat broader portfolio participation.

The retail position was made up of three specialty retailers. Circuit City Stores was, in our view, the class of consumer electronics retailers. Pier One Imports, a retailer of exotic and unique home furnishings, principally from underdeveloped countries, was the only national force in the business. Burlington Coat Factory, an almost national retail outlet, merchandises a wide range of coats and other apparel—the only company to do this on a near national scale. We had had our eyes on this segment for some time. Even as other investors were still mesmerized in late October by a plunging market, my Windsor colleagues and I gang-tackled the retail merchandising sector in search of the likeliest winners. In that, we succeeded. ***Outcome:*** *Circuit City became a star performer in 1988. Its price rose by 115 percent, compared to 11 percent for the S&P 500. Though less impressive by these standards, Pier One and Burlington Coat also delivered exceptional performances that far outpaced the market and the specialty retail group, which advanced 28 percent.*

After a particularly good January, fashioned significantly by recovering financial intermediaries, we sank back a bit into ennui. We had braced for this, simply because the market works in a characteristic ebb-and-flow fashion. But we were not satisfied. We had to concede some disappointment, particularly in the financial intermediaries, where we felt that Citicorp and Bankers Trust, for example, were sharply undervalued at a bit over four times earnings and yielding 7.2 percent and 6.1 percent, respectively.

The multiline insurance industry's first quarter results showed continuing significant pressure on earnings, except for Travelers, which scraped bottom in late 1987. Improvement seemed inevitable, if only because 30 to 40 percent rate increases were being implemented. We conceded that the multiline insurance position was a "slow case" rather than one promising instant gratification in bottom-line earnings. On the other hand, our auto industry unfolding was, if anything, better than our optimistic outlook. The airlines were garnering good fare and traffic increases, and Boeing's backlog continued to build gratifyingly.

A Turn for the Better

Results turned quite decent in the third quarter, up 9 percent for the Fund versus just over 2 percent for the S&P, and a smidgen higher versus the competitive group. On the more extended time plane of the year to date, we were a little over 12 percentage points better than the S&P and almost 13 points ahead of the competitive group. We weighed in with a 22 percent total advance, which represented a pretty good comeback after a somewhat disappointing 1987. Improvement stemmed largely from our outsized position in banks, autos, airlines, and Boeing, which together represented about half of Windsor's portfolio.

Company	Price Appreciation 12-31-87 to 8-15-88
Bank America	100.0%
Circuit City Stores	97.3
Boeing	61.9
Ford	40.4
Delta	36.0
First Interstate	34.2
Citicorp	33.3
General Motors	30.8
AMR	30.1

It was gratifying to note the contributions to performance by brand-new 1987 areas of emphasis. The most laggard area was multiline insurance. However, second-quarter earnings statements encouraged our turnaround in the group health side, particularly for Cigna. With Wall Street's ever-present proclivity for compressing performance in a relatively short period of time, particularly upon inflection points, we looked forward to banking noteworthy multiline insurance price advances.

Seeking Wider Diversification

We were still trying to broaden our diversification without prostituting our standards more than a little bit. We were prepared to accept somewhat lower-than-average standards of portfolio appreciation in new areas; however, we wanted to remain faithful to our total return relative to p/e standards. Until prices dipped in mid-August, however, we did not have much luck. We were a little uncomfortable with the somewhat narrow diversification we were giving to our shareholders in the Windsor portfolio—a concern that we communicated to the shareholders. We never flew under the "closet index" banner, but it seemed appropriate to share at least that insight so that shareholders would be able to incorporate our "out" position in their financial planning and risk taking.

It is always hard to be too penetrating or too precise about the outlook for the market in general. In the dog days of 1988, I guessed that we would fuss around for a while in the vicinity of a Dow at 1,900 to 2,000, at least until concerns about interest rates, inflation, and the business expansion had a longer period of gestation. Our perspective was that interest rates were in the high end of a range for the year, and inflation would continue to come in around the 4 to 5 percent range, even though business continued to expand moderately. A cyclical decline did not seem in sight over the near horizon. This was not the consensus perspective. Even at Wellington, a school of thought had inflation quantum jumping and interest rates spiraling upward.

If we were right, we expected the market to move eventually upward and out of its somewhat narrow trading range, reflecting how well earnings had advanced and dividends had grown. Our 1989 projection called for a moderate earnings advance of some 5 percent, even so late in the business expansion.

By far the largest sale during the third quarter was Boeing. We had created this position in 1987, mostly before October 19. Our Boeing stake represented 4½ percent of the Windsor portfolio. After a 40 percent relative move from the purchase price, we sold into the strength of a major move of a big stock that was rather suddenly discovered by Wall Street aerospace analysts. They highlighted most of the same virtues that had attracted us a year earlier and were subsequently confirmed by very significant bookings of new aircraft.

You don't need to have too many of these successful, outsize, conviction-laden positions to measure up. If you accept our target of snaring four percentage points or more annually in excess of the market (on average, of course, not every year), the 4½ percent position in Boeing would result in 1.8 percentage points of relative performance.* This was almost half of what we targeted in a single year, and we still had the other 95½ percent of the portfolio working for us. The trick was to hold our losers to a minimum in the portion of the portfolio that was underperforming, and come close to getting our money back even when our initial model of expectation broke down.

Commodities Again

During the fourth quarter of 1988, we were a little more successful in broadening our quite narrow diversification via new purchases in the general cyclical commodity segment. We had not been represented in this sector since 1987, when we eliminated the last of our large and successful aluminum positions. New investments included Dow Chemical, Great Northern Nekoosa (paper and forest products), Phelps Dodge (metals), Potlatch (paper and forest products), and two oil companies, Amerada Hess and USX (by dint of its stake in Marathon Oil). After languishing for almost two years, the market prices implied that earnings power was not durable. We took issue with this prevailing opinion. Our below-consensus inflationary outlook (which was becoming more the consensus) held that basic cyclical pricing would not erode sharply.

Unlike some other institutions, we made no special effort to tilt Windsor toward wider participation in the accelerating leveraged buyout trend. In fact, we were driven by the same earnings, yield, and growth rate evaluation framework that had always guided us. We were not evolving an approach based predominantly on cash flow or asset value. In short, we were still basically low-p/e equity investors, though we were always on the lookout for areas where the chance of being taken out fostered a serendipitous "free plus."

We snagged just such a winner in Great Northern Nekoosa. This paper and forest company featured a broad, well-positioned product mix plus an improving balance sheet. Atop a doubling of earnings in 1987 versus 1986, we expected a further 74 percent jump in 1988, followed

---

* A 40 percent move by 4.5 percent of the Windsor Fund enlarges the whole portfolio by 1.8 percent. The arithmetic is simple if you convert 40 percent to .4, its fractional equivalent: $.4 \times 4.5 = 1.8$.

by a more nominal, but still attractive, 15 percent in 1989—an almost fivefold earnings increase over four years. This vault in earnings reflected a physical increase more than commensurate with growth in the economy, but the lion's share of the earnings increment was due simply to better pricing. We thought, with the possible exception of newsprint, that the supply-and-demand relationships would remain tight in most other paper products for at least a couple more years. Such was our confidence that we bought 4.4 million shares, nearly 8 percent of the company. *Outcome: We never got to find out. When Georgia Pacific swooped in and bought Great Northern Nekoosa in 1989, we took our 63 percent advance and ran, happy with a gain that outpaced the S&P 500 by three-to-one, and the paper and forest products group by four-to-one.*

Phelps Dodge was another participant in the basic industrial commodity sweepstakes. Although copper still represented an overpowering percentage of the company's earnings, significant acquisitions in other industrial areas, such as carbon black and truck rims, buttressed performance. The real sizzle was that Phelps reduced the cost of mining copper by some 30 to 40 percent. Its cost position was then virtually as low as anybody else's in the world, particularly considering the predictability of operations. At around $1.50 a pound, the going price of copper was way too high to last, in contrast with other commodities. We figured, however, that even at a more reasonable price of $1 a pound, Phelps would earn $10 in 1989. At a purchase price in the high $30s and with a dividend that had just been doubled, Phelps Dodge cried for notice in the marketplace. *Outcome: Patience was a virtue. In 1990, Phelps surpassed the lackluster nonferrous metals group and the S&P 500 by whopping margins. Phelps's price advanced by 57 percent, compared to a gain just shy of 30 percent for the S&P 500 and 13 percent for the competitive group.*

Windsor finished calendar 1988 up 28.7 percent, a 12 percentage point edge versus the S&P 500. We weathered the 1987 inflection point with aplomb. All told for 1982 through 1988, Windsor shareholders outpaced the S&P benchmark by just over 29 percentage points. An investment dating to my taking Windsor's reins celebrated a 41-fold increase, versus the market's 16-fold increase. Herein lies my case for a low p/e investment strategy. No further facts are required.

13

~

GOOD GUYS PERSEVERE

1989–1993

WE PLUNGED INTO the post 1987 era with gusto and confidence. In calendar 1988, Windsor's 30th year, results achieved attention getting magnitude—28.6 percent, or 12.2 percent better than the market. Vanguard chairman, John Bogle, spared no praise for our efforts in that year's annual report, crediting Windsor with a superlative record achieved "not by flair or by excessive risk, but by concentration on security analysis and investment fundamentals." I guess my message was clear. It's good Bogle expressed such confidence when he did, because the next couple of years were not so glorious as we struggled with a hefty commitment to financial intermediaries including embattled Citibank. This period underscored the market's harsh unpredictability. It punished some of our old friends with surprising ferocity. But after a severe beating, culminating in predictions of obsolescence for low p/e investing, the very moves that landed Windsor in the crucible steered us once again to market-beating performance. All it took was another inflection point to bring the market to its senses about the underlying importance and financial strength of our good guys. In calendar 1992 and 1993 Windsor advanced 49.8 percent to 18.5 percent for the S&P 500. These were not quite of the magnitude we would have liked, but in the worst of times Windsor took a lickin' and kept on tickin', as old ads for Timex watches used to claim. On the other side of inflection points, frenzies end, fundamental prevail, and every tub sits on its own bottom.

1989: BACKING AND HAULING

Considering the adrenaline-spurred marketplace, which was capped by an 86 percent annualized rate of advancement in January, Windsor held up pretty well in early 1989. As investors embraced the airlines and some of our other positions, we accommodated them by selling this merchandise. Although we also managed to find undervalued securities on the other side of the market's enthusiasm, sales outpaced new purchases significantly. Moreover, after reopening Windsor to individual investors for the first time since 1985, receipts ran two and a half times ahead of the pace we had anticipated. As a consequence of proceeds from sales and new shareholders, cash rose quickly to 11 percent of the Windsor Fund.

This development was not so troubling as it might sound. Our cash position was not disquieting in a marketplace that had already logged the advance we had guessed it would log for the whole year. Put another way, if our projection of a 10 to 12 percent total return for 1989 was realistic, we reasoned that the market would tread water for the rest of the year.

Intel, a new holding, represented the cutting edge of innovative semiconductor—actually, microprocessor—technology. We had admired Intel from a distance for some time, never quite thinking that it would qualify as a Windsor type of "yardstick" investment. However, never say "Never" in the wonderful world of stock market fluctuations. In November, the 286 and 386 families of microprocessors were found to be in abundance in users' inventories—the result of stockpiling at a feverish pace during most of 1988. A significant markdown in Intel's fourth-quarter earnings followed. When the announcement came, the stock market broke sharply from 23½, well down from the 37½ high earlier in the year. The price fell below $20 per share, but only for a couple of days.

Everybody immediately marked down 1989 numbers. Final demand for personal computers, workstations, and the like seemed to still be on a positive growth track of 10 to 15 percent a year, so our best guess was that both Wall Street and the company were overcompensating with reduced earnings. All of a sudden, Intel became a low p/e stock with a 16 percent growth rate thrown in for good measure. ***Outcome:** The market soon came to its senses and Windsor pocketed a 70 percent price advance.*

We began to take profits in General Motors following an approximately 60 percent absolute advance and a 35 to 40 percent relative move.

We were working the margin a bit in our auto holding, but, at 22 percent of assets, and with Ford and Chrysler so much more attractive, it was only prudent to hit General Motors. We followed our usual script by selling GM after the gain represented 70 percent of the portfolio's appreciation potential. Nevertheless, the autos still comprised a fifth of the Windsor Fund.

Gradually, the battle to slow the economy became less intense by late spring. This took some of the pressure off the inflation side, in respect to both labor supply and pricing of basic commodities. Grains moderated a fair bit as moisture levels normalized in several important geographic areas, and there was still reason for hope on the winter wheat front. Some of the more exaggerated areas of commodity price excess started to moderate—most notably, crude oil and copper—and even some of the plastics and chemicals had receded from their highs.

A Wrong Judgment

By the third quarter, the economy and inflation were unfolding very much along the lines we had predicted. Each was moderating quite satisfactorily; long-term interest rates came down more than one percentage point. The Fed was even getting a few kudos in the media and on the Street for anticipating rather than reacting. Despite some concerns to the contrary, it was our judgment that the economy would continue to expand moderately and that a recession was not lurking around the corner.

So we thought.

As we progressed to the fourth fiscal quarter of 1989, Windsor began to lag badly. Four reasons lay behind this poor showing:

1. Awful performance of the major concentration in the autos.
2. A rising cash position.
3. The burgeoning position in commodity cyclicals that we were building all year; save for one or two exceptions, these cyclicals had not gone much beyond our purchase prices.
4. An adrenaline type of year in the stock market outdistanced our more ordinary merchandise.

Still, we had rather good responses in major segment areas such as the airlines, the banks, and the savings and loans. With the possible exception of the autos, I did not think we had anything major to apologize for.

We remained convinced that the market was wrong and that the Big Three auto companies would show representative earnings in 1990, particularly if we were correct in our projection that car and light truck sales would be on a par with 1989.

Outsize gains in supersafe and predictable (at least if you bought the conventional wisdom) areas, particularly consumer nondurables, characterized 1989. To us, the latter area, broadly speaking, represented sharp overvaluation. We avoided it like the plague. This was another facet of our underperformance, but, if we were right, it also represented considerable future opportunity. The irony of the cyclicals was that their poor performance occurred in the face of a consensus judgment that we were in for a "soft landing" in 1990, instead of a recession. We not only held that same view but we believed in it; cyclical stocks comprised one-third of Windsor's assets. The eternal dilemma was: Would this perspective come to pass in 1990, and would pricing in these industry segments allow continued good earnings to result?

Windsor's stock purchases edged out sales by a small margin in the final quarter of 1989. A critic might have asked, with reason: "Why did you do so much selling if you were trying to increase your invested position, particularly with friendly priced equities available?" I need only cite what ensued afterward. Weeks after we cashed out of AMR, Digital Equipment, Phelps Dodge, Delta Airlines, IBM, and the savings and loans, their prices were down 15 to 30 percent from the prices Windsor garnered.

Ignoring the rising tide of troubled real estate and construction loans, we loaded up on banks. We could well have been accused of gilding the lily by adding to our bank holdings; we already had an outsized 16 percent stake. Even though banks clearly faced more potential landmines, we believed that banks and other financial intermediaries would show a noticeable earnings thrust in a lackluster (or a depressed) corporate earnings environment. This earnings thrust, in combination with moderate multiples and good yields, represented very desirable investment characteristics in the difficult earnings environment that we foresaw. We were partially right. As it turned out, the circumstances turned worse before getting better.

We set the stage for better days by repurchasing recently relinquished shares of Delta Airlines. We paid 17 percent less than our sale price earlier in the same quarter.

1990: THE CENTER DOES NOT HOLD

It was difficult to generalize, at this somewhat discouraging point in early 1990, why we weren't garnering better results in the market, but it's always tough to try to fully explain market behavior. The financial intermediaries had a flash point in the widespread consternation over construction and commercial real estate lending. Our largest bank holdings—Citicorp, Bankers Trust, and BankAmerica—had about 9 percent in this area, versus 20 to 30 percent for the garden-variety regional bank. Our two biggest savings and loan holdings, H. F. Ahmanson and Golden West Financial, issued almost wholly "cookie cutter," 1–4-family residential loans that were likely to survive the worst of California residential concerns. Our bottom line: We did not think ordinary homes in California were going to take a 20-percent-plus shellacking, as a lot of the financial press had predicted.

Amid a bevy of pricey European pharmaceutical companies, we found a frugal entry point. Akzo was a Netherlands-based chemical company that offered a synthetic fiber and even a drug business. This was another cheap, accomplishing company that we had uncovered while trying to broaden our international focus. Incidentally, we had built up almost 5 percent in international stocks, which included Telefonica in Spain, National Westminster and Barclays in U.K. banking, and British Steel. (I don't include our approximate 5 percent holding in Alcan. It was based in Canada and had a far-flung international business, but so did a lot of Windsor's domestic companies.) ***Outcome:*** *Realization captured Akzo's 63 percent move in late 1993. British Steel registered a 151 percent price advance in 1993, outpacing steel stocks by more than a threefold margin, and the S&P 500 by 14-to-1.*

Hints of Rebound

Good 1990 performance was experienced in the autos (except Chrysler) and the airlines. Even the aluminum and copper equities poked their heads up. But financial intermediaries continued to plague Windsor. It was hard to be dogmatic, at that juncture, about where and when they would bottom out. In such stalwarts as BankAmerica, Bankers Trust, and our better savings and loans, we thought we spotted some signs that they had found their bottoms. Then again, hints of a rebound might have been only knee-jerk reactions from an overly depressed base.

This point in the banking crisis is easily forgotten. To serve as a reminder of how tough it really was, our four large, high-quality California savings and loans, which represented three-fourths of our total S&L holdings, turned in first-quarter earnings increases averaging 33 percent versus 1989. Such earnings momentum in a lackluster corporate earnings environment usually triggered unusual market response. However, to show how spooked the market was, the leading institutional firm's analyst, who was not only the premier S&L analyst and accordingly the principal influencer of institutional opinion, withdrew all his buy recommendations rather than face serious consequences. His superiors, both the market gurus and the technical strategists, accordingly willed their exclusion from the recommended list, fundamentals be damned.

This was not very professional by our standards, but it depicts how convoluted the reasoning was. The perspective in overruling a securities analyst, in effect, dealt essentially with an appraisal of how turned off or indifferent potential buyers were, not only to the marketplace but also to the future path of California residential real estate prices. This struck me as a masterstroke of doublethink or doublespeak. We have always maintained that opportunity is born of such circumstances, and we conducted ourselves accordingly. In the case of the savings and loans, it was probably surprising how well the "good guys" held up, despite the adverse headlines, opinion, and confusion that prevailed.

We continued to vote not only in our economic outlook, but also in how we were running Windsor Fund. Expectations of a soft landing for the economy guided our decisions. We noted mounting evidence that the wary consumer could be lured into buying on the good old American basis of price. This was not always positive for the bottom line (lower prices usually meant lower profits), but it still represented our system as working pretty much as intended. Automotive production rebounded from a virtual shutdown in January and gained successively better levels in February, March, and April.

Some of the basic commodity cyclical industries experienced either stabilized or moderate upticks in their selling prices. Earnings in the first quarter were reasonably satisfactory, and the outlook in the second and third quarters was a fair bit better. We were ready to concede that our aggressive earnings estimates were not wholly realized for the year, but the Wall Street estimates were, for the most part, being increased.

Besides, we expected further increases in later quarters. This out-in-front strategizing may be a somewhat difficult way to make money, but, perhaps too often, we choose that path and some hoped-for encouragement from a few of our industry representatives enjoying a mild bounce from their lows. Economic activity, as measured by the Federal Reserve Board Index of Industrial Production, jumped a couple percent from the January lows when the operating rate and the economy moved up as well. Meantime, factories were running at near-peak capacity.

Keeping Our Heads

Along with this optimism, there were unknowns and risks in the economy, particularly because the credit structure of some companies and components of our economy was pushed to extremes. Accordingly, there were more black holes and potentially negative surprises. Commercial real estate, with a national vacancy rate of 19 percent in office buildings, was a concern, as was the fallout of the bank examining process in this area. In effect, as credit tightened, monetary policy was being made, in some considerable part, by examiners.

The whole high-yield sector, the province of junk bonds, experienced a sharp correction. Interestingly, some considerable carnage had been wrought in this area, but our economy and our marketplace had absorbed it with considerable resiliency. We never wanted to become complacent, but at least this experience showed how well our financial system's self-correcting process seemed to work. This excess eventually tumbled by its own weight before government could get overly involved. Carnage is never pleasant, but it reminded people of the penalties awaiting imprudence and illicit activity.

The tender of the remaining successful holding of Great Northern should be noted: We realized almost $118 million and an appreciation of 58 percent for a holding that was not even a year old. At a particularly poor moment for Windsor, this success showed that value, or low p/e, investing, could pay off in individual securities.

While somewhat discouraged, we were not distressed. We had known and survived "rough patches" before. With confidence that low p/e philosophy and right seem to eventually win out, we were determined, as always, to keep our heads while others seemed intent on losing theirs.

An Undiscerning Market

We continued to be discriminated against, it seemed, in the marketplace. Our companies, for the most part, were measuring up rather well in a difficult environment. Among the banks, BankAmerica and Bankers Trust turned in formidable earnings results, and the consumer side of Citicorp was up in excess of 20 percent.

Our portfolio strategy at this somewhat chancy point in time had not changed. The economy continued to measure up by our standards, although not by everybody's.

All bets were off, however, after Kuwait was overrun by the Iraqis. If this had become a permanent arrangement, some four million barrels of OPEC oil per day would have been under the control of a not-so-benevolent despot. With the price of oil at about $28 a barrel, the United States would have been pushed into a mild recession, and the 4 percent inflation would have escalated to 5 percent or more.

We did not allow a lack of success to constrain sales, which outpaced new purchases by almost two-to-one. This differential reflected a marketplace that seemed a little happier in its enthusiasm than fundamentals otherwise suggested. With the pressure to bring the Dow to 3,000, this momentum seemed somewhat out of character in several fundamental respects: a lack of thrust in the economy or in corporate profits; few corporate mergers; and stubborn interest rates that were unlikely to recede. In this climate, we found more to sell than to buy, particularly because we were not dedicated to increasing our positions in areas where we already were aggressively represented. Put another way, we were usually skilled at exploiting an overdepressed industry about which the market was not very discerning, thereby turning losers into winners and upgrading our concentrations.

Objects of Our Affection

By our standards, BankAmerica was not only a current winner, at five times current earnings, but actually would show, with a reasonably high degree of assurance, attention-getting earnings gains not only in testy 1990 but also in 1991 and 1992. Not unlike Citicorp, BankAmerica offered the whole book of business to the consumer. Besides a competitive edge in traditional areas such as credit cards and installment lending, these two banks filled the void in California left by moribund S&Ls that were unable to finance mortgages and home equity loans. *Outcome: In the second quarter of 1993, appreciation in Windsor's BankAmerica stake garnered a 159 percent return.*

Citicorp, of course, was the other object of our affection. We continued to maintain a 5 percent position in this outstandingly run company in its consumer lending, even though it was not faring so well in the rest of its business, at least over the near term. Fearful of much-publicized bad loans to Latin American countries and to U.S. real estate developers, many investors retreated. We saw continued excellent growth from the consumer sector. Problem loans were adequately provided for. A lackluster economic environment dampened hefty LBO fees, and the consumer segment required fresh investment. We thought, however, that some refocusing and restructuring, plus an improving climate in some downtrodden parts of the business, would build on the solid consumer earnings. The stock looked to us like a big winner.

The wherewithal for these two additions came not from losers but from two bank stocks that, during our relatively brief holding period, had excellent records. These were our two U.K. representatives, National Westminster Bank and Barclays Bank, where we banked a 25 percent-plus profit and a good yield. When we recycled these proceeds into depressed BankAmerica and Citicorp, we had some fortuitous help from the British pound. We didn't expect it to go down, although that seemed to be the consensus when we bought the British banks' stocks, but, somewhat surprisingly, it strengthened.

Among our realizations on our investments, General Motors was noteworthy. We had been capitalizing on this stock for more than a year. (It gained a maximum position after October 19, 1987.) GM shares had been fetching increasingly attractive prices for a while, and we were not shy about handing shares over as the drumbeat intensified. In so doing, we reduced our large and overweighted dependence on auto stocks. Where we once had over 20 percent in autos, a combination of the GM sales (which took over four points out of this position) and the underperformance by Ford and, particularly, by Chrysler, now lessened our dependence to 12 percent.

Other profit taking was reflected in the aluminums. Reynolds Metals had a decent, although hardly remarkable, success at a 24 percent appreciation plus an average yield. This was workmanlike for basic cyclicals. Alcan was somewhat more restrained at only a 9 percent appreciation. We decided that discretion was the better part of valor for this outsized holding. Its earnings were not measuring up as well as those from the banks and autos. We still retained an approximate 8.6 percent position in the aluminums, and the price of ingot finally moved up about 10 percent. This move was more in keeping with our fundamental case for this industry.

Success was still eluding us; ours truly was the loneliness of the long-distance runner. We were being severely tested, not unlike the experience in 1971–1973. The market, particularly in some of our equities, seemed not only irrational relative to the fundamentals, but bordering on panic fashioned by Wall Street gloom and doom, in concert with experts from academia and analysts on ABC's *Nightline*. We were in no position to guarantee when the market would turn or even that it *would* turn one day, but we refused to be whipsawed and to cave in at the bottom. We continued to represent Windsor shareholders with our usual prowess and professionalism.

Good Guys Persevere

We felt a bit put upon. In our perspective, the marketplace had not been very discriminating in its evaluations of banks, savings and loans, and multiline insurance companies. Admittedly, we were in a period of considerable stress in these areas, particularly commercial real estate and construction lending. However, we continued to highlight some "good guys" who were persevering. We were confident that they would eventually provide the grease for the total economy and, in the bargain, they would enjoy a place in the sun. The market overlooked quality competitors who had sufficient capital, good ability to generate more capital under adversity, cutting-edge technology, and, of course, critical mass. These were very viable survivors.

Meantime, all but Citicorp measured up fundamentally. The bank had been tarred with the same brush as all the other companies in the arena that were failing or, at best, just surviving. If our judgments were at all close, Windsor shareholders were due for a just reward after some rough sledding.

1991: BATTLING BACK

We had a little better time in early 1991, despite a bit of liquidity (8½ percent) at the start and considerably more (17 percent) at the end. This better result was led by our "good guys" within the financial intermediaries: BankAmerica (+57 percent), Golden West Financial (+55 percent), Great Western Financial (+52 percent), Aetna (+43 percent), and Bankers Trust (+40 percent). Finally, there was a bit of recognition and differentiation for what we had been calling accomplishing survivors. There was also some resurgence in the basic commodity chemicals; they were not as spectacular as the "good guys," but they were noticeably better than the S&P 500.

I would like to be able to point to a specific inflection point or two and say that we built our confidence on the durability and continuance of better performance, but singling out specific examples is difficult. A consciousness on the part of the Bush Administration, plus the attitudes of the bank examiners, contributed some moral suasion and a recognition that driving the banks into oblivion was not wise policy when the goal is to thwart an impending recession. Also, the "groupthink" on the Street and in the marketplace encouraged excesses both over and under the true evaluation. Price trends in individual stocks and industries took on a life of their own, but not forever.

The General Motors holding was on its way out; its elimination was completed in early February. We did not turn in a remarkable performance, but it wasn't terrible, considering the fundamentals and the good dividend return over our holding period. We did a lot better with our earlier sales of 90 percent of the holding. General Motors had disappointed us. In previous years, GM had turned out cars and trucks that were styled more dramatically and differentiated more markedly from one model to another. In addition, GM's inability to recover any noticeable market share, even with heightened incentives, had to be a longer-term concern. The company continued to be pressured in its downsizing efforts, as well as in the overlay of difficult industry conditions.

We were a little puzzled as to why the market was so animated as 1991 progressed. It was particularly curious for us because we were more optimistic on the economy than most observers. Even so, we ended up with evaluations that were on the high side. That left us unable to explain why the majority of investors, who seemingly bought the conventional wisdom of an extended recession and the concomitant fallout, were so optimistic. The Dow was within sniffing distance of 3,000. Yet, six months after closing twice at 2,999.75, on July 16 and July 17, 1990, the Dow still had not managed to cross the next milestone.

Well-selected financial intermediary stocks represented the most undervalued part of the market. In May, we added modestly to our Citicorp position, in order to bolster the financial intermediary position following sales of some of Windsor's regional banks and small savings and loans. Of our eight "good guys," Citicorp was the one that failed us on both the earnings side and the capital adequacy side. We thought, however, that improvement was already visible. First-quarter earnings were disappointing, but we expected revenues to improve with the economy. Credit card charge volume, mortgage originations, and credit losses were likely to improve from their high first-quarter level. In April, the bank reported some encouraging signs on the loan delinquency front. The first-quarter expense performance was promising. The all-important Tier I capital ratio,* under the most rigorous rules, exceeded the required level, thanks to proceeds from the initial public offering of Ambac, a Citibank unit that provided insurance for fixed-income securities. We had Citicorp earning over $4 a share in 1994, which the stock, at $16, clearly was not buying.

Our basic commodity position of a little over 18 percent was down from a high of about 25 percent. This reduction reflected sales of such successful holdings as British Steel, Federal Paper Board, and Phelps Dodge, as well as continued sales of Alcan, which was not measuring up. (The market was giving us the opportunity to get out of Alcan at our purchase price.) Directionally, the decline in our basic commodity position was not altogether uncomfortable because the economy was weaker than we would have thought at this point in time. We had been looking to consumers to lead us out of the recession. The signals were mixed and muted: modest recovery in housing sales, airline traffic, and, maybe, soft goods, but no improvement in auto sales. This latter item was not great near-term news for purveyors of basic commodities like aluminum and steel, especially weaker industry factors like Alcan.

---

* As a consequence of the banking crisis in 1990–1991, regulators required banks to shore up their capital structure.

On the other hand, with a vehicle population age that was at the high end of the historical range, at about 7.5 years, we still thought that trend-line automotive demand was something like 7 million cars and 4 million light trucks, some 25 percent above the April sales rate. We felt that we could get back to these levels if consumers' current expectations of a better future were realized. An end to declining employment and to widespread fear of job loss seemed to us like a trigger point for more consumer spending. A slowing in the decline in payroll employment in April was encouraging in this regard. In any event, the longer car and truck sales remained at low levels, the more pent-up demand accumulated, which promised a stronger recovery than otherwise. When we envisioned the recession as not so bad and not lasting so long, we also had a very modest recovery in mind. Given the prospects for recovery, it looked like we might have to mark up our estimates. This would bode well for the Alcoas, Lyondells, Phelps Dodges, and other low-cost quality factors that were still well represented in our remaining 18 percent basic commodity position.

Traversing 3,000

On April 17, 1991, the Dow finally muscled its way across the 3,000 mark. "Propelled by lower interest rates and by expectations that the recession will end soon, the Dow gained 17.58 points, on strong volume of 246.9 million shares, and closed at 3,004.46. It has risen 27 percent since October 11," *The Wall Street Journal* reported. Elation was short-lived, however. It slipped below 3,000 in the next session.

The market, which we thought was high going in, advanced over 4 percent in the quarter. Our equity ratio of 71 percent was lower than we would have liked, but we continued to think that our shareholders would be best served by keeping our powder dry for more Windsor-priced opportunities down the road.

The buy side featured:

1. A modest addition to Citicorp.
2. Price-opportunistic additions to our Aetna and Telefonica positions.
3. A further fleshing-out of the energy thrust.
4. A big $100 million-plus addition to our Bayer AG position, a stock that was "working" and was still cheap, literally by orders

of magnitude, versus equivalent U.S. companies. We expected this gap to close as the investment business became more global.

Defensive Posture

Our portfolio strategy remained a bit on the defensive side. We expressed clear recognition (although it seemed clear only to us) that the market was more than a bit on the high side, particularly because pushy 1992 earnings were being revised downward, to 16 times earnings for the S&P. This, in combination with the 3.1 percent yield, seemed not the stuff of near-term market enthusiasm. Long-term rates had come down a half of one percentage point, and it was hard, in our judgment, to make a further case for an eye-catching decline from these levels. The economy seemed mired in an essentially stagnant period, and we were not so sure that our lackluster, moderate economic outlook wouldn't evolve into a moderate advance or, stated more clearly, hardly any advance at all.

The most unusual, if not puzzling, transactions were both purchases and sales of Citicorp, with the sales coming after the purchases and at a lower price. Here's the explanation. In the interim, the bank had completely eliminated its dividend, which was all we had to show for one of the most dismal investments in Windsor's history. The price had declined some 50 percent from our original cost. We obviously had been wrong to that date on Citicorp. We had severely miscalculated the carnage related to commercial real estate loans, which had become coupled with pressure on the consumer loan portfolio, thanks to the 1991 recession. The biggest aberration, however, appeared on the cost side. Employee costs had been allowed to run amok due to arrogance, if not a macho perspective on the company's ability to grow willy-nilly on the global commercial banking side.

However, even after all this bloodletting, we thought that the company's franchise, on the consumer side as well as in most aspects of corporate banking, was very much intact. With employee costs reduced by almost $2 billion, plus an eventual reduced need for the provision for bad debts, the path of future potential earnings enhancement seemed clear.

In our view, earnings would come tumbling out at $2, $3, $4, and $5 a share in 1992, 1993, 1994, and 1995, respectively. Meanwhile, the insufficient capital position would build to a respectable 5 percent of assets by the end of 1993. The elimination of the dividend would allow these earnings to forcefully surge through to create an improved capital position, so we did not look for any substantial asset growth during that period. In fact, a few timely and rewarding dispositions were likely. We tried to avoid being doctrinaire, particularly with our poor track record, but Citicorp struck us as being somewhat in the same position as BankAmerica was in 1987: It subsequently appreciated by a multiple of about 8 times. The "8 times" part of the analogy was not appropriate in respect to Citicorp, but if we were right about the $4–$5 of earnings power in 1994–1995, the stock stood to triple or quadruple.

The subsequent sale switched a portion of our outsized holding into the Citicorp convertible preferred, where we believed the dividend was safe (although we had said that about the common stock dividend as well). This helped considerably in replacing at least a portion of the lost dividends that made up about 7 percent of our income stream. Although this convertible preferred sold at a substantial premium (around 48 percent above the common equivalent), the power of the 11.7 percent yield meant that we would recoup our premium in 2.7 years. This was a somewhat cowardly move, but, besides adapting to changing circumstances, we try not to be cowed or intimidated by our own lack of success. This does not preclude our admission, in other cases, that we were wrong.

The most recent example was our elimination of Ford and General Motors earlier in the calendar year. We don't wear blinders, and it's not an ego thing in our view and perspective, but we believe that a business's risk investment could and should be very rewarding for Windsor's shareholders. We have to be correct on the fundamentals, of course.

Two things should be remembered about this experience at its low point: (1) however big our holding in Citicorp, it was a little less than 4 percent of Windsor, which meant we owned over 96 percent in other things; and (2) however unsuccessful Citicorp had been to date, our Bankers Trust and BankAmerica holdings were as gratifyingly exceptional on the upside as Citicorp had been on the downside. The Windsor Fund was a *portfolio*, even with its concentrations and diversification. Of our "good guys," seven out of eight was not a perfect score but it was rewarding for the shareholders.

We built a big position earlier in the year in the USX-Marathon Group; in combination with its appreciation, it was our largest holding. We took a bit off the top and, after a move that was appropriate against a lackluster marketplace, we weighed in with a 22 or 23 percent total return over an approximate six-month holding period. It's always hard to generalize, but one underlying theme was that we still found some investment opportunities over the near term that did not have gigantic price targets but were quite serviceable when, to us, the marketplace looked a bit long in the tooth. Other good realization was evidenced in Phelps Dodge and USX-US Steel Group. A couple of junk bonds also worked out well.

After ending fiscal 1991 with a slight edge over the S&P 500, Windsor lost ground by calendar year end. Our 28.6 percent gain marked a slight deficit to the S&P, which garnered a 30.4 percent gain. All things considered, however, Windsor measured up reasonably well in 1991, when supersafe stocks in general continued to captivate investors. Short of claiming victory, we nevertheless felt gratified. By sticking to our principles and maintaining our equilibrium amid the inexorable passage of panic, Windsor had kept its footing. In particular, our beleaguered band of financial intermediaries, after taking it on the chin for so long, chipped in with a weighted annual appreciation of nearly 70 percent. This was a welcome relief and a sign that the merits of our low p/e strategy were still intact.

1992: BOUNCING BACK

Sharp upward moves of 43 percent for Citicorp and 22 percent for Chrysler gave Windsor a big boost. Though a long time in coming, the marketplace responded to the virtues we had been extolling. Even when we were right, we did not expect a one-way street to glory. At the risk of sounding vindictive, we took a little pleasure, not only in the move, but in seeing the short sellers squeezed a bit in each of these stocks. Short sellers forced to buy may have accounted for part of the move, a development that is not uncommon in marketplaces captured and captivated by momentum.

There was, particularly in the month of January, a battle raging as to whether we had hit a market inflection point. Cyclicals were beginning to gain favor, as opposed to the growth stock groupthink of the previous few years. One had to be careful, particularly with the economy's lackluster, to not become overly jubilant. Enthusiasm, or lack of it, seemed to ebb and flow almost from day to day. We thought there were some positive arguments for value winning out in the basic commodity cyclical area. Even more compelling, in our judgment, were financial intermediaries. The difference was that the financial intermediaries were not overly economy-dependent; instead, they fulfilled basic needs in the marketplace. Broadly speaking, this meant cheapness and accomplishment (as manifest in the "good guys" with strong capital positions), as well as attention-getting growth rates buttressed by handsome yields. The specter of commercial real estate—more particularly, office buildings—hung over the financial stocks, especially in insurance and banking areas. We did not want to demean the reality of these circumstances, but we thought it had been largely absorbed and reserved against. However, at such times, no one can speak with absolute certainty.

The Right Moves

The economy was progressing a little slower than we thought, and we were pretty much on the low side of expectations. On the other hand, it seemed to us that the Fed had made most of the right moves and the Administration at least had not lost its link with reality, to judge by President Bush's State of the Union proposals. Congress, of course, was the wild card in all of this. It could always do something foolish against the backdrop of an already onerous budgetary deficit in the neighborhood of 7 percent of gross national product (GNP). What struck us as being fundamental was the Fed's moves to make residential housing so much more affordable. The media notwithstanding, an observer could not forget that the other side of 7 percent unemployment was 93 percent employment. We were hardly overhoused in this country, and the desire for one's own piece of turf beat lustily in the hearts of most Americans. We had just finished a year in which 1 million housing units were started. The number had been as high as 1.8 million in 1986 and 2 million in the early 1970s. A pop to 1.25–1.30 million in 1992 seemed like a good guess, and, as this goal developed into an actual count, it stretched out into several raw material support industries and created concomitant positive economic effects.

The other depressed mature area that cried for improvement was the automotive industry. Sales of around 6 million domestic cars plus 2 million or so foreign cars were some 1 million below scrappage (the rate of replacement). Ordinarily, in the longer-term scheme of things, the car population *grew* moderately. But ordinary demand, on top of pent-up demand, implied faster-than-usual growth. Moreover, consumers had built cash meaningfully in this area; auto installment debt outstanding had declined almost 8 percent in two years. Recovery here promised a positive effect in a great number of basic commodity cyclical industries.

This, in turn, meant much higher operating rates in these industries—steel, chemicals, paper, or aluminums—than in previous recessions. Price happiness would undoubtedly happen sooner and would achieve greater magnitude than the going consensus predicted. Accordingly, our representation in financial intermediaries and basic commodity cyclicals was about 54 percent of Windsor's assets.

The sales side was studded with realization in diverse areas—S&Ls, EDP, retailing, telephone, and homebuilders—but most prominent were American among the airlines, and Bankers Trust. The savings and loan profit taking was interesting because this was a much-maligned area, as more than a few shareholders' letters attested. We had experienced a disaster or two, but the sales during the quarter followed a 123 percent appreciation.

Our Kind of Music

The marketplace was singing our song at last. Basic commodity cyclicals as well as consumer cyclicals, exemplified by the autos, surged. These gains would only endure if economic recovery unfolded and solid earnings gains followed. So far, so good, on each account. Additionally, some of the financial intermediaries were continuing to kick in, even on top of an excellent 1991. With their earnings gains (in a testy earnings climate), very reasonable p/e ratios, and often outstanding yields, the "good guys" among financial intermediaries were beginning to command the market's attention. As marginal rivals were purged, a more benign competitive environment returned to the financial segment. Capital was king, and the quality competitors were adding to it through retained earnings. Additionally, there was an overlay of cyclical recovery, highlighted by stronger loan demand and reduced loss experience in an improving economy.

For reasons that we were not bashful about proclaiming, Windsor unfurled the banner of natural gas producers. Short of capturing attention in the marketplace, this broad area had at least started to receive a little attention as spot prices increased by 30 to 35 percent from the late winter lows. This movement was partially aided by (finally) some colder-than-normal weather in the eastern section of the country in March and April. Storage totals were pulled down sharply. At the same time, natural gas was priced in a friendly manner relative to crude oil. We thought we were "locked in the candy store" over a 2- to 4-year period. We expected natural gas prices to double and an eventual stock market enthusiasm to unfold. This was not our characteristic type of investment; current earnings were lackluster, to say the least, and current p/e ratios were not so low. We noted, however, that natural gas providers were selling at great discounts—around 50 percent of market value—and that the p/e ratios were low on prospective 1995 earnings.

Disappointing June employment numbers prompted the stock market to retreat somewhat to growth stocks and out of cyclicals, which reversed some of the year's rotation in the other direction. We continued to believe that the economy was in a gradual, steady recovery, and we hung our hat on the housing starts and auto production numbers. June new-home sales and mortgage applications for home purchases showed clear signs of life in housing demand, which as would be expected, was stimulated by the low prevailing mortgage rates. Domestic car and truck sales for July, hot off the press, came in better than for any of the first four months of the year, and suggested to us that a good, solid, albeit modest, three-month rebound was under way.

It may seem simplistic that we focused on these two industries as measures of the economic recovery. Each was clearly important to the economy, especially in view of its ripple effects. Overall car and truck sales were recovering, but we judged they were still a good 15 percent below the normal trendline at the top of 1991, when they were even more below normal. As this pent-up demand accumulated, it made likely a higher and higher level of future sales at some point, which would lead the economic recovery. Housing had the same potential, though we were less doctrinaire about the level of sales being subpar. But even if sales were "normal," there was still the earlier period of subpar sales to be "recouped," à la the autos.

This was not to say that June employment numbers did not count. They served as a reminder that the recovery would be gradual. American industry, it seemed, was going through a transition to a slower-growing, more globally competitive period, chiefly marked by shrinking payrolls. As these layoffs occurred—and were well publicized by the media—they were bound to dampen consumers' propensity to spend. The personal debt level, while improved, was still historically high. So, with all said and done, we saw some recovery, but it was gradual and moderate.

The hesitation in the economy was a negative factor, given our commitment to cyclical participants, notably exemplified by commodity producers such as the aluminums, chemicals, and steels. Other cyclicals, such as Citicorp, also surrendered some earlier gains. Chrysler, though, continued to roll along with 131 percent appreciation for the year to date. Its superior sales and earnings results rode right through cyclical qualms.

More Noise Than Substance

In our judgment, the economy was about to lift gently, removing some of the cyclical apprehension. More importantly, however, a number of our holdings, which owed us a great deal, were disturbed, if not distressed, by particular issues that contained more noise than substance. Because our kinds of goods always needed special understanding, noise was easily misinterpreted and it caused a temporary disregard of fundamental values. To be specific, significant tumbles from the year's highs in Telefonica, Commonwealth Edison, USX-Marathon, Aetna, Cigna, and Citicorp took their toll. But, in our judgment, these stocks, particularly in aggregate, represented future positives.

In some fairness, however, these assertions had the aroma of opinion; they needed to be proven in the marketplace. We were a little bothered that we had given back more than in the "olden days." In most past comebacks, we had enough important winners to more than make up for weak performance leading up to inflection points. This pattern did not orchestrate quite as well through the first three-fourths of 1992.

We had a little better luck uncovering attractive common stock equity prices. In a marketplace that really hadn't declined all that much, there was some fairly significant carnage in individual stocks, which the readers of *The Wall Street Journal* witnessed on any given day. "Black holes" opened up, owing to somewhat lofty valuations in the marketplace and disenchantment with cyclicals. In this climate, our kind of fare became attractive to us. For example, the stocks in our quarterly buying program were purchased at an average price that was about 27 percent below their highs for 1992. This was not necessarily a determinant of value, but *somebody* paid these prices during this year, and 27 percent was a pretty good markdown, particularly in a marketplace that has been kind of "same-ish."

Philips NV, the Dutch-domiciled international electronics company, had been very much out of favor. Our average purchase price was $13\frac{5}{8}$, quite a bit below the high for the year of $21\frac{7}{8}$. In the throes of a potentially major turnaround, Philips was experiencing considerable consolidation in its laboring consumer electronics operation in Europe, where it competed primarily against the Japanese. It was our perspective that this problem area would be brought under control, not only as a result of the introduction of new product, but also by the rationalization of current manufacturing facilities. Also, there was an opportunity for better pricing because the Japanese had all kinds of reasons for being less price-aggressive in Europe than previously. Lighting and semiconductors were among the company's many other solid areas. The real substantive and overlooked determinant of "giveaway," in our judgment, was the 80-percent-owned Polygram operation, a world leader in recorded music as well as allied entertainment areas. This company's growth pattern popped right out of the growth-stock textbook. It featured regular earnings increases in the 15 percent area and a not unreasonable market valuation at 13 times prospective earnings. This market capitalization of Polygram's earnings power accounted for virtually all of Philips's capitalized value in the marketplace. The rest of Philips was almost free. On another scale, we looked for eventual earnings—in, say, 1994 and 1995—of around $3.75, which made the stock "compelling" at our purchase price. For 1992, we expected Philips to report only moderate operating earnings and maybe even a loss after restructuring, but we were looking for something in the neighborhood of $1.50 in 1993. *Outcome: Philips logged a 90 percent price gain in 1993, twice the advance by the conglomerates group and eight times the gain garnered by the S&P 500.*

Seagate Technology, the largest disk drive entity and a principal supplier to the personal computer industry, was actually growing even more aggressively than the sum total of personal computers, laptops, and workstations. As a component supplier, the company had not been without its rocky moments. It posted only breakeven results in fiscal 1989 and nominal earnings in some other years. However, the company, which was now very well financed and better run, in our judgment, promised to show impressive earnings in the fiscal year ending in June 1993. This was reflective not only of the company's better management and control but, in a product group that bordered on being a commodity, the relationships of capacity and demand was in much better balance than in earlier years. Even more importantly, it looked as though the industry's expansion of capacity was less aggressive than before. We paid a little over four times earnings for Seagate and established a significant position. *Outcome: In 1993, while its competitive group slid by more than 20 percent, Seagate advanced by 50 percent. The S&P 500, meanwhile, gained 12 percent.*

1993: ON A ROLL

We looked a good bit better in the performance derby when the last quarter of 1992 came in more than eight points better than the S&P. Results in the trailing 12 months were almost ten points superior. Competitive group comparisons were almost that good, although, interestingly, the competitive group average beat the S&P nominally for both periods. This suggested that value—or, as we defined it, low p/e—got a somewhat better break in the marketplace than in periods just passed. Much of this I attributed to the very poor performance of the drug stocks and IBM. As a matter of fact, for the calendar year, if you owned neither the drug stocks nor IBM, you would have beaten the S&P by about three points. This illustrated the occasional advantage gained from what is *not* owned.

It seemed, anyway, that the "big Mo" (momentum) in respect to the consumer nondurables had been broken. If anything, this area was apt to oversuffer fundamentally. We expected camp followers to desert the area. It became increasingly unfashionable, if not uncomfortable, to have to explain it in quarterly reviews.

We were basking in the warmth of putting up better numbers. We were also wary of becoming too "giddy" as a result; we knew full well that marketplace emphasis can change overnight. Witness the rough patch we suffered in the middle of 1992, when there was some noteworthy indigestion in the commodity cyclicals and financial intermediaries.

Our biggest challenge at this point was a familiar one: staying invested. We were approximately 21 percent in cash equivalents, which was one percent more than our targeted maximum. We interpreted the cash equivalents a little more broadly than before. As of June 1992, we had taken almost three-quarters of a billion dollars of the cash and extended maturities, by about three years, in Treasury securities. We garnered a return that was about two percentage points higher than the return we were getting in traditional short fare. We didn't think we were inviting much risk of principal, because of the shape of the yield curve.* In fact,

---

* Bond yields represent the stream of fixed income investors receive. Yields would be a snap to calculate if everyone paid the face value for newly issued bonds, but it's not quite that easy. Bond prices and yields go up and down like two ends of a seesaw. When prices go up, yields go down, and vice versa. If you pay $1,000 for a bond with a stated interest rate, or coupon, of 6 percent, what happens if interest rates rise? Another investor might then pay

we subsequently experienced an approximate 3½ percent capital gain. These securities were included in cash, by our standards.

We managed to keep the purchase side reasonably active even with increasingly lofty valuations in the general marketplace. However, a lot of our overlooked, misunderstood, and out-of-favor holdings had captured the market's attention. Recognizing the size of these positions, we accommodated demand at the margin. This pulled down our invested position by about five points, and we were scrambling on the buy side.

The economy continued to perk along a bit better. The evidence was particularly strong in retail movement. This augured well for a continuing moderate build in industrial activity. Combined with good productivity, particularly as a result of the Fortune 1000's continuing purge of middle management personnel, we expected to see corporate profits rise.

This was a favorable market climate for us. The big consumer nondurables stocks were still laboring. In a lackluster period for the S&P (up only 1 percent for the first four months of 1993), Windsor displayed some extraordinary results in these divergent stocks:

Citicorp	+24.7 percent
Philips NV	+38.4
Aetna	+13.7
Burlington Resources	+22.5
Enserch	+32.7
Pennzoil	+25.0
Bethlehem Steel	+24.6
British Steel	+66.7

Our biggest challenge was to stay 80 percent invested, but for different reasons than usual. We were able to find sensible Windsor-like investments, even in an elevated market. Exceptional market enthusiasm

---

$1,000 and receive 7 percent interest. To ensure that the income on your bond represents a 7 percent rate of interest, the price must fall. The new price of your bond would be only $857.14, if you decided to sell it. (If you don't sell, you just keep collecting the original percent rate of interest.)

Bonds vary in credit quality, according to the likelihood of their being repaid, and maturity. For bonds of a particular credit quality, yields also vary, depending on the time until repayment. Usually, the longer a borrower waits, the higher the interest rate. Plotting interest rates for a bond at various points in time depicts a curve. This is the yield curve. It doesn't predict the future. It simply shows how much General Motors, or the U.S. Government, or any other borrower, must pay in the current market to borrow money for one year, thirty years, or any length of time in between.

for our previously out-of-favor holdings was impossible to resist. As always, we often took out-of-favor positions of considerable size. When the market embracement happens, we are obliged to accommodate that kind of market happiness.

A Good Question

Critics could legitimately ask: "When was Windsor going to find larger or more broadly based extensive buying opportunities?" Our answer: That would come as a result of seemingly inevitable market indigestion. Until then, we struggled along, at times, only 78 percent invested. There wasn't much penalty for uninvested funds when the market did not seem to be going anywhere. Put another way, in a market that was up one percent in the year to date, there were obviously opportunities to lose money in individual stocks, and, arrogant though it sounds, we preferred cash to stocks that were going down.

The economy was pausing a bit. This happened not only because of a difficult winter, but, more importantly, because of some hesitation by consumers, as seen particularly in the sales of the general line merchandisers. In my view, this was reflective of some loss of confidence in the new Clinton Administration because of: (1) onerous taxation proposals for those who have the ability to spend, and (2) some floundering, if not ineptness, because the new leadership was trying to do too much at once and was forgetting the need to justify the new programs, particularly with a Congress that included a significant Republican minority.

In the previous eighteen months or so, we had been getting a little better shake from a more level playing field. Supersafe consumer nondurables of whatever label had come under considerable market stress. The pendulum had swung too far in a positive direction, reflecting Wall Street's never-ending ability to overemphasize and overcapitalize a good thing. To state the obvious, 1989 and 1990 were no fun for us. Although we made some fundamental mistakes during this period, there really was not much of a performance defense. We did stay loyal to our principles. We didn't panic, and we tried to represent our shareholders rationally and skillfully within the longer-term scheme of things. I wish a better lesson could be learned from the 1989–1990 experience—other than: Don't make fundamental mistakes—but I am not quite sure what that lesson would be.

Reviewing our annual report for 1990, after we had performed so miserably, I found, to my surprise, that it actually read pretty well as things turned out. Particularly in the investment area, it is always interesting to review one's pronouncements after a meaningful passage of time.

I guess the message was—and is—that value or low p/e investing can win the day if and when the fundamentals unfold positively as a more discerning marketplace embraces the stock. Moreover, low p/e can sometimes garner instant gratification—if not through a leveraged buyout phenomenon similar to the late 1980s, then by straight corporate purchase. Some 2½ percent of Windsor's assets resulted from such developments.

The economy continued to track along our model of expectations fairly well. In particular, consumption picked up in a broad way, which supported our sustained moderate-growth view. After a pause in the summer months and September, car and truck sales picked up nicely in October, registering the best annual rate for 1993 and exceeding the pace a year earlier by 14 percent. New housing sales seemed to break out in September, some 17 percent ahead of the year's average pace and 13 percent ahead year to year. General merchandise sales improved in September and October, though with some weather-influenced abatement in the latter part of October. Importantly, we thought these trends were sustainable, given some pent-up demand for cars and trucks and for housing, and given the likely broadening of consumer confidence to the nondurable side of things.

The sales side consisted predominantly of favorable realizations. Not least of these was a very quick turnaround on shares of Burlington Northern, after a robust move. We also sold down our Citicorp stake at very attractive multiples of cost. Interestingly, we were selling six of the eight foreign stocks Windsor owned, totaling nearly 9 percent of the Fund. When we bought the likes of Bayer, critics carped, "Well, it's dirt cheap, but it always has been, and what's going to change that?" Our answer: Other American institutions would discover it later, like we did, and be drawn to its cheapness relative to U.S. alternatives. We said that Windsor would make out as our industry, the U.S. investment business, globalized. That appears to have been an important driver of the strength in foreign, especially European, markets in 1993. Windsor obligingly sold into that strength. *Outcome: Initial sales of Bayer garnered 50 percent gains; on later sales we doubled shareholder's money.*

Summing Up

As the market entered a new cycle, my final two years at Windsor were not stellar. Suffice it to say that we lagged the market by roughly six percentage points, all told, in calendar years 1994 and 1995. The final account requires a later chapter, one that encompasses an inflection point beyond my tenure. I look forward to reading it. I fully expect renewed vindication of low p/e investing.

14

DÉJÀ VU

IT WOULD BE nice to be able to invest yesterday, but investors don't have that option. You can spend your time regretting that you didn't buy Cisco before a tenfold rise, or you can organize for future performance. That's the nature of the daily investment challenge. You can't invest yesterday; you have to invest today. How do you rise to the occasion and still keep the odds in your favor?

Stock tips don't fall within the purview of this book. But because the investment process is supposed to generate investment ideas, and also because today's market is more familiar to readers than past epochs, the market in June 1999 is a good backdrop for showcasing my low p/e principles within a framework of Measured Participation. I've stuck my neck out before. I'll do it again here, just to illustrate my way of surveying the investment horizon. Needless to say, I reserve the right to change my opinions as markets change.

At 28 times earnings and about a 1.1 percent yield, the current market is the most highly valued that I've ever experienced. It resembles two previous markets that exceeded 20 times earnings and eventually folded dramatically: in 1986–1987 and, before that in 1971–1973. High price earnings this time manifest an economy and a country that are doing unbelievably well versus the world. I readily concede that I'm a big fan of this economic boom, even though, after 100 months, it's double the duration of the longest average business expansion since World War II.

The typical areas of excess—capital expenditures, inventories, and consumer debt—all look pretty good to me. Consumer debt has troubled some observers, but not me—so far. In this robust economic climate, consumers can afford to ratchet up debt levels a bit. And consumers have not been stupid; lately, according to government figures, they have moderated their appetite for debt even as lower mortgage rates have increased their disposable income. Less credit card solicitation has helped ease the overall growth in consumer debt. After distributing credit cards almost willy nilly, lenders became more cautious and took this prudent step.

With no signs of excess visible in these areas, a recession seems unlikely; however, over the intermediate term, we always have to remain alert to other excesses that are not measured as acutely. The market itself suggests excess. The so-called "wealth effect" represents a question mark. It's not clear how much a high stock market prompts consumer spending, which lately has obliterated savings. With corporate America awash in cash flow from operations, savings are not needed to keep companies well oiled. But if a down or even a flat market were to influence consumers to cut spending, thereby choking cash flow, a ripple effect could gather force.

Here is how an economic assessment becomes an investment strategy. Average price–earnings ratios in the neighborhood of 28 times are justifiable only if the outlook for earnings is outstanding. But we seem to be in a part of the business cycle that favors moderate growth at best. Insofar as overall growth governs even demand for the spiffiest high-tech products and services, it seems foolish to predict that those areas will continue to expand at an exceptional pace. Along with improvements in productivity, we must weigh prospects for wage increases, which have been trending upward lately. Meantime, a hotly competitive environment across most sectors hampers price increases. All things considered, it's almost axiomatic that earnings are going to grow slowly.

So, should we pay 28 times earnings for 3 to 4 percent growth? Red-hot NASDAQ stocks seem most exposed to reality checks, particularly because five stocks command almost 40 percent of the market capital of the NASDAQ 100 index. Four of these five stocks advanced more than 140 percent in 1998. This growth is quite unsustainable. Even if growth had been less than 140 percent, that's impressive, to be sure. My point is: They have enjoyed superlative growth for several straight years. Does the market believe they'll grow in excess of 30 percent for the next five years? I don't. And as we've already seen at Dell, sales growth is outpacing earnings growth, which suggests that profit margins are shrinking.

If there is any classic lesson in the marketplace, it's that, at some point, reversion to the mean occurs. Sooner or later, something happens and growth, particularly high-magnitude growth, is diminished. If these stocks are being hailed as 20 to 40 percent growers, any diminution of their growth rates will be dealt with quite severely in the marketplace. Besides those easy five, lots of others fall into the same fragile category. Still more egregious are the fledgling Internet stocks that are valued at ludicrous levels and constitute about 8 percent of the total market value of all U.S. stocks. Two factors will KO this segment. First, the Internet is not the exclusive province of Internet companies. The Fortune 1000 are going to be big on the Net, simply because the profit potential is so enormous. CEO Lou Gerstner of IBM reported, in May 1999, that nearly one-fourth of IBM's sales were Internet-related. He described all but two or three of the Internet swarm as fireflies darting about before the storm. Needless to say, his comments were aimed at promoting IBM stock, but they waved a caution flag at legions of Internet groupies. Moreover, any similarity to the Nifty Fifty ends with one very important distinction: Those companies had earnings.

Exit strategies also will trip the Internet racers. The holders of Internet stocks who plan to get out as soon as possible are legion. They are venture capital firms, founders, and employees with tremendous paper fortunes. Even corporations have big stakes; expect them to cash them in when possible. Delta Airlines owns a stake in Priceline.com worth about $2 billion.* Those proceeds represent a lot of airfares. All these people are near the cusp of cashing in, but the initial offerings are too recent. They have to hold on for a while, to satisfy underwriters.

With so many investors poised to sell, who will be the new buyers? There are roving bands of Internet day traders, but, as day traders, they aren't likely to help sustain the stock price for more than 24 hours.† Already, these stocks have begun to labor and lose momentum. Is the jig up already? Time will tell. Meantime, people who are sucked into day trading eerily suggest the investors of 1929. A dazed and confused public has been persuaded that investing is easy and that stock prices only go up.

---

* As of June 1999. Highlighting how fast things change, two months later this stake is worth $1.3 billion.
† If day traders really get out before the day is over, who owns those stocks at the end of the day? I've never quite gotten an answer to that question.

HIGHLY RECOGNIZED GROWTH CANDIDATES

No Current Candidates

In this climate, constructing an investment portfolio that is guided by Measured Participation is difficult but not impossible. We can quickly pass over the highly recognized growth category, though it will undoubtedly resurface after the next inflection point.

MODERATE GROWTH CANDIDATES

REITs

Consistent with late stages of adrenaline markets in the past, few solid citizens populate the moderate growth segment. One area stands out, however: REITs, or Real Estate Investment Trusts. This area has been bruised, maligned, overlooked, and misunderstood. I like office buildings and apartments; retail properties seem like shakier propositions. Office buildings and apartments have good supply-and-demand relationships that have been preserved a bit by recent tightness in credit availability (which may curtail new supply requirements within a couple of years). A few units, added or due this year, are manageable, and the demand side looks pretty sturdy.

Accordingly, I expect a 4 to 5 percent increase in basic revenue per unit. Besides doing a good job on the expense side, sellers have enlarged the range of fee-generating ancillary services in each unit: office equipment in commercial buildings, cable TV in residences. The typical yardstick for earnings in REITs is called FFO: income "from financial operations." That's essentially earnings plus depreciation—the deductions companies must make on their ledgers to account for yearly wear and tear on plant and equipment. The Flat Iron Building in New York City is still full of people after more than a century. The old twelve-story Society Bank Building in Cleveland, on Public Square, was built in the 19th century without steel support. It's stone on stone and still has occupants. This depreciation is not as real as for typical industrial corporations. Machinery wears out and technology becomes outdated, but well-maintained buildings can last long beyond their depreciated life.

The great buttress of a yield, plus the growth rate, supplies about a 16 percent total return, slightly more than half the going rate in the same marketplace where plenty of 15 percent growers with a 1 percent yield fetch 40 to 50 times earnings. Go figure. I'm banking on exceptional performance when the market shakes off its high-tech stupor. If increased earnings materialize along with expanding multiples, I foresee good appreciation potential in these stocks.

Financial Intermediaries

Among moderate growers, aka solid citizens, financial intermediaries, in my estimation, have some running room. These are mainly banks and savings and loan institutions. Many are selling for 10 to 16 times next year's earnings, and some feature quite good yields—2 or 3 times the market's 1.1 percent average yield, which currently prevails. Put yields of 2, 3, and 4 percent together with a 10 percent growth rate, and a total return of 12 or 13 percent is available for prices in the vicinity of 10 to 14 times earnings. That's not twice total return, the old Windsor benchmark, but it's attractive relative to prevailing relationships. Some observers argue that below-market multiples are appropriate for financial intermediaries, owing to the black holes that continually emerge and KO earnings: excessive Third World debt in the early 1980s, and profligate real estate lending at home in the late 1980s, to name two recent fiascos. Still, as I see it, so far so good. Maybe lessons have been learned, as evidenced by the recent pullback from wanton credit card distribution.

Fundamentals for financial intermediaries center on asset growth and income resulting from asset growth, but some new wrinkles have emerged. Net operating income used to be calculated by subtracting interest costs from interest income. In recent years, banks have found ways to boost non-interest income from an array of new services and charges—from premium checking accounts and gold credit cards to mutual fund management and other premium services for high-net-worth customers. Net operating income from asset growth on the moderate side, from 4 to 6 percent, may be constrained somewhat by fierce competition for financial assets. Supplement that performance with fee income, and the best run banks can post earnings growth of 10 percent, or thereabouts, if accompanied by workmanlike results on the expense control side. One ratio that garners a lot of attention is expense as a percentage of revenues; 55 percent seems to be the desired target these days. Expense control reflects an answer to a question I raised repeatedly over the years: When do the banks cash in on productivity from massive investments in electronic data processing? The means to greater productivity were handed to them by the IBMs of the world. To lure deposits, especially into corporate checking accounts, which did not bear an interest rate, banks gave away services gratis. But now they are becoming more adroit at pricing those services for a pot-pourri of potential customers.

LESS RECOGNIZED GROWTH CANDIDATES

Home Builders

Bargains have not vanished entirely from the less-recognized growth sector. Many stocks of home builders feature price–earnings ratios more than 75 percent below going market multiples. Five that I own feature multiples ranging from 5.3 to 7.7 times 1999 earnings. Looking ahead to fiscal 2000, which ends in September or October 2000 for three of them, the multiples range from 4.9 to 6.8 times earnings. Honest differences might arise over classification: Are these stocks cyclical growers or less recognized growers? To the degree the economy stays solid, and absent too many excesses, I think the thrust will continue. So long as mortgage interest rates avoid a quantum jump, home owning will remain affordable. Lust for one's own piece of turf still beats heartily in virtually all Americans who will either buy homes for the first time or move up to more luxurious homes.

Thanks to the advent of large regional and some national home builders, housing may turn out to be considerably less cyclical, and multiples will expand in tandem with greater earnings. These publicly owned home builders enjoy at least three basic advantages over fragmented, mom-and-pop home builders: (1) better availability of credit even if credit tightens, (2) enough clout to compel price concessions from suppliers, and (3) sufficient resources to exploit expensive technology. With the aid of computers, sellers can show customers their virtual dream houses, replete with profitable extras. And don't forget that big home builders can command the loyalty of plumbers, carpenters, and electricians as markets become more competitive for these tradespeople.

These are some of the several indications that home builders behave less like cyclicals and more like less recognized growth stocks, coupled with 80 percent discounts to prevailing price–earnings ratios. To some degree, this discount reflects a very lofty market. But to buy stocks in this arena at 5 to 7 times earnings is remarkable. I'm among the minority who think that these stocks will behave more like less recognized growth stocks than like cyclical stocks. Not everyone agrees. Therein lies opportunity. What if I'm wrong? An awful lot of stocks at 28 times earnings have some taint of cyclicality. They'll get pronged very badly versus home builders that are selling around book value in a marketplace where market-to-book multiples equal to 5 or 6 times prevail.

CYCLICAL GROWTH CANDIDATES
(THE GOOD, THE BAD, AND THE UGLIES)

Airlines

A worthy case for airlines can be made in this climate. These stocks, I would say, have cyclical growth. Most still fetch single-digit p/e multiples; a few are inching up into double digits. They have pretty well turned back the underfinanced discount airlines. The price competition of a few years ago has subsided. Leisure travelers will fly at odd hours in exchange for very friendly airfares. They get to travel cheap, and the airlines get some return on seats that are otherwise empty. Seats are perishable commodities, in a very real sense. When the plane pulls back from the gate, empty seats become worthless. Internet services have helped fill seats. Priceline.com, for instance, lets travelers bid for seats. It's no surprise that Delta owns 10 percent of Priceline.com.

Though cyclical, airlines are to some degree a growth industry. Growth keys off consumers' increasing disposition to travel. Productivity also increases from one cyclical peak to the next. Newer planes are more fuel-efficient and require less maintenance. By dominating certain hubs, airlines can differentiate themselves from competitors while ensuring some level of traffic, even in a downturn.

Petroleum Marketers and Refiners

My old friends in the oil sector, basic commodity cyclicals, derive their earnings from two sources: (1) production and (2) refining and marketing.

The price of crude has virtually doubled in recent months, so crude earnings are due for an increase. But the market price appears to anticipate and discount these higher earnings. Until Texaco shelved its proposed merger with Chevron, mergers promised to introduce some additional efficiencies that could boost earnings further, but these seem like marginal gains at best.

A more interesting participation, and one I've been mulling, pertains to companies that strictly refine and market gasoline and heating oil. These companies have been squeezed between the rising price of crude and unrewarding prices at the pump. Though operating near peak efficiency, they have not been able to lift prices enough to realize normal earnings. A basic commodity cyclical play would be in these refiners' strategy book. Right now, the margins are next to nothing. It seems almost inevitable that they've got to get decent margins, or else capacity will become inadequate. In fact, a small refiner in the middle of Michigan, a so-called "teakettle" refiner, recently shut down permanently. This closing probably nudged the industry even closer to capacity output by a small but not trivial amount. These stocks are on their can today, but some improvement in earnings seems inevitable.

EPILOGUE

RIVERS AND MARKETS

October 1994

"You cannot step twice in the same river."
Heraclitus, Greek philosopher circa 500 B.C.

FOUR MONTHS BEFORE retiring from Windsor, I joined my son Stephen for a rafting trip down the Colorado River. I envisioned an opportunity to survey several hundred thousand years of geological history while reflecting on a career spent navigating a different sort of river.

Some similarities seemed obvious. Like the brown Colorado, markets move at their own pace. Both entail risks that can be managed and reduced today, but not eliminated. We had a great big sausage boat that basically consisted of four very large pontoons strung together. Like a well-constructed portfolio, this arrangement gave our square, 18-passenger vessel excellent stability in rough water. The last time one flipped was in the mid-1980s, and that was before a few improvements in the design. Short of capsizing, riders nevertheless faced the risk of getting drenched by very cold water, or getting thrown overboard, or, in the worst case, getting caught in the raft's center if rapids drove the two sides of the raft upward, causing it to fold in half. My feet were exposed to this hazard. When the risk seemed apparent, the river guide and raft pilot cried, "Suck rubber!" and we knew to pull our feet up high, away from the crease.

A scale from one to ten denotes the ferocity of river rapids. Ten is maximum and virtually unnavigable. The Colorado subjects rafters to some pretty good risks, including a few eights and nines. Each rapids has a different character. Like the 1987 market crash, Hermit, a No. 9 rapids, is short and scary. Waltenberg, also a No. 9, is somewhat less violent, but more prolonged, like the character of market performance in 1980–1981. There were always obstacles. Chunks of lava cover the riverbed near Lava Falls. This wreckage came from the natural dam formed when lava flows plugged up the Canyon. We had to hold on for dear life or else get thrown right out of the raft.

In this spectacular environment, almost everyone becomes a naturalist. Except for rapids, the River is serene, remote, and spiritual. The Canyon has remained much as it was when the first millennium rolled to a close a thousand years ago. The whole geology was awe-inspiring and the region's history was humbling. We knew that Major John Wesley Powell led an expedition along the same route in 1869. I could imagine him in the quiet stillness broken occasionally by the sounds of rapids, birds chattering, or the occasional head-butting of mountain sheep in the cliffs above.

It was easy to conjure the terror experienced by the men who traveled the Colorado under Major Powell. He and his companions didn't know whether mere rapids or a 500-foot drop awaited them around each bend. Powell had lost an arm in the Civil War, which made him rather unsteady in rapids. So the men lashed him to the mast. His relentless determination to brave any risks demanded too much of several men. They deserted by trying to scale the mile-high canyon walls and were never seen or heard from again.

In addition to its visible benefits, our trip supplied an object lesson in the pitfalls of excessive regulation. Tampering with nature's balance (or free markets) tends to trigger a Law of Unintended Consequences. The Glen Canyon dam was built to control Lake Powell and avoid the annual peaks and dips in the rate and velocity of water. Efforts to manage the flow upset the sand and rock discharge that had created landings along the river. As a consequence, there were few places to land with so many people. The dam also lowered the river's water temperature, because it releases water from the bottom of the lake. This water was too cold for many species of fish, and they didn't survive. Wiser for the experience, regulators have since tried to replicate the river's natural flow, with favorable impact on landings and on the remaining species of fish.

Long stretches between rapids left plenty of time for reflection. I wasn't uncomfortable going into retirement. I had given Windsor my all. I was going out while I still had a lot left, which had been my intention. I wouldn't have given shareholders a tired job; I have too much hard-earned pride. After 31 years, however, it seemed that it was time to head for the exit while still doing well and still contributing.

Looking back, several professional accomplishments stood out. Two meant most: best effort and integrity in my capacity as Windsor's portfolio manager, and fulfillment of an obligation to the community.

I owed each day to Windsor shareholders. I now often read about portfolio managers hopping from one fund to another. I wasn't so inclined. An investment in the Windsor Fund represented—in part, anyway—an investment in its management. I was the principal manager, so I took each new investment quite seriously. Any desire to dabble in personal investments raised a simple question: Was it appropriate to spend time analyzing investments that were not suitable to Windsor? I thought not.

Perhaps I was obsessive in my attention to markets, but it never seemed that way to me. I remember a trip to Israel with a small group from Philadelphia. We found ourselves at Masada, where, in a moment's lull after two hours or so of examining the very moving site, I opened up the section of *The Wall Street Journal* that I customarily carried with me. Two of my companions were also in the investment business, and they quickly got on my case for looking at a newspaper at such a dramatic place. By coincidence, a third tourist from another group overheard and asked if I was the Windsor Fund's Neff. I answered in the affirmative. "Look," he said, "I've got a six figure investment in the Windsor Fund. You go ahead and read your *Wall Street Journal*."

Fairness to shareholders meant low transaction and investment management fees, coupled with incentives for exceptional performance and penalties for dismal performance. We met these hurdles at Windsor. Unlike funds that receive fixed annual percentages of assets under management, performance governed Windsor's compensation. Similar incentives and penalties are scarce because most managers lack confidence in their ability to do well.

Lighter investment expenses are like a lighter jockey in a horse race. After the late Seventies, Windsor never assessed an up-front load. All of the proceeds we received from investors, we invested on their behalf. As for annual fees, whatever a fund charges it has to earn back, over and above its market performance, to stay even with the market.

Our base investment expense was 16 basis points (100 basis points comprise one percentage point). If Windsor outperformed the S&P 500 by 4 percentage points a year, stretched over 3 years, we received an additional 10 basis points of compensation, or 26 basis points (.26 percent). If we underperformed by an equal amount, we gave back 10 basis points. Thus, we earned 6 basis points when results were poor and 26 basis points when Windsor flourished. Unlike mutual funds that assess fixed–percentage fees every year, regardless of performance, we felt an obligation to deliver. For a fund with $10 billion, the difference between superior performance and inferior performance was $26 million versus $6 million. The difference—315 basis points superior to the S&P 500—was very significant to our investment health and to Windsor shareholders.

Fairness to Windsor shareholders meant taking up the cudgel against companies that shortchanged them. I wrote, in 1979, in *Institutional Investor* magazine, that big investors would not always be able to continue to vote with their feet when stocks underperform. I never thought institutional concern would reach current proportions, with state and other public pension fund systems attempting to steer the management process. The California Public Employee Retirement System alone manages more than $100 billion, and many other state funds now lobby for their own agendas.

We were always eager to offer opinions in areas where we felt we had some special insight or expertise. Given Windsor's yield-oriented thrust, we frequently weighed in on abrupt, adverse changes in dividend policy. In January 1991, we fired both barrels at Citicorp. Windsor had 22 million shares at stake. "However relatively laudatory management's steering of the corporate ship may be, the recommendation to slash the dividend is flawed, inconsistent and completely lacking in credibility." Later events lent support to Citi's decision, made at a point of crisis fanned by regulatory pressure. USX–Marathon chairman Charles A. Corry heard from us in like manner after the oil company slashed its dividend in November 1992. "This probably does not come as a new revelation to you, but you have done a severe disservice and injustice to the USX–Marathon shareholders by more than halving the dividend. It is particularly perplexing, frustrating, and hard to understand. . . . "

We rarely became embroiled in any kind of management selection process. But sometimes we had no choice. Disaffection with a former CEO of First Interstate led us to push for his retirement, despite his inclination to stay on beyond the bank's customary retirement age. He seemed increasingly insufficient as time went by. Unable to talk for twenty minutes without contradicting himself, his tenure was not a great moment for an orderly mind.

Another succession issue we lobbied for was at Chrysler. In the mid-eighties, CEO Lee Iacocca didn't seem as interested in Chrysler's predicament as in sundry noble but distracting activities, like refurbishing the Statue of Liberty. With the company in crisis, it needed a full time CEO. We pushed for change in the CEO's office, and the title soon went to Bob Eaton. Later, Eaton and Chrysler's directors invited me to join Chrysler's Board amid a hostile takeover bid by Kerk Kerkorian, the largest shareholder of MGM Grand, Inc. I remained on the Board until Chrysler's 1998 acquisition by German carmaker Daimler Benz.

As for repaying the community, I began managing the University of Pennsylvania's endowment fund in 1980. Penn Trustee Paul Miller, a good friend, extended the invitation. Instead of the usual route—joining the committee and working my way up the ladder—I received a battlefield promotion on the spot. One trustee raised objection to my instant assumption of sole responsibility, but after my presentation on the merits of low p/e, he became one of my staunchest supporters. The $170 million endowment, meager by Ivy League standards, was floundering at the time and needed help. Applying low p/e principles reversed its fortunes. Over the next 16 years, net inflow was $125 million after the University's withdrawals. Nevertheless, we achieved nearly an elevenfold increase, to $1.8 billion.

My involvement at Penn eventually introduced me to the Philadelphia Scholars program. Parts of Philadelphia today remain underprivileged urban neighborhoods. Increasingly, students from the inner city are succeeding in entering colleges and universities around the United States. I recognized a special need for a so-called "last dollar" program. The program provides up to $2,000 to local high school graduates accepted into college, to cover the price of books and other costs that routinely come up but are not normally anticipated in scholarships or student loans. Many of these students come from families headed by mothers, which, as might be suspected, has some resonance for me. It's a democratic program; every accomplishing high school graduate accepted into college is eligible for support. Since starting with three schools, the program now has grown to encompass college-bound graduates at nine local high schools.

We reached our destination on the fifth day of our river trip. A helicopter met us and lifted us out of the Canyon. As the helicopter gained altitude, we captured a far better glimpse of the river's course than was visible at water level. Next to countless millennia of geologic history visible from the Colorado, my three decades at Windsor seemed few. And yet, thirty-one-and-a-half years represented not only the length of my tenure at the Windsor Fund, but half of my life and most of my career. I have been fortunate in most respects, investment performance not the least. I attribute success not to genius or blinding insights, but to a frugal nature and lessons well learned. Therein rest my enduring principles, stamped indelibly with the merits of low p/e investing.

APPENDIXES

Appendix A

THIS CHART SHOWS the Windsor Fund during my watch, from year-end 1964 through year-end 1995, when I retired. During my 31-year tenure, Windsor beat the market 22 times. Each dollar invested in 1964 grew nearly 56-fold by the time I retired. Windsor's total return, a gain of 5,546.4 percent, outpaced the benchmark S&P 500 by more than two-to-one. Years through 1994 are calendar years; 1995 data are for Windsor's fiscal year, which ended on October 31.

Windsor vs. the S&P 500
on My Watch

Period	Per Share Data*				Total Investment Return			
					Windsor Fund			S&P 500
Year Ended December 31	Net Asset Value	Capital Gains Distributions	Income Dividends	Value with Income Dividends & Capital Gains Reinvested	Capital Return	Income Return	Total Return	Total Return
Initial (6/30/64)	$ 7.75	—	—	$ 7.75	—	—	—	—
1964	7.79	$ .24	$.06	8.09	+3.6%	+0.7%	+4.3%	+5.4%
1965	9.42	.49	.11	10.44	+27.6	+1.5	+29.1	+12.5
1966	8.28	.66	.15	10.10	-4.8	+1.5	-3.3	-10.0
1967	9.43	1.19	.21	13.28	+28.8	+2.7	+31.5	+23.9
1968	10.27	.90	.21	16.12	+18.9	+2.5	+21.4	+11.0
1969	9.19	.52	.21	15.51	-5.7	+1.9	-3.8	-8.4
1970	9.48	.02	.24	16.49	+3.4	+3.0	+6.4	-3.9
1971	9.34	.50	.29	17.73	+4.3	+3.2	+7.5	+14.2
1972	9.39	.57	.29	19.54	+6.9	+3.3	+10.2	+19.0
1973	6.64	.14	.32	14.65	-28.0	+3.0	-25.0	-14.7
1974	5.25	—	.31	12.19	-20.9	+4.1	-16.8	-26.3
1975	7.77	—	.32	18.83	+48.0	+6.5	+54.5	+37.1
1976	10.68	.22	.38	27.56	+40.7	+5.7	+46.4	+23.8
1977	9.77	.56	.40	27.84	-3.0	+4.0	+1.0	-7.2
1978	9.12	1.01	.48	30.28	+3.8	+5.0	+8.8	+6.5
1979	9.72	.85	.53	37.10	+16.4	+6.2	+22.6	+18.4
1980	10.42	.79	.59	45.50	+15.7	+6.9	+22.6	+32.4
1981	9.92	1.49	.69	53.12	+9.9	+6.9	+16.8	-4.9
1982	10.36	.99	.62	64.66	+14.8	+6.9	+21.7	+21.5

1983	11.69	1.03	.70	84.10	+23.0	+7.1	+30.1	+22.5
1984	12.64	.48	.76	100.47	+12.4	+7.1	+19.5	+6.2
1985	14.50	.74	.79	128.63	+21.1	+6.9	+28.0	+31.6
1986	13.95	2.59	.85	154.70	+14.3	+6.0	+20.3	+18.6
1987	11.11	2.21	.87	156.61	-4.7	+5.9	+1.2	+5.2
1988	13.07	.55	.63	201.55	+22.6	+6.1	+28.7	+16.5
1989	13.41	.85	.75	231.83	+9.2	+5.8	+15.0	+31.6
1990	10.30	.32	.74	195.89	-20.8	+5.3	-15.5	-3.1
1991	11.72	.84	.57	251.82	+22.7	+5.9	+28.6	+30.4
1992	12.74	.38	.49	293.37	+12.0	+4.5	+16.5	+7.6
1993	13.91	.89	.37	350.20	+16.3	+3.1	+19.4	+10.1
1994	12.59	.86	.44	349.67	-3.3	+3.2	-0.1	+1.3
1995 (10/31)	15.55	—	.20	437.59	+23.5	+1.7	+25.2	+29.3
Cumulative Total							+5,546.4%	+2,229.7%
Average Annual Total Return							+13.7%	+10.6%

* This period reflects my tenure as Windsor's portfolio manager.
* Adjusted for the 2-for-1 stock split, April 29, 1969.
Note: No adjustment has been made for income taxes payable by shareholders on reinvested income dividends and capital gains distributions.
© The Vanguard Group. All rights reserved. Reprinted with permission of the Vanguard Group.

Appendix B

W E A P P R A I S E D T H E Windsor Fund's performance each year with a report card. This sample report card, from 1981, shows that even in an excellent year for Windsor, some results were below par. Overall, however, winners outweighed losers. In addition to avoiding the institutional fetish for market-weighted and larger positions in oil and oil-related technology stocks, three other factors contributed to positive results. (1) We enjoyed the blossoming and maturing of our large positions in supposedly dull, moderate-growing, high-yield, interest-sensitive areas such as banks, foods, insurance, telephone, and electric utilities. (2) Windsor collected extraordinary gains from a broad array of holdings that had required some imagination in the first place. Among them were McDonald's, Denny's, Northwest Industries, U.S. Shoe, Whirlpool, Brown Group, Consolidated Freightways, Levitz Furniture, Overnite Transportation, Delta Airlines, and the Washington Post. *(3) We happened to own a very large position in Conoco when three suitors came calling. Dupont ultimately prevailed, and Windsor shareholders banked a significant profit.*

Windsor Fund's 1981 "Report Card"

Industry Groups	Percent of Net Assets	S&P Group Percentage Change*	Performance of Meaningful Windsor Positions (In Order of Size)	Grade	Critique
Aluminum	4.8	-34.2	Reynolds Metals (-29.9), Kaiser Aluminum (-33.3)	D–	Very poor 1981 result—should be a real winner with economic recovery.
Apparel	4.1	-7.1	Interco (-3.6), Blue Bell (-9.8)	C	Average performances.
Banks	12.8	+11.7 (Non-New York City Banks) +29.2 (New York City Banks)	First Interstate Bancorp (+27.2), First Natl. Boston (+19.4), Ameritrust (–0–), Pittsburgh Natl. Corp. (+36.2), Phila. Natl. Corp. (-5.7), Seafirst Corp. (+32.3) Mercantile Bancorp (-1.9), Virginia Natl. Bankshares (+54.1), South Carolina Natl. Corp. (+32.9), Natl. City Corp.(-13.1), Bancorp Hawaii (+21.3), First Tennessee Natl. Corp. (+36.5)	A–	Finally paid off in big way—both concentration and selection, on balance, was excellent.
Conglomerates	2.5	-2.7	Northwest Industries (+67.4), Scott & Fetzer (+26.1)	A	Northwest, our oil well equipment participation, was "right on."
Consumer Durables (Household Appliances)	1.6	+12.6	Whirlpool (+30.7)	A	Excellent selection in lieu of autos; should be further heard from.
Containers (Metal & Glass)	1.7	+7.1	Anchor Hocking (-17.4)	D	Not our finest moment.
Finance (Personal Loans)	2.2	-10.7	Household International (-15.6)	D	Poor. Declining short-term interest rates should help in 1982.
Foods	6.4	+14.8	General Foods (+6.5), Dart & Kraft (+17.5), Consolidated Foods (+26.7)	B+	Good group, though General Foods behind the parade.
Insurance—Multi-Line	4.6	+22.3	Aetna Life & Casualty (+21.3), Travelers Corp. (+27.1)	A–	Workman-like Windsor result.

Media	1.1	+23.9	Washington Post (-25.7)	A	Good lesser-recognized growth choice plus fortuitous recent ABC purchase.
Oils	19.4	-19.0 (Internatl.) -17.5 (Composite)	Royal Dutch (-32.8), Exxon Corp. (-20.2), Gulf Oil (-9.7)	B+	Actually championship considering huge gain on Conoco, which was bought and sold during the year, and profits on heavy purchases at spring lows.
Paper	1.6	-8.1	Mead Corp. (-10.6)	C-	Another economic recovery participation.
Restaurants	4.3	+36.0	McDonald's (+58.2), Church's Fried Chicken (+2.9)	A	Outstanding McDonald's result plus other significant profit taking.
Retailing	5.8	+5.9	Melville Corp. (+4.0), U.S. Shoe (+103.8), K-Mart (-12.3)	A	Superb U.S. Shoe result; Levitz sold at large profit.
Shoes	0.4	+5.8	Brown Group (+29.1)	A	Our kind of grind-out.
Telephone	3.8	+20.7	AT&T (+19.6)	B+	Telephone an excellent big market cap stock.
Tire & Rubber	1.2	+4.4	Goodyear (+5.1)	B	Another auto substitute.
Trucking	1.3	+10.2	RLC Corp. (-30.4), Consolidated Freightways (+48.7)	A	Came of age, although RLC owes us a lot; Delta & Overnite sold at eye-catching gains.
Utilities—Electric	1.7	+9.4	Central & SouthWest (+10.9), Houston Industries (+11.1), Consolidated Edison (+37.8)	A-	Good selections in a positive group.

* Compares with overall S&P change of -4.4%

Appendix C

THE WINDSOR FUND *portfolio in 1981, as indicated by the annual report for that year, highlighted the stocks we owned within the measured participation framework (see page 101). Virtually all of the stocks we owned fell into four categories (listed in descending order of emphasis): (1) Cyclical Growth, (2) Moderate Growth, (3) Less Recognized Growth, and (4) Recognized Growth. As usual, Windsor was notably light in the Recognized Growth segment, which tends to captivate mainstream investors. Our four Recognized Growth holdings represented less than one-tenth of the Windsor Fund. Moreover, the Windsor Fund approached $1 billion, but we owned only about 100 stocks—and for us, that was a fairly high number.*

Windsor Fund Financial Statements
Statement of Net Assets—October 31, 1981

Common Stocks (99.2%)	Shares	Market Value (000)*	Common Stocks (99.2%)	Shares	Market Value (000)*
Recognized Growth Companies (9.0%)			United Virginia Bankshares, Inc.	10,000	351
International Business Machines Corp.	371,800	$ 19,055	Virginia National Bankshares, Inc.	202,802	4,335
K Mart Corp.	634,100	10,700	Washington Post Co.	141,200	4,148
McDonald's Corp.	529,000	37,030	**Group Total**		**$232,539**
Xerox Corp.	416,200	16,960	**Moderate Growth Companies (31.5%)**		
Group Total		**$ 83,745**			
Less Recognized Growth Companies (25.0%)			American Fletcher Corp.	140,000	2,117
			American Telephone & Telegraph Co.	577,258	34,347
Aetna Life & Casualty Co.	654,000	27,958	Ameritrust Corp.	350,000	10,325
Ahmanson (H.F.) & Co.	112,000	1,652	Anchor Hocking Corp.	550,000	8,456
American Greetings Corp.	112,900	1,969	Brown Group, Inc.	125.300	3,681
Atlantic Richfield Co.	38,000	1,829	Central & South West Corp.	438,300	6,136
Bancorp Hawaii, Inc.	169,748	3,278	Consolidated Edison Co. of N.Y.	122,200	3,956
Blue Bell, Inc.	357,400	9,426	Consolidated Foods Corp.	110,000	3,327
Central Bancshares of the South Inc.	280,000	2,625	Exxon Corp.	1,523,200	46,267
Church's Fried Chicken	116,300	3,140	First Hawaiian, Inc.	55,000	1,719
Colonial Penn Group, Inc.	200,000	3,700	First Interstate Bancorp	820,046	29,727
Dart & Kraft, Inc.	467,700	22,800	First National Boston Corp.	340,244	14,928
Deposit Guaranty Corp.	20,100	540	General Foods Corp.	1,004,800	31,023
First Alabama Bancshares, Inc.	25,000	644	Gulf Oil Corp.	647,300	23,222
First Tennessee National Corp.	177,254	3,157	Household International Inc.	1,373,800	20,435
First Union Corp.	91,871	1,803	Houston Industries, Inc.	202,500	4,050
Interco, Inc.	577,000	27,335	Manufacturers Hanover Corp.	81,100	2,879
Internorth, Inc.	250,000	7,063	Maryland National Corp.	98,500	2,167
Kroger Co.	211,800	4,633	Mercantile Bancorporation Inc.	210,000	5,434
Leaseway Transportation Co.	40,400	1,172	Mid-Continent Telephone Corp.	39,800	697
Leslie Fay, Inc.	81,029	1,124	National City Corp.	130,000	3,867
Lucky Stores, Inc.	219,300	2,769	Philadelphia National Corp.	277,600	8,085
Melville Corp.	361,300	13,955	Phillips Petroleum Co.	260,000	10,725
NCR Corp.	280,000	12,460	Pittsburgh National Corp.	314,000	8,714
Pennzoil Company	189,900	8,688	Sun Co., Inc.	105,600	4,145
Pillsbury Co.	66,000	2,623	Texas Utilities Co.	84,059	1,744
Pitney Bowes Inc.	560,000	12,880	**Group Total**		**$292,173**
Seafirst Corp.	201,446	6,194	**Cyclical Growth Companies (33.1%)**		
Squibb Corp.	43,700	1,245			
South Carolina National Corp.	161,000	4,226			
Supermarkets General Corp.	141,300	2,596	Aluminum Co. of America	350,000	8,444
Transamerica Corp.	74,400	1,832	Amerada Hess Corp.	853,700	21,236
Travelers Corp.	300,000	14,587			
U.S. Shoe Corp.	394,350	13,802			

Windsor Fund Financial Statements *(Continued)*

Common Stocks (99.2%)	Shares	Market Value (000)*
American Broadcasting Cos., Inc.	162,400	6,049
American Stores Co.	152,700	3,856
Amstar Corp.	250,600	6,547
Brockway Glass Co.	178,400	2,475
Cone Mills Corp.	18,300	538
Consolidated Freightways, Inc.	114,400	4,233
Emhart Corp.	174,800	5,178
Federal Co.	290,000	5,764
Ford Motor Co.	142,800	2,303
Getty Oil Co.	95,000	6,009
Gifford Hill & Company Inc.	29,100	575
Goodyear Tire & Rubber Co.	636,300	11,374
Hyster Co.	14,100	474
Ideal Basic Industries, Inc.	142,700	3,015
International Minerals & Chemicals Corp.	273,800	9,309
KDT Industries Inc.	223,100	1,088
Kaiser Aluminum & Chemical Corp.	950,000	15,438
Kidde, Inc.	14,800	651
Libbey-Owens-Ford Co.	300,000	8,025
Mead Corp.	650,000	15,113
National Can Corp.	242,500	4,729
Northwest Industries Inc.	183,372	11,048
Pennwalt Corp.	58,200	1,695
RLC Corp.	630,700	6,307
Reynolds Metal Co.	800,000	20,200
Royal Dutch Petroleum Co.	1,402,300	48,204
Scott & Fetzer Co.	225,000	6,525
Sperry Corp.	225,000	7,369
Staley, A. E. Mfg. Co.	920,600	17,952
Texaco, Inc.	300,000	9,825
Union Carbide Corp.	412,120	19,679
U.S. Truck Lines, Inc. of Delaware	20,000	228
Jim Walter Corp.	63,000	1,063
Whirlpool Corp.	608,100	14,898
Group Total		**$307,416**
Miscellaneous (.6%)		**$ 5,418**
Total Common Stocks (Cost $873,328)		**$921,291**
Temporary Cash Investments (3.6%)		

	Face Amount (000)	Market Value (000)*
U.S. Government Obligations		
U.S. Treasury Notes		
13.25%, 4/15/88	$6,000	5,648
14.0%, 7/15/88	6,000	5,760
Commercial Paper		
Caterpillar Tractor Co.		
14.70%, 11/2/81	2,000	1,989
General Motors Acceptance Corp. 14.875%, 11/25/81	4,000	3,950
Repurchase Agreement		
Merrill Lynch Pierce Fenner & Smith 13.75%, 11/2/81 (Collateralized by U.S. Treasury Bills 11/19/81–4/29/82 and Federal Farm Credit Bank 11/25/81–3/1/82)	16,300	$ 16,300
Total Temporary Cash Investments (Cost $33,926)		33,647
Total Investments (102.8%) (Cost $907,254)		954,938
Other Assets and Liabilities (−2.8%)		
Other Assets—Note C		$ 13,467
Distribution Payable	$(156,583)	
Less Estimated Amounts to be Reinvested—Note E	135,428	(21,155)
Other Liabilities—Note F		(18,465)
		$ (26,153)
Net Assets (100%)		
Applicable to 96,504,817 outstanding $1 par value shares (Authorized $100,00,000 shares)		$928,785
Net Asset Value Per Share		**$9.62**

*See Note A to Financial Statements

INDEX

INDEX